Public Reason

Public Reason

Mediated Authority in the Liberal State

Fred M. Frohock

Cornell University Press   Ithaca and London

First published 1999 by Cornell University Press

Cornell University Press strives to utilize environmentally responsible
suppliers and materials to the fullest extent possible in the publishing
of its books. Such materials include vegetable-based, low-VOC inks,
and acid-free papers that are also either recycled, totally chlorine-free,
or partly composed of nonwood fibers. Books that bear the logo of the
FSC (Forest Stewardship Council) use paper taken from forests that
have been inspected and certified as meeting the highest standards
for environmental and social responsibility. For further information,
visit our website at www.cornellpress.cornell.edu.

Printed in the United States of America

Library of Congress Cataloging-in-Publication Data

Frohock, Fred M.
    Public reason : mediated authority in the liberal state / Fred M.
    Frohock.
        p.   cm.
    Includes index.
    ISBN 0-8014-3677-X (cloth)
    1. Political science—Philosophy.   2. Reason.   I. Title.
JA71.F68   1999
320'.01'1—dc21   99-29687

Cloth printing   10   9   8   7   6   5   4   3   2   1

Contents

Acknowledgments

Early versions of Chapter 2 and Chapter 3 appeared in journals: Chapter 2 as "The Boundaries of Public Reason" in *The American Political Science Review* 91, no. 4 (December 1997), and Chapter 3 as "Conceptions of Persons" in *Social Theory and Practice* 23, no. 1 (Spring 1997). I am grateful to the editors of these journals for permission to reprint this material here and for the comments by the anonymous readers selected by the journals to evaluate the work. I am also grateful for the critiques provided by the set of readers used by Cornell University Press as I slowly brought this work up to its present level. It is impossible to exaggerate the importance of such critical commentary for the author as a book like this one is being written and rewritten. I thank two colleagues, Manfred Stanley and Jonathan Bach, who read and commented on selected chapters in a very early draft of this work. I also thank Marian Paules for helping me with the final, bibliographic stages of the research. The patience and effectiveness of Roger Haydon of Cornell University Press in the review process, which sometimes must have seemed endless to him, were remarkable. Basically, I mugged him with constant revisions even while the readers were trying to do their work. In the course of this unstable time (when the manuscript was truly a moving target) he taught me again what a good editor is all about. For my wife: regrets for the lost days and evenings we might have spent together in the years I worked on this book. I have seen yet one more time that the costs of the writing vocation are absorbed mainly by the partner of the author. Maybe now, Val, with the book finished, we can find ways to retrieve some of those missed experiences. For my two daughters, Renée and Christina, and son-in-law, Harry: the good conversations over the years were all that I could ask for and handle as demonstrations of the powers of public reason in private settings. I think I lost most of the arguments. But please be impressed with this book if you want me to cut some slack in trying to convert you to the right point of view over dinners in New York City.

Public Reason

Introduction

It does not take long in any conversation to discover that arguments are often short on reason and long on passion, even among those who are pleased to be called intellectuals. The pattern is familiar: special pleading overrides impartial logic; emotional appeals dominate judicious uses of evidence and inference; ad hominem attacks replace objective appraisals. This is not to say that passion is a bad thing. Intensity of belief is refreshing not least because it seems to be an endangered species in academic circles, and the irrational has always had its dark attractions. Sometimes nothing works better at getting the point across than the intimidation of a powerful and dishonest (well, devious) argument. Conversely, a disinterested survey of "facts" and their various implications can be sudden death for an intuitive exploration of counterfactuals and ideal states.

But the approbative force in the terms *rational* and *reasoned* represents long-standing beliefs that the powers of reason are the most reliable guides to sound reflections and actions. These powers are typically regarded as directions for a full understanding of social thought and practices: rationality and reason have long been designated as the indicators of human identity, the resources for discovering or deriving governing principles, the instruments that provide access to a full range of experiences, and more. The assignment of such standing to reasoning may explain why it is so startling to encounter impeccably framed and deployed rational arguments intractably opposed to one another. The pattern is equally familiar: not the absence of reason in favor of passion or intuition, but the spectacle of dispassionate and objective presentations unable to reach rational closure on their differences.

The absence of closure in rational discussions can be explained in many ways, including the shortcomings of disputants. But the more likely explanation is that reasoning is a skill that relies on open languages, and as a consequence arguments can easily move in different directions. Adversaries who differ on rudimentary understandings of human experience seem chronically inclined to use rules of evidence and inference in opposing ways, with the result that reason is collapsed to mutable contexts and its legislating powers limited to particular points of view. The correlates of these familiar patterns are also well known: rival criteria and indicators, and the obvious influence and occasional dominance of background conditions (such as capital) over the normative powers assigned to reason. This simple story accords with postmodern theories of language, which attest to the natural openness and instabilities of all terms, including (so it seems) one of the basic concepts in political languages.

The story, however, does not eliminate reason from our intellectual landscapes. It accommodates instead two different theories of rational powers. Both accept the fact of incompatible arguments and conceptions of reason. But one theory maintains that these arguments and conceptions can be rationally ordered by an adequate concept of reason. This theory begins with the efforts of classical political philosophers to develop an account of the state and of justice drawn from the assumption that human reason can discover an objective reality at least partially outside human conventions. This reality is represented in Plato's theory of forms, which attempts to name the fixed and universal ideas of being. The form of the state is an ordered and harmonious arrangement of constituent parts. Reason is the skill that discloses and reflects this arrangement.

This first belief in the settlement powers of reason continues in different ways in the theories of the great liberal political philosophers of the seventeenth and eighteenth centuries. Here reason becomes an instrument of decision, not of discovery, and rational choices in hypothetical conditions satisfy objectivity. The state that originates in consent has defining values and purposes that rule out a range of community actions, and perhaps of beliefs as well. But it is also to be noncommittal on certain kinds of truth, allowing persons the freedom to define the good for themselves (provided that these conceptions of the good are reasonable). In attempting a kind of moral distance from at least some definitions of the good, the liberal state differs from the communities it houses, which are free to subscribe to an inventory of the whole moral life. Both versions of the first story of reason follow the paths cut by objective vocabularies, however, for reason in both classical and modern political theory is to provide arguments with strong retentive powers, reasonably free of partisan interests, and generalizable across member communities. This is the good dream in which reason adjudicates rival claims to truth and power.

But there is another account of reason and the state. It is found in those subterranean political traditions initiated by Thrasymachus in Plato's *Republic*. In this account reasoning is influenced and sometimes even controlled by distributions of power and interest in human communities. The explanations for this deconstruction are both interesting and persuasive. They include the dominance of culture in all languages (especially evident in multicultural settings where languages serve as instruments of partisan movements), the sensitivity of (especially) moral and political vocabularies to rival definitions, the powers of reflection to generate anomalies (Moore's "open question" argument; the hostility between completeness and consistency demonstrated in Gödel's theorem; Quine's underdetermination thesis, which allows rival theories to account for the same empirical data), and more. Many contributions in various fields—some formal, others anecdotal—support critical legal studies, feminist critiques, postmodern skepticism, and other approaches that view the objective, consistent, and general languages identified in the first account of reason as little more than chimeras, not real, not possible, and finally delusions that harm by missing the realities of power. This story is the bad dream in which reason is dominated by political forces. Incompatible claims are not rationally ordered but are regarded as an incorrigible condition of political societies.

Both stories are critical to a full understanding of public reason. The first develops the vocabularies and sensibilities of objective judgment commonly expected in any effective use of reason. The second story recognizes the connections between reason and those partisan disputes that it is charged with resolving. But however vital both traditions are to definitions of reasoning, they are mutually antagonistic. A skill or principle that governs successfully insofar as its meaning is insulated from partisan disputes must be regarded as compromised if disputing factions can control what it means, and, conversely, disputes cannot be rationally intractable if reason provides criteria for an objective ordering of claims.

Classical principles and the social contract are part of the political cultures of their historical time and place, and each is characterized by gradual and sometimes rapid introductions of content, of cultural interpretation and modification, to their sparer formal machinery. But the objective reference points are always abandoned reluctantly, for they are crafted to exclude unwelcome and sometimes unthinkable alternatives. If reason is no more than another partisan instrument, nothing remains to evaluate and order the many rival claims to power and truth found in any political society. To the pessimist, conflict itself may be the first and last resort when reason folds into the disputes it is designed to address, indemnifying by default Thrasymachus's warning that indeed *might* does make *right* in the real world of politics. The sad possibility is that a failure of reason also appears to risk a workable concept of justice.

The assignments in any political philosophy are unmistakable once competing accounts of reason are recognized. One is to pass judgment on the accounts. Is there a persuasive case for the objective ordering of claims? Or does the strategy that stresses relativity and power dominate? A second is to settle on the implications for political philosophy of the superior account. If rational objectivity is possible, what is an objective version of public reasoning and what does it do? If relativism prevails, what is left of reason as a legislating concept? What devices are available to adjudicate the inevitable disputes that define political experience?

No one can pretend to answer these questions completely in any imaginable time span. But they can frame an agenda to examine the powers of reason in areas of political life. The areas I will explore here are the theories of public reason found in contemporary liberal political philosophy. My primary guides (and occasional targets) are the versions of liberal political philosophy developed by John Rawls in both *A Theory of Justice* and *Political Liberalism*. Although many of my arguments extend beyond the concerns of these two works to address other considerations in public reason, Rawls's work has strongly influenced my thinking even when I disagree with it. I regard political liberalism as the strongest version of contemporary liberal political theory, and this conviction guides the discussions here away from alternative theories. I also have almost nothing to say (except in passing) about the concepts of reason found in compositional utilitarianism, largely because I believe that methodological individualism fails rational and other expectations in well-known ways that others have set out ably. One of the casualties in this failure is the production of a social good from individual utilities. In particular, the main body of rational choice theory, by demonstrating some remarkable problems in mapping from individual choices to collective outcomes, undermines the utilitarian reliance on arithmetical composition rules.[1]

---

1. This statement on utilitarianism is of course hyperbolic, though like many exaggerations it expresses a modest truth. My reservations are about the standing of bottom-to-top utilitarianism given the substantial work in rational choice theory that identifies so many interruptions in the conceptual paths between descriptions of individuals and aggregates. For an elegant defense of utilitarianism as a program for human welfare that relies on select ver-

The derivational (noncompositional) powers of contract theory promise a sounder rational connection between parts and wholes in political systems, though my arguments lead to renewable agreements in ongoing conversations rather than those formed in the more static and differentially privileged conditions of the state of nature or the original position. This unsavory union of respect and radical change makes me the worst kind of critic, I suppose, one who is inspired to revolutionize the subject precisely because it is so attractive. Leavening this dour assignment is the possibility that the sketch of public reason I offer at the end of this exercise may be the prize that restores liberal values to their proper high station, though (unavoidably) in attenuated form. At manic times I am even able to convince myself that my work is a natural extension of contract theory to more adequate structures that complete the program of political liberalism. I just wish that these structures were more closely aligned with the accounts of public reasoning and the state found in modern liberal theories. But if a reflective examination means anything, it must mean that a theory stands or falls on the terms of such examination, not whether it presents a desirable cluster of statements. I am aware that currently such examinations are not completely held in favor, in part because of the convincing attacks on objectivity that are among the main topics of my work here. But I still assume that scholarly work can be objective, at least in the fine sense that demarcates wants and wishes from conclusions drawn through careful attention to argument and evidence.

The version of public reason developed in the arguments here will suggest a skeletal account of the state joined to a minimalist theory of political morality. I will argue that what I call merit public reasoning is incoherent in the presence of communities that disagree about the foundations of human experience (ontology exceeding the reconciling powers of computational reasoning). Avoidance mechanisms, among them perhaps certain types of reconciling narratives, are devices that meet criteria of rational governance in conditions of extreme pluralism. Public reasoning produces conclusions in these conditions through mediated dialogue that is controlled by the referring framework of collective arrangements. The argu-

---

sions of rational choice, however, see Russell Hardin, *Morality and the Limits of Reason* (Chicago: University of Chicago Press, 1988). Donald P. Green and Ian Shapiro have also written so thoughtful a critique of the applications of rational choice theory to political conditions, *Pathologies of Rational Choice* (New Haven, Conn.: Yale University Press, 1994), that some of the theory's corrosive effects on utilitarianism (strangely enough) may be blunted: if rational choice theory is incoherent, then it cannot be either an effective critique or a formal expression of a political philosophy justified at least partially on independent grounds.

ments on these themes are of course conceptually biased (though I hope rational), but one notable bias is my conviction that we do not have a concept of the political sufficiently "thick" to allow the demarcation of state and community needed in liberal theory. The result is a collapse of that distance between public reason and community values regarded as necessary to ensure impartiality. But we do have (or so I argue) workable distinctions between individual and collective that can secure a more realistic set of political domains, and these domains contain forms of public reason that meet certain expectations of political morality.

The overall aim of the book is to provide an intelligible account of public reason on the acceptance of post-Wittgenstein theories of language. Roughly the first third of the work is an effort to show that no computational version of public reason is coherent in conditions of extreme (or what I call deep) pluralism. The reasons are familiar, and organized on the thought that political languages chronically admit rival and reasonable interpretations (meaning that the standard admonition of liberal governance—"Be reasonable"—will not work). The first chapter is an inspection of terms (equality, liberty, harm) that illustrate the openness of political languages. Chapter 2 consists of a set of arguments (with examples) outlining how and why merit forms of public reasoning fail, and suggesting that the pluralism expected and celebrated in liberalism can extend to the governing languages of the state.

The next two chapters of the book begin developing an alternative version of public reasoning. Both explore some defining concepts in public reasoning and the methods of reasoning aligned with them. Chapter 3 is a study of various theories of the person, in which I argue that liberalism depends on property and practice dualism. I suggest here that a narrative account of the person may be a more productive way to proceed in public reasoning. In this chapter I offer the possibility that the person can merge with certain processes, which I label (with others) *dialogue* and *discourse*. This part of the book undermines what I call linear models of reasoning in liberal theory by attacking and rebuilding their foundations in certain concepts, of which the most important are those of the *self* or *person*. In Chapter 4 I argue for mediation as a central part of public reasoning, in part by recognizing the need for translation and guidance once the direct, transparent and accessible text is abandoned. The setting for mediation is to be uncoerced dialogue on the model of a conversation. I elaborate this model in terms of the intersections of political and moral reasoning described in Chapter 2, and I try to say some things about the way freedom and coercion can be joined in these conditions.

Chapter 5 tracks (in reasonably succinct form) the standing and implications of the version of public reasoning based on mediated speech acts that is the central theme in this work. This chapter develops a set of variations on an Oakeshott (or Feyerabend) orientation to theory: a defense of a political order with no a priori content. In this chapter I discuss the pragmatic techniques of oblique reasoning and the uses of analogy and maxims in public reasoning. But I also maintain that public reasoning is deliberation on the proper collective arrangements for the political society, and on these grounds combines moral and political reasoning at the highest levels. Chapter 6 describes some of the implications for politics of combining noncomputational reasoning and collective references in a single account of public reasoning. I try to link breakdowns in public reason to the open nature of the self, and I revisit the differences between contract and mediated dialogue models of public reasoning. Extensive notes complete the package.

The critiques of liberalism I develop here are not for the timid. I maintain that the defining languages and proposals of liberal programs are flawed in the most general ways: liberal distinctions between the right and the good are difficult to make, and sometimes are just plain specious; the neutral state is a fiction, though the state and its reasoning powers are distinct from the communities that constitute the political system; political and moral languages are elastic enough to permit multiple and rival interpretations among reasonable persons; public reason must be conducted in conditions of risk and uncertainty, and at least occasionally in social contexts so pluralistic that incompatible ontologies are introduced to public space; narratives are needed to complete and sometimes to supplant the failures of linear versions of public reason to govern rationally; the person in political theory can be conceptualized in different ways, these different concepts have striking effects in political theory, the concept of a person in the liberal state folds easily into the practice and narrative selves of a reconstructed public reason, and the term *public* can only be defined in terms of access crafted on open "sidebar" languages whenever the liberal state is composed of disparate subcultures.

My positive suggestions (there are several) accept limited generalizing powers for liberal concepts. But I argue that the only salvation for liberalism is found in the dual strategies of abandonment and amendment. The vocabularies of neutrality, impartiality, and the concept of a distinct and fully defined political domain must be given up. The amendments require the introduction of various holistic terms as a framework for that mediated dialogue which can serve as a standard for the public reasoning of the liberal state. Always attached to the frames and dialogues of public reason, however, is the potential or actual exercise of power. Power is an unavoidable property of the state, and any adequate account of public reason must find areas of congeniality between the coercive powers of the state and the liberty of its citizens.

The problems I address emerge precisely as coercion is directed at persons whose liberties allow them to define and redefine the governing apparatus of the state. The fact is that any item is a potential candidate for political dispute in conditions of genuine freedom. The interpretive powers of liberty extend the natural pluralism of liberal conditions to the center of public space, opening even the most revered principles to critical inspections and shifts in meaning. Members of liberal political systems can and do disagree about the fundamental things in life (as time goes by). Some of the more acrimonious and important political disputes have been over justice, the common good, and the proper way to govern divergent beliefs. This seemingly unlimited range of interpretive powers denies us the traditional shaping concepts of justice and the public good to govern the pluralism of self-interest. Politics is so much more complicated than these frames admit, arriving often in unwrapped packages of issues with the power to appropriate the languages used to adjudicate differences. I propose an understanding of public reasoning as a kind of unrestricted discourse that can yet bring the multiple dialogues of political life to reasonable, though only provisional, closure.

The methods and conclusions of this work may not satisfy. I consciously ignore many types of widely accepted (and convenient) distinctions. The differences between descriptive and evaluative statements, for example, will not easily be found here, inasmuch as the work itself is both an empirical account of public reason and an affirmation of its discursive forms of communication. I argue that public reason just *is* a form of mediated speech oriented by collective nouns, and that this model meets the needs of political morality. Nor do I recognize current antagonisms between liberalism and democracy, and philosophical and political judgments. This indifference to theoretical conventions is sure to irritate even readers of good will. But the theoretical conventions cannot be maintained, at least as controlling guides for the work at hand. I argue that political languages always offer the possibility of rival interpretations, that disagreements can always slide toward essential contestability, that discussion is easily moved from dialogue to discourse, and that the only (and always provisional) halting points in public reasoning come about through mediated speech acts organized by those collective references that define and order political talk. All theoretical conventions, every concept and principle, must be exceedingly tentative on these terms. Cherished distinctions are simply targets for critical inspection and redefinition.

Anyone developing these arguments can offer only stratagems and narratives as rest stops along that unwelcome slope extending from a rejection of classical and modern rationality to the nihilism of a state without reasoning powers. It will quickly be evident that these rest stops are not as comfortable as those provided in the stories of classical truth and contemporary moral realism. I wish I could do better. But, as one of my philosophy professors used to say, gifts that do not exist cannot be given even by Santa Claus at Christmas. I hope that the work here can find justifications in the political realities that are the only true guides for theories of the state and of public reason.

1 Political Languages

The issues and problems that enter the domains of public reason can originate in events that move individuals in contrary directions within social practices. In 1991 Timothy Quill published a note in the *New England Journal of Medicine* that poignantly told the story of Diane. Diane was one of Dr. Quill's patients. She visited Quill one day complaining of fatigue. She also had an annoying rash. His medical instincts led him to run blood tests, and then bone marrow tests, which revealed acute leukemia. After exploring the treatment and survival rates Diane opted for no therapy (on her conviction that she would die anyway in a great deal of pain—a not unreasonable forecast). Quill arranged for hospice care for her. A week later Diane asked Quill for barbiturates to help her sleep. In their conversation it was clear that she wanted the security of having enough barbiturates to commit suicide at an appropriate time. Quill wrote a prescription generous enough to help her die. Months later, at the end, and in pain and dependency, Diane said good-bye to her friends and family. She promised Quill "a reunion in the future at her favorite spot on the edge of Lake Geneva, with dragons swimming in the sunset." She died peacefully using the barbiturates and, in Quill's report to the medical examiner, of the acute leukemia that had ravaged her body but not her mind.[1]

In the years after Quill's note was published physician-assisted suicide evolved into one of the more profound moral issues in health care, especially in the United States. It has properly been seen as quite different from justice-oriented issues such as health coverage for the unemployed and the influence of market forces on medicine. Assisted suicide is a material and a

---

1. Timothy Quill, "Death and Dignity: Case of Individualized Decision Making," *New England Journal of Medicine* 324 no. 10 (1991): 691–694.

metaphysical issue, touching the meanings of the person, of the healer, of life and death, and so has implications for almost all aspects of health care. And because many of the issues of assisted suicide occur among the elderly, and because women far outnumber men in this age group, the practice is gender sensitive, representing in this sense an intertwining of morality and fairness in the care of our oldest citizens. How we regard assisted suicide, whether we reject it as a medical practice or accept it as a standard alternative in a complete inventory of medical treatment, influences every trend in health care in most political democracies. The ways in which we resolve or manage disputes like those over physician assisted suicide also illuminate the types of public reasoning found in democratic arrangements.

One enduring approach to the issues in any area of public reason is decomposition, in which actions are broken down to simple and basic (uncompounded) parts in a kind of Aristotelian exercise. The surface structure of physician-assisted suicide is a triad. The two primary agents are the physician and the patient, with (and here is the strange part) lethal assistance rather than healing as the connection between the two. On the physician's side are the medical norms that seem to forbid the provision of deadly means, including the Hippocratic Oath's "Do no harm" injunction. The patient's side of the arrangement spells out what it takes to be a patient in the transaction: one must be terminally ill and competent, and must genuinely give consent to the act. In its agreeable form assisted suicide consists of a dying patient requesting a lethal drug, which the doctor then provides. The outcome of the act is the death of the patient from the drug. In legal vocabularies the patient must be competent and terminally ill (in the language that made assisted suicide legal in the state of Oregon, "capable" and with "an incurable and irreversible disease that . . . will . . . produce death within six months"). Procedures governing the act typically require the judgment of at least one consulting physician to confirm the medical opinion of the attending physician.

Privacy is the overarching principle that sets the stage for assisted suicide. Individuals own their bodies in liberal traditions of law. In the metaphor used by Robert Nozick, selves are within a hyperplane of moral space that cannot be invaded without the consent of the occupant.[2] Any trespass without consent may be battery or assault. Like the refusal of unwanted attention in so many areas of life, the competent patient's *no* on treatment must be honored. Assisted suicide raises fresh questions about the individual's authority, the scope and logic of that hyperplane of moral

2. Robert Nozick, *Anarchy, State, and Utopia* (New York: Basic Books, 1974), 57.

space established by privacy. The question is not whether individuals can refuse treatment and die, but whether they can ask for and receive what is necessary to hasten death. The escalation is dramatic, from "Doctor, help me" to "Doctor, let me die" to "Doctor, help me to die." What makes assisted suicide so strange on the surface (and it is strange) is the same oddness that attends those scenes of doctors assisting in state executions of prisoners: a healer as part of the team that brings death—in some instances in the past, doctoring to kill.

It is this oddness that invites us to think about a balance, an equilibrium, among the constituent parts of assisted suicide which can meet legal, moral, and medical needs. The problem is that there are multiple arrangements of the parts with no easy way to rank order them. Two federal courts have sought and found different arguments to overturn laws that prohibit assisted suicide. In *Washington v. Glucksberg* the United States Court of Appeals for the Ninth Circuit, basing its decision on the due process clause of the Fourteenth Amendment, found that there is a "liberty interest in choosing the time and manner of one's death." The Second Circuit Appeals Court, in *Vacco v. Quill*, relied on the equal protection guarantee of the Fourteenth Amendment. The court noted that there are two sets of terminally ill persons: those on life-support systems, and those who are not reliant on life-support machinery that can be disconnected. The former can legally have their support systems withdrawn to bring about death, but the latter do not have the right to accelerate their impending deaths. Because, according to the court's reasoning, the two sets of persons are similarly situated under the law, equal protection requires that the latter set must have a right to physician assistance in hastening their death.

In June 1997 the U.S. Supreme Court reversed both Circuit Court rulings, to the disappointment of the Hemlock Society and the lawyer for that well-known figure Dr. Kevorkian. The court held that states may continue to ban physician-assisted suicide if they wish to do so. But the decision does not prohibit states from legalizing physician assisted suicide if they wish to do so. The opinions written by the justices were almost engraved invitations to keep talking and bring other cases before the court. The vote on the two cases was unanimous, but the reasoning was almost a case study in pluralism. The justices interpreted key phrases in the Constitution in different ways, and found and weighed data differently. Even the conclusions of the Supreme Court seem to be partial judgments on matters inasmuch as the justices occasionally suggested that they would be inclined to consider different arguments in future cases. They left the legal standing of assisted suicide in a tentative state.

Those who continue to argue for assisted suicide as a legal practice in medicine do what Quill does so well: they construct a narrative that reminds us that the interests of the patient require a medical compassion that will help the dying avoid suffering, maintain dignity, and so speed the journey toward death when all else has failed. This narrative trades effectively on the premise that doing good for patients requires an understanding that death is sometimes best, and that assistance to achieve this best end is on occasion the humane thing to do. Almost every doctor can relate extreme cases of pain and loss in their terminally ill patients that seem to demand the compassion that Quill delineates. The arguments for physician assisted suicide summon the very impulses that create healing practices in human communities, which seem to be morally centered in the thought of doing good for others.

But the reservations about assisted suicide for opponents of the practice are also persuasive. They appear in vivid form when we try to imagine a counter-narrative: the shape and logic of medicine in the future with assisted suicide as a standard alternative in health care. The counternarrative also checks off other wide considerations in assisted suicide: concerns about the effectiveness of consent in the practice and about differential patterns of assisted suicide according to morally irrelevant criteria. Put simply, consent might be sought differently from among the very best patients and the very worst in terms of intelligence, education, wealth, contributions to society, moral virtues, and other traits and inclinations.

Worries have also been expressed on how parents might change their views about their chronically ill children, whether adult children will see and understand their aged parents differently, how nursing homes and hospices would be regarded if assisted suicide were given legal imprimatur as a legitimate alternative in health care. Would health care and death become more or less humane if patients could (in the words of Kathryn Tucker, the attorney representing the plaintiffs in the *Washington* case) seek and get "a peaceful, humane, dignified death" through medication?[3]

3. All quotes are from the *New York Times* summary of the oral arguments (January 5, 1997). So many good arguments have been published on these issues. Among the better immediate pieces at the time are Ezekiel Emanuel, "Whose Right to Die?" in *The Atlantic Monthly* (March 1997): 73–79; (no author cited), "The Euthanasia War: Last Rights," *The Economist* (June 21, 1997): 19–22; and (in the magazine's usual high octane style of writing) David France, "This Doctor Wants to Help You Die," *New York* (January 13, 1997): 25–29. See also "The Philosopher's Brief," *New York Review of Books* (March 27, 1997): 40–44, and the thoughtful work in Ira Byock, *Dying Well* (New York: Riverhead Books, 1997) and Timothy Quill, *A Midwife Through the Dying Process* (Baltimore, Md.: Johns Hopkins University Press, 1996). Also helpful is a collection of essays in Michael M. Ulmann, ed., *Last Rights: Assisted*

2

The inquiries found in physician-assisted suicide illustrate the patterns of public reason to be explored here: the welcome elasticities of languages, the wide scope of debate over issues and problems, the ways in which discussions continue without obvious points of closure, and the compelling needs to reach provisional agreements about practices that represent the moral and political principles of a political society. These themes introduce the union of theory and practice that must be contained in any complete account of public reason, and they are the main concerns of this book.

A distinction in current philosophy between the rules and tokens of language may provide the most useful way into the discourses of public reason. All languages have semantic and syntactical rules. But these rules cannot provide meanings for the linguistic tokens that are speech acts. The meaning of an utterance is not only a function of the rules of language, but also the intentions of the speaker, the audience, and background factors like levels of understanding, traditions and conventions, social structures, and so on—culture, in short. Linguistic tokens are one of the domains of indeterminacy in language, for there is no reason to think that the meanings of tokens can be precise or durable given the natural instability of the variables that constitute speech acts.[4]

The indeterminacy of language is not much of a problem in ordinary communication. Speakers continually adjust for misunderstandings and breakdowns, revising patterns of speech to accommodate uncertainties and relying on tacit understandings to facilitate communication. Close-knit members of groups are notorious for speaking in economical phrases often impenetrable to outsiders. But communal understandings are local by definition. They cannot resolve indeterminacy in a language that is to extend across disparate communities. The liberal state governs in conditions of pluralism, and so requires a political language that communicates effectively across diverse communities each of which may have its own indige-

---

Suicide and Euthanasia Debated (published jointly by Washington: Ethics and Policy Center, Grand Rapids, Mich., and William E. Erdmans Publishing, 1987).

4. John Searle reviews these elementary points (with devastating effects on some of Derrida's literary theories) in "Literary Theory and Its Discontents," *New Literary History* 25 no. 3 (Summer 1994): 637–667. Habermas's blunter distinctions between a speech act (which attends to the lifeworld) and its setting (the system) allows him to differentiate communicative (oriented to mutual understanding) and strategic (oriented to outcomes) rationality. But he follows the modern (and standard) linguistic perspective in providing dense frameworks and contexts for language usage. In Jürgen Habermas, *The Theory of Communicative Action* (Boston: Beacon Press, 1984). The requirements that actions impose on words is noted (first?) by John Austin in *How to Do Things with Words* (Cambridge: Harvard University Press, 1975).

nous form of communication. The central problem of public reason is to craft a governing language that allows and employs vernacular languages while yet binding into a political system the subcultures constituting the political domain.

The need for a public language is found in the liberal premise that justifications for the state's use of coercive power be accessible to all citizens, and especially to those who are coerced. The language of governance in this moral program must be no less precise than the conditions required to satisfy an action-directive, which are that the action be specified by the words and the directive generally comprehended by the participants. The pragmatic adjustments of ordinary uses of language must be sharpened with a provisional rigor that makes a settlement actionable (in the logical sense) and public in the minimal sense of generally comprehensible.

The standing question is how political languages can help manage differences, and reach settlements enforced by the state, in conditions of strong pluralism. What are the forms of public reasoning that can produce authoritative conclusions and political closure when the society is divided and participants disagree on fundamental matters?

The literatures are dense with alternative ways to answer these questions. What is arguably the most prominent version of public reason today is advanced by John Rawls in *Political Liberalism* and later papers. Rawls's account, working from a social contract model, presents a loose and complex amalgam of (a) top-to-bottom reasoning (from languages that govern the relations we have with one another "down" to the issues and problems that enter public spheres), and (b) the traditions of discourse or open dialogue that seem to represent the leveling powers of politics at its best and worst. But Rawls's theory of public reasoning is strict on the virtues of certain partitions. Public reasoning occurs in a political domain separate from civil society in terms of its own deliberative languages, rules, and reasons. Partisan values are to give way to the political values drawn up from "a political conception of justice" accepted by all reasonable persons, and the outcomes of public reason are conclusions settled within the overlapping consensus that establishes and represents the political domain. This deliberative engagement permits a reciprocal satisfaction of interests among citizens who disagree on profound issues and problems.

The version of public reason I will develop here is different. My arguments rely on a political domain supremely influenced by the values and arguments, and political interests, of the larger society, even as the state is distinct from other social domains by virtue of its orientations to power and collective arrangements. One consequence of accepting lines of influence between public and civil (and uncivil) reasoning is that the shields in liberal thought ensuring merit orderings are abandoned. I argue that the model for public reasoning is not a deliberative ordering of claims framed on a social contract, but rather a mediated conversation among participants open to historical and social dialogues and employing skills of composition.

My controlling assumption is that mediation is the more natural form of political discourse, more deeply embedded in civil languages than the social contract (which, by comparison, seems to be an artifact of Western legal and political theory superimposed on political cultures). In contemporary Western societies the mediator is a familiar figure in contractual breakdowns: the settlement of labor disputes, disagreements over medical care, the advisability of caps on million-dollar salaries in professional sports. But "mediator" is a strikingly generic term, with referential powers in many cultures. Walter Burkert in *Creation of the Sacred* uses the term *mediator* to refer to "the seers, the oracles, the shamans, the medicine men, the rabbis" in ancient Greek culture, those who "know more" and thus can "provide a frame of interpretation for women and men confronted with evil," who "make sense" of texts and experiences by restoring a mental world that has broken down. The mediator in the public reasoning of liberal democracies may do all of these things but also do little more than assist in translating among different languages while using criteria of relevance to guide conversations. These efforts need not include enforcing a contract or even securing an accord among beliefs. The conclusions of what I call *mediated speech acts* are often just fragile and provisional settlements, regarded more accurately as resting places on the endless journey of political talk rather than the destinations suggested by the language of settlements in contract versions of public reason.[5]

---

5. Walter Burkert, *Creation of the Sacred: Tracks of Biology in Early* Relisions (Cambridge: Harvard University Press, 1996), 116–118. See Seyla Benhabib, "Toward a Deliberative Democracy," in Seyla Benhabib, ed., *Democracy and Difference* (Princeton, N.J.: Princeton University Press, 1996), for a treatment congenial with the program I offer here, though also quite different (as will be clear in the text). See also Evan Charney, "Political Liberalism, Deliberative Democracy, and the Public Sphere," *American Political Science Review* 92:1 (March 1998): 97–110 for a helpful discussion. The textual summary of Rawls is drawn from *Political Liberalism* (New York: Columbia University Press, 1993). Benjamin M. Nelson cites the mediation of cultural cues by individuals who present themselves or others as models, and the roles of mediatorial elites in elaborating patterns of thought in *On the Roads to Modernity: Conscience, Science and Civilizations* (Totowa, NJ: Rowman & Littlefield, 1981), especially in Part II.

3

One truth acceptable in all versions of public reason, and indicated again and again by issues such as physician-assisted suicide, is that disputes are possible, and perhaps even common, among reasonable persons in a political system. Persons can have conflicting preferences, interests, understandings of reality (ontologies), and ideologies, any of which can lead to disputes that reach the political domain. The causes of social disputes are multiple. Theorists are inclined to distinguish between rational and material variables.[6] The items constituting dialogue and discourse are typically classified as rational, while a variety of explanatory variables outside the reasoned offerings of agents populate the material category.

Two material considerations are star attractions in social theory. One is structural. Certain social settings can provide explanations for a variety of disputes, usually as we identify rival interests created by the settings.[7] A second is psychological. Various identities or characteristics of persons may represent differences that account for disputes.[8] But the distinctions between the rational and the material begin to dissolve when we realize that another material consideration may be discourse itself. Ideas and their expressions can present a cultural frame that affects perceptions and understandings of experience over historical time, and perhaps structures realities. Put simply, embedded reasons can cause beliefs, and these beliefs can conflict with one another, leading again to political disputes.[9] This explana-

6. See Andrew Mason, *Explaining Political Disagreements* (Cambridge: Cambridge University Press, 1994), for a discussion of these matters. Mason also draws a distinction between political disagreements explainable by the imperfection conception, in which at least one party to the dispute is mistaken, and the contestability conception, in which political terms allow for a variety of different interpretations. Mason goes to develop a hybrid of these two explanations. He allows for the idea of moral truth and error, but denies that disputes are resolvable as a correction of error. He rather defends a version of moral cognitivism in terms of the norms of morality that make rational resolutions of disagreements possible.

7. This is an argument found in unsophisticated Marxism. But note the nuances in Karl Marx and Frederick Engels, *The German Ideology* (New York: International Publishers, 1970).

8. Carol Gilligan, for example, has argued that gender differences explain many disagreements in human experiences: *In a Different Voice: Psychological Theory and Women's Development* (Cambridge: Harvard University Press, 1982). See also Nancy Chodorow, *Feminist Psychoanalytic Theory* (New Haven, Conn.: Yale University Press, 1989).

9. Alasdair MacIntyre, in maintaining that disputes are explainable in terms of inherited moral beliefs that may be incoherent and at odds with contemporary experience, offers an idealism that is opposed to Marx's materialism, though as I say in the text I am not convinced that these terms are helpful any longer in drawing distinctions among social theories. Inspect *After Virtue: A Study in Moral Theory* (Notre Dame, Ind.: University of Notre Dame Press, 1981), and, for versions of relativity and resolution, *Whose Justice, Which Rationality?* (Notre Dame, Ind.: University of Notre Dame Press, 1988).

tion requires that we regard rational considerations as types of material explanations, an integration of causal types accommodated by reductionist sympathies.

Why disagreements persist is not the same as why they occur. Material origins of disputes are causal, and may be generalizable to some degree across political societies. But the prolongation of disputes, their tractable or intractable natures, may be tied to regimes and be eminently contextual. An authoritarian state may admit no intractable disputes, resolving all political differences with effective force. A theistic state, governed by truth, may regard all disputes as occasioned by error on the part of some or all of the disputants. Corrective mechanisms follow the imposition of a theory of truth. In liberal regimes, however, the acceptance of pluralism rules out simple force and a controlling truth as available options. A language of public reason must prevail.[10] The contestable view is that this language admits multiple reasonable interpretations, which leads to the chronic presence and intractability of political disputes. But contestability may not be a product simply of language, but of a political setting that resists conclusions. The powers of regimes to activate or suppress the elastic possibilities of terms are important variables in determining whether language is contestable. Is the relationship between language and political disagreement a rational or a materialist explanation on this account of contestability?

The problem is that we do not have an adequate account of rational and material considerations that will allow us to ponder how to integrate them. The liberal reluctance to explore background variables in adjudicating disputes may be based on a separation between the rational and the material that needs to be abandoned rather than closed with an integrated model. But the capacities of governing terms in liberalism to admit competing reasonable interpretations is undeniable, whether explained in terms of rational or material considerations, some fusion of the considerations, or an abandonment of distinctions between the two. The simplest and perhaps unavoidable starting point for characterizing political disputes is that concepts and principles are clusters of various indicators that (a) may be rationally arranged in different priority orderings, and (b) constitute an open set that may be extended, contracted, or redefined in rational ways.[11]

Provisional distinctions between material and rational variables can be arranged more successfully on a larger canvas. All liberal models of the

10. John Rawls is persuasive on this point, in *Political Liberalism*, Lecture VI.
11. Mason, in *Explaining Political Disagreements*, describes these differences. Persons can disagree on the ordering and emphasis of indicators in a term, or (more broadly) contest the sense and reference of the term itself.

state must address two influential critiques. One is represented by an assignment of priority to background conditions (such as economic structures). This line maintains that any adequate account of the state must attend to material origins in the establishment and interpretation of governing principles, and usually concludes with the view that liberalism neglects structures in its preoccupations with the surface forms of institutional arrangements. The second line is critical of rational possibilities because political languages are open to rival and reasonable interpretations. On this theory rational variables must be indeterminate in specifying which actions are to dominate or exclude others. One extreme consequence is the effective elimination of rules and principles as governing languages.

Evidence for both lines of theory is abundant in contemporary social practices. The effects of background conditions and the indeterminacy of governing languages are commonplace in a modern world accustomed to the influence of social/economic structures and multicultural experiences in political settings. But the theoretical lines yield mutually independent critiques of liberal theory. The problems identified in the second theory, for example, cannot be resolved with a settlement of the problems raised by background conditions. The neo-Marxist claim that capital influences the formation, uses, and perhaps meanings of rules and principles is plausible. Also plausible is the critique that liberal partitions between political discourses and economic conditions are porous. Some forms of economic equality may even be required for political justice. But unless one maintains that background conditions are deterministic in all important respects, halting problems in discourse still occur even if social conditions are shaped into acceptable forms. A social order that meets the background conditions for adequate political discourses will still have to address indeterminacy in public reason. Nor, to turn the theoretical lines in the opposite direction, will a language crafted somehow for closure cancel with those powers alone the effects of background structures.

An acceptance of indeterminacy in language admittedly enlarges the possibilities of background influences (if, that is, one subscribes to them in the first place). Critical legal studies, for example, is organized by two sets of arguments. One set is developed on the proposition that legal texts are elastic, which permits a variety of interpretations that are each consistent with the law but inconsistent with one another. The second set offers arguments that are more complex and diffuse. They assert various relationships between interpretation and distributions of power and interests. The latter arguments depend (to some degree) on an acceptance of the former. But a measure of independence nevertheless distinguishes the two arguments.

One, acceptance of open or elastic languages does not require an acceptance of background influences of any particular form or in general. Two, therapy for one set of problems (iniquitous background influences, indeterminate languages) is not necessarily therapy for the other set. Again, the indeterminacy of language may not raise problems of communication in a range of background conditions, in particular the natural consensus found in cohesive groups. But the liberal mission to formulate a rational language of governance that can resolve or manage differences in conditions of pluralism is bound to fail if language cannot provide political closure, no matter what the sources of these differences may be.[12]

4

John Rawls lists some of the main explanations for why individuals reach different conclusions in the exercise of judgment. Among these are conflicting and complex evidence, different weights that might reasonably be assigned to rational considerations, the indeterminacy of our concepts, the effects of our total experience on judgments, the existence of rival normative considerations, and the need for forced choice among several cherished values. On these conditions and possibilities even the most conscientious persons, exercising their full rational powers, may not arrive at the same conclusions.[13]

There is little doubt that divergent judgments can be explained in terms of such "burdens of judgment," including especially the unreasonable assignments we give to evidence in the face of its incompleteness, inconsistency, and resistance to simplifying efforts. Evidence seems typically difficult and complex, in the data needed in mundane judgments and, especially, in supporting those judgments that range over the natural heterogeneity of even a restricted set of human experiences. But another

12. The standard references on contestability are W. B. Gallie, "Essentially Contested Concepts," *Proceedings of the Aristotelian Society* vol. 56 (1955), 167–198; William Connolly, *The Terms of Political Discourse* (Princeton, N.J.: Princeton University Press, 1993); and John Gray, "On the Contestability of Social and Political Concepts," *Political Theory* 5 (1977), 331–348. If political principles are open to rival and reasonable interpretations they cannot be used, in Rawls's phrase, "to assign basic rights and duties and to determine the division of social benefits" in the political society, at least not without some assistance. In *A Theory of Justice* (Cambridge: Harvard University Press, 1971), 11. For a helpful exposition of critical legal studies, see Mark Tushnet, "Critical Legal Studies: An Introduction to Its Origins and Underpinnings," *Journal of Legal Education* 36 (1986): 505–517, and the survey and critique in Andrew Altman, *Critical Legal Studies: A Liberal Critique* (Princeton, N.J.: Princeton University Press, 1989).

13. Rawls, *Political Liberalism*, Lecture 11, section 2.

source of divergent judgments is the tendency of theory to yield rival explanatory and interpretive frameworks in reasoning. In social inquiry these frameworks can be the products of a theory not fully determined by data, but they also arise from methodological disputes over proper evidence. Whether, for example, a study should rely on written documents, behavior, utterances, background factors like demographic data, and/or social structures contributes to differences in judgment. Another divisive influence on judgment is the set of background items that funnel into interpretations of experience. Conflicts among identities, including sect, race, religion, nationality, can bring competing attitudes, preferences, interests, and other variables into judgments. Given that individuals also have rival ontologies (for whatever reason), and these contrasting theories of reality can yield radically different views on the uses and meanings of both evidence and theory, it is a marvel that any convergence is found in the conclusions that individuals reach in the exercise of judgments.

In any list of explanations for divergent judgments, however, the indeterminacy of governing vocabularies must be stressed, even granted that this indeterminacy is activated by other considerations. It is not just that our concepts can be elastic and multiple in helping us arrive at judgments, but also that the guiding languages that constrain our choices—the principles that restrict and force choice in political arenas—contain the possibilities of rival interpretations that may be selectively appropriated for partisan uses even among native speakers. One might even speculate that the elasticity of political languages in liberal regimes, given that they are offered as brakes on divergent actions, accelerate the tendencies of individuals to arrive at different judgments as the braking systems so easily fail.

The capacities of languages to allow rival interpretations are recorded at foundational levels in legal and political theory. John Gray has argued that a two-stage process cripples liberalism: principles are indeterminate due to the open texture of their central concepts, and this indeterminacy invites incommensurable values into the liberal project.[14]

Look first at the minimum principle in all liberal states, even those that begin and end with the principle. A liberal political domain, whatever else it does, must protect the lives and physical well-being of its members, pri-

14. John Gray, *Post-Liberalism: Studies in Political Thought* (London: Routledge, 1993); "Agonistic Liberalism," *Social Philosophy and Policy* 12 (1995): 111–135, and *Liberalisms: Essays in Political Philosophy* (London: Routledge, 1989). This section of the text—on political principles—parallels, and perhaps follows, Gray's contributions in these cited works. Also J. Raz, *The Morality of Freedom* (Oxford: Clarendon Press, 1986) and his "Multiculturalism: A Liberal Perspective," *Dissent* 41 (Winter 1994): 17–79.

marily by sanctions against physical assaults. The logic is transparent. A political philosophy that begins with a celebration of persons and their communities, that originates in the thought that individual persons are the most important and real items in experience, is bound to ensure the physical integrity and existence of its citizens. The methods and practices that are effective in doing this are varied and controversial. But a *harm* thesis must be a part of any liberal conception of the political.[15]

Two additional principles, and their interpretations, are found in all liberal political domains. One is liberty. The other is equality. The presence of these two principles is hardly surprising. Together they state the conditions of individualism. Liberal persons have natural liberty and are generally regarded as moral equals. A governing arrangement without some robust form of liberty would be contrary to liberal starting points and ideals. Similarly, equality is a first principle that can be amended only on overriding arguments. Equality of opportunity is typically the first amendment of equality. It urges the realization of natural talents, with the expected inequalities of outcome, as a fulfillment of both individualism and social utility.

The underlying principle of harm, and the more explicit principles of liberty conjoined with various iterations and emendations of equality, are the main principles in the liberal state. The governing authority of these languages is typically drawn from the consent of member communities. The dominant contractual explanation of the liberal state is that it is an artifact resulting from an agreement. The agreement is to establish relatively

15. The obligatory references here on libertarian theory are John Stuart Mill's *On Liberty* (Indianapolis, Ind.: Hackett Publishing Company, 1978) and Robert Nozick's *Anarchy, State, and Utopia* (New York: Basic Books, 1974). All libertarian theories are inclined to start and stop with the role of the state in protecting individuals from physical assault, though a welfare state may be seen as a logical result of libertarian premises and arguments. See, for example, James P. Sterba's "From Liberty to Equality," in Sterba, ed., *Morality in Practice*, 4th ed. (Belmont, Calif.: Wadsworth, 1994), for an argument that the celebration of liberty in a libertarian state leads to a universal right to welfare and that the recognition of this right leads to an equalization of resources characteristic of a socialist state. Sterba discusses (in one argument) the possibility that rational imperatives require the wealthy to provide social welfare to the desperate poor as a way of "buying" security against the attacks (and forced redistributions) sure to follow from those in extreme poverty. The problem with this assertion of self-interested generosity is that too often it is false: the powerful can effectively maintain dominance over the less well off without losing sleep over organized attacks on their security. Also, since power can take the form of co-optation, the poor may be deluded into thinking that radical inequalities may really be in their best "systemic" interests. On some of the subtleties of power, see Russell Hardin. for example, in *One for All: The Logic of Group Conflict* (Princeton, N.J.: Princeton University Press, 1995), especially Chapter 2. Liberal theories usually assign large responsibilities to the state up front, but do not (contrary to rumors) abandon the primal state functions of protecting persons from physical assaults.

coordinated relations among individuals and communities who may be irrevocably opposed to one another on all other understandings of a good and proper life, but find it mutually advantageous to construct a political domain to adjudicate their differences.

The book values of liberal vocabularies can be initially set by displaying the ease with which these three dominant principles permit multiple interpretations. The regulation of harm-to-another, the minimum condition in even the sparest libertarian state, is notoriously open-textured. Mill offers several prominent considerations to limit the governing scope of the state. These include the now widely distributed arguments that the evils of constraint far outweigh errors made by individuals as final judges of their own actions, that individuals will be punished by the consequences of their wrongdoing through social censure without the intervention of law, and that the interference of the public will likely be in error when regarding purely personal conduct. Mill means to limit the state severely with these arguments and recognize a zone of unexceptional state regulation created by the need to prevent harm in the civil society.[16]

The core idea in libertarianism is that individuals are free and rational creatures who can, on the whole, live their lives in reasonable coordination with each other. When this natural equilibrium breaks down, when persons harm one another, then the same impulses that deny the advisability of state regulation now summon it to restore the desired balance. Individuals are so important that liberties of thought, expression, of tastes and pursuits, of plan of life, and of association must be respected by a minimal state that governs only to prevent individuals from harming each other.

Harm for Mill is a necessary, not a sufficient condition, for state regulation. Many forms of harm in human societies—broken hearts, failed vocations, market dislocations—are not Mill's concerns. The harm that justifies government regulation for Mill is that which affects interests that should be considered rights.[17] The paradigmatic form of harm for all followers of the libertarian tradition is the direct and physical harm represented by assaults and homicides. The libertarian state has historically been charged with the protection of its citizens and their property from attacks, and little else.[18]

But it is not clear why state regulation must be indifferent to other harms even on libertarian theories of the state. Offensive actions, especially

16. *On Liberty*, Chapter IV, primarily.
17. *On Liberty*, Chapter V.
18. Nozick, *Anarchy, State, and Utopia* for a well-known defense of these limits.

those that verbally and graphically attack beliefs and status, can be as harmful (on some views) as physical assaults. Pornography, for example, can be regarded as an assault on all women (as individuals categorized by gender) that is both intrinsically harmful because defamatory and causally harmful in encouraging physical abuse of women.[19] Insults to deeply held beliefs, especially religious convictions, are regarded by victims as at least occasionally worse than physical assaults. Hate speech, for example, can be gravely harmful.[20] Nor is it always a settled matter that all physical assaults are harms that the state should regulate. Euthanasia and physician-assisted suicide may be defined as necessary goods in the context of Western medical treatment. There is not even a widespread agreement currently on the identification of *another* in a "harm to another" expression of Mill's thesis. Abortion is one extreme case of a dispute in which the participants on either side may all subscribe to the harm thesis but not agree on whether there is "another" there in pregnancy to be harmed by an abortion.

An absence of consensus on the scope of the sentient community also complicates disputes over care of badly damaged individuals in a variety of medical practices, in areas of animal rights, and in concerns for the potential persons in future generations. Then there are the influential nonlibertarian traditions that maintain that market disequilibria are among the more dreadful harms, and that social conditions can structure reality and distort "free" choices. Obviously these critical perspectives will offer a radically different understanding of harm than the one found in Mill's libertarianism.[21] The harm thesis, on the surface a minimal and noncontroversial principle of governance, is in fact an open-ended principle that invites a wide range of interpretive disputes.

A similar pattern of contentious interpretation is also found in the other two principles of liberal governance. Liberty, a first principle in many liberal theories of the state, is divisible along two axes. One is negative versus

19. Rosemarie Tong, "Feminism, Pornography and Censorship," *Social Theory and Practice* 8 no. 1 (Winter 1982): 1–17. For the more controversial suggestion that the Fourteenth Amendment ought to be used to restrict free speech in areas of pornography, see Catherine MacKinnon's *Only Words* (Cambridge: Harvard University Press, 1993). See also Judith Butler, *Excitable Speech* (New York: Routledge, 1997).

20. Kent Greenawalt, "Insults and Epithets: Are They Protected Speech?" *Rutgers Law Review*. 42 no. 2 (Winter 1990): 287–307. See also Mara J. Matsuda, Charles R. Lawrence, Richard Delgado, and Kimberle William Crenshaw, *Words That Wound* (Boulder, Colo.: Westview Press, 1997).

21. Mill is aware of these problems of interpretation. See, for example, *The Subjection of Women*.

positive.[22] As every beginning student of political theory knows, negative liberty informs the shields against the state and others that permit those freedoms that are central to classical liberalism. Positive liberty invites the state (and others) to provide those conditions in the absence of which freedom cannot be exercised. The first type of liberty favors a minimal state, the second an interventionist state. The second axis is formed by another pair of poles: liberty as a general good pursued in some formal arrangement, and as a power to act. The first permits a maximum of freedom for all individuals in a formal equilibrium governed by certain rules (such as Robert's Rules of Order). The second, as the power to act in certain ways, is typically not maximized but traded off against other forms of free actions. The first liberty is desirable for its own sake, but may still be selected later than other goods (the means for economic survival, for example). The second is desirable only on an inspection of what others are using their power to do.[23] A rational choice of liberties to act must always be a balance of opportunities and denials. Some basic liberties are even in a zero-sum relationship with each other. To the student of politics, the question is more immediate and uncomfortable: Which of these (and other) senses of liberty meets tests of rational governance and justice?

Equal opportunity fares no better in producing a single or dominant interpretation. Among the many interpretations of this principle, two easily demonstrate the point: One is fair competition, the other equal access. Equal opportunity in the first sense is satisfied if individuals are given the chance to compete for desirable goods or positions. If equal opportunity is interpreted as equal access, however, fair competition may not satisfy the principle. An individual's talents or skills may consistently exclude her from competitive rewards. A social practice of periodic and guaranteed access to rewards may be needed in this second sense of equal opportunity. Rotation, for example, can lead to a balanced distribution of goods and positions not even remotely possible on a fair competition interpretation of equal opportunity. Which sense of equal opportunity is more just?[24]

22. A distinction attributed originally to Isaiah Berlin in *Two Concepts of Liberty* (Oxford: Clarendon Press, 1958). There are impressive efforts in the literature to collapse this distinction, e.g., Gerald MacCallum's "Negative and Positive Freedom," *Philosophical Review* 76 no. 3 (July 1967): 312–334.

23. H. L. A. Hart, "Rawls on Liberty and Its Priority," in Norman Daniels, ed., *Reading Rawls* (New York: Basic Books, 1974).

24. These points are still argued best in Douglas Rae's *Equalities* (Cambridge: Harvard University Press, 1981).

5

Coherence accounts of political languages call attention to distinctions between terms that seem to be in our power, bending according to the points that speakers intend to make with them, and certain empty or formal terms that seem more nearly to constrain the speaker because of their positions in language. In the latter category are found procedural limits that are to check the powers of the state in liberal democracies. These brakes do not depend on principles, but on rules of languages and perhaps discourses. They may be found only after a long conversation about their meanings, but if they cannot be found at all in any way then the constraints on power that they are to provide do not occur. It is an easy concession to say that such limits can be found. But they are not the usual suspects.

It may seem that the logical or formal standing of some terms is a natural shield from partisan control. A requirement, for example, that a law must be standing and general (one of Locke's provisions) would appear to be an adequate protection against capricious and arbitrary governing. But the shield works only if there are fixed, or essential, or at least resistant definitions of "standing" or "general." Suppose that a valid law is passed and repealed on successive days. Does this action violate "standing" requirements? Whether a law is standing varies with any of several conventions. "Generality" is similarly open. The only clear exclusion from "general" laws would seem to be proper names. But the scope of any general rule is a function of definition and interpretation. Laws may be valid in any of several political jurisdictions that limit generality to identifiable localities. Laws also are typically general to class or family resemblance items, such as age, condition, qualifications, and so on, of the law's subjects. Because these criteria and conventions can oppose one another, the use of "standing" and "general" is a matter of selecting some meanings over others, and so is contestable.

Opening formal restrictions to variable interpretation is an important qualification on the stability of government. Such restrictions are easier to identify and so are harder to frame as partisan. They depend on a logic that is more nearly resistant to rival interpretations. But even when the language is firmer in setting out limits the provisions may still allow discretion in use. Ex post facto laws and double jeopardy, for example, are contested and manipulated in practice. Some laws are retroactive for good reasons, and crimes may be broken down and redescribed for "second" indictments and trial, or shifted intact to a different law that effectively tries the same infraction again.[25] Jurisdictional assignments are excellent case studies of spatial and functional categories that are open to partisan use. A separation of powers and the assignment of political cases to a venue of governing can be an effective check on the state. But the spectacle of political disputes over jurisdictional assignments is also well known. Control over the definition of a political case, with subsequent direction over where it is to be resolved, is an important political influence on jurisdictional constraints. Procedural or formal checks in politics seem to be as open to interpretive variance as governing concepts and principles are.

Even reasonably stable languages, those, for example, based on time (ex post facto stipulations) or space (jurisdictional specifications), may still be interpreted, and manipulated, for partisan purposes. The burden is at once intriguing and considerable. Reason must prevent the state from devolving to anarchy or one of many versions of nihilism while accepting the interpretive variability of governing languages along multiple axes of discourse. This task requires the identification of at least provisional points of rational closure that allow the coercive powers of reason to dominate interpretation.

The instability of terms exhibited as one shifts from one level of a principle to another, or across linguistic and social domains, also seems typical in the rational derivation and use of political principles. It requires no intuitive leap of faith to believe that rational persons in Rawls's original position (OP), for example, can agree on both the principles of justice they are said to agree on, and on a lexical ordering of the principles. Given the description of the original position, with both liberty and equality built into its conditions, it would be counterintuitive to expect a radically different

25. George Fletcher has pointed out that two serial trials in the United States now circumvent prohibitions of double jeopardy: acquittal on criminal charges, for example, leads to a tort action for the same offense (as with O. J. Simpson and Bernhard Goetz); and a not-guilty verdict in a state criminal court still permits a federal trial on violation of civil rights for the same actions (a tactic used in the second prosecution of the police officers who beat Rodney King and on several occasions by federal prosecutors during the 1960s in the South for racial crimes). In "Justice for All, Twice," *New York Times* (April 24, 1996). For the record, even the consent basis of the liberal state is open to critical interpretation. Studies of serial selves indicate that individuals can agree to one thing at one time and in one set of circumstances, and to another thing at a different time or in different circumstances. Examine the papers in Jon Elster, ed., *The Multiple Self* (Cambridge: Cambridge University Press, 1986). The influences of conditions on consent vary in importance and meaning almost from one social theory to another (from Mill to Marx, in one extreme contrast). It should come as no surprise that consent can also be the subject, rather than the resolving instrument, of disputes. It should also be no surprise that tacit consent has been a surrogate for full and satisfactory consent since Plato's *Crito*. Locke had the temerity to allow legitimacy for governments *worthy* of consent, meaning those that rule in accord with natural law.

set of selections.[26] But if different interpretations of the principles were mapped back into the selection set, it is not clear what the "right" choices would be. Nothing at an impartial level of reasoning favors restricted or expansive senses of harm, negative or positive liberty, fair competition or equal access. *These* choices can only be made when additional empirical content is introduced behind the veil of ignorance, for the different interpretations speak to particular not general interests. Absent knowledge of talents, for example—a famous condition in OP choice—and rational (and even reasonable) persons cannot settle on the advisability of choosing one interpretation over others.

The belief in liberal thought that deeper interests cut across all human differences, establishing a kind of property that all humans share qua human, *and* that these interests can be discovered with devices like an "original position" of choice, may have to give way to another, harder truth. There may be no interest that can be generalized across disparate regions, nothing that is free of fundamental differences. And if this chasm holds, then the only formal or hypothetical agreements on justice may be at the most general level possible and only on condition that affinities in these areas not be known to the individuals making choices. The harder truth undermines the social contract. Map the separate and rival understandings of human experiences back into the conditions of choice and no agreement is possible. Keep the differences out with a device like the veil of ignorance and expect acrimonious disputes when the veil is lifted.

These observations are neither original nor surprising. Nor are they confined to contract theory. They address, and cripple, all efforts in liberal theory to ground justice in formal or objective conditions. They also undermine principles of reason as impartial governors of individuals and their relations to one another. The observations do not deny that persons can agree on the meanings of political terms. They do indicate that the agreements cannot be explained by the governing powers of the terms to mandate sense or reference.

6

The breakdowns in political languages identified here occur in liberal practices. The obvious and interesting problem is whether the political setting for indeterminacy can be given a determinate definition. Defining any

26. Remember that OP people are all equal to one another and free to select governing principles. It is not surprising that freedom and iterations of equality find their way from the selection mechanisms through the veil of ignorance to distributive arrangements.

political term is difficult for several reasons. But *liberalism* is an especially troublesome concept. So many versions of this term can now be identified that a complete definition (in the traditional sense of necessary and sufficient conditions) is an unlikely contribution. David Johnston, for example, identifies three major contemporary forms of liberal political theory, which he labels rights-based liberalism, perfectionist liberalism, and political liberalism.[27] Other versions of liberalism, based on different sets of distinctions, are possible and support the thought that defining the term may itself present a halting problem.[28]

A more unsettling possibility is that more than one concept may be present in the term, with the consequence that all definitions expand in multiple directions along many axes of theory. The risk in this type of conceptual pluralism is that definitions are not critically examined, and the possibility of common foundations is dismissed prematurely. The main business here is with political liberalism. But the arguments are focused on certain features of liberalism—concepts of public reason, the person, coercion and liberty leading the list—that are general to different forms of liberal theory. In an odd way these deeper features of liberalism must be retrieved to explore the implications of multiple concepts. The retrieval action is unintelligible if there is no single manageable account of liberalism to begin the discussions.

Lexical definitions are usually safe starting points. Liberalism is an arrangement known for a kind of mythic generosity, dutifully noted in all dictionaries. The word *liberal* is usually defined by phrases that include "following policies or laws that favor the freedom of individuals to act or express themselves in a manner of their own choosing," "tolerant of the ideas or behavior of others," "bountiful," "an emancipation from convention, tradition or dogma," and (perhaps more revealing) favoring "nonrevolutionary progress and reform." If the definitions found in dictionaries

27. David Johnston, *The Idea of a Liberal Theory* (Princeton, N.J.: Princeton University Press, 1994).

28. A helpful discussion is in Steven Kautz, *Liberalism and Community* (Ithaca, N.Y.: Cornell University Press, 1995), J. Donald Moon, *Constructing Community: Moral Pluralism and Tragic Conflict* (Princeton, N.J.: Princeton University Press, 1993), and the treatment of Habermas and deliberative democracy by Simone Chambers in *Reasonable Democracy* (Ithaca, N.Y.: Cornell University Press, 1996). Fortunately, my arguments here are not in a transactional mode of dialogue, meaning that I am not in a productive or even polite conversation with other theorists over the meaning of liberalism and do not provide a survey of contemporary liberal theory. I am engaged in a simpler task, which is to make a set of arguments that depend on several excellent theoretical literatures that are not brought explicitly into the text for the usual inspections and emendations.

controlled our understandings of human experience most of us would be considered liberal in at least some of these senses.

But dictionaries cannot control the current instabilities of political terms, which is not surprising given the heterogeneous conditions and multiple understandings of truth that modernity encourages. All sufficient definitions of liberalism may have to be stipulative, meaning that they can only clarify particular arguments and never extend to all political theories labeled as liberal. Early liberals, for example, were far more concerned with the promotion of virtue, tradition, moral education, and moral personality than was allowed for in later "minimalist" versions of liberalism.[29] But a skeletal definition of liberalism can be provided that is unaffected by these important jurisdictional disputes. The priority of persons, for example, is central to all versions of liberalism. One might regard it as a necessary condition of the modern liberal state. From its acceptance follow other properties of liberalism, including the liberal principle (LP) that Richard Flathman has proposed: "It is a prima facie good for persons to form, act on, and to satisfy and achieve desires and interests, objectives and purposes."[30]

A parochial view of the liberal state can be expressed with four minimal propositions.[31] First, and a contemporary view that is much in dispute, the liberal state rests on some version of the proposition that reasonably empty procedures dominate claims for the good, or the values representing (and perhaps promoted by) the state are appropriate for managing the political domain and not the private activities of members of the political system. This means that rules, principles, and *political* norms are the primary influences in governance, not conceptions of the good life for individuals and communities. Second, and in part a consequence of the first proposition, the state in liberalism is to be reasonably distinct from other institutions and practices. Unlike the classical assumptions of fusion between state and society, with resulting distributions of political authority throughout social practices, the liberal political domain is in some way different from the communities it houses, accommodates, and at times governs. The thought

29. Gottfried Dietz, *Liberalism Proper and Proper Liberalism* (Baltimore, Md.: Johns Hopkins University Press, 1985).

30. In Richard Flathman, *Toward a Liberalism* (Ithaca, N.Y.: Cornell University Press, 1989), p. 6, and throughout the essays collected in the book.

31. I am influenced in this stipulative sketch by Alasdair MacIntyre's *After Virtue* and *Whose Justice? Which Rationality?*, and by Michael Sandel's *Liberalism and the Limits of Justice* (Cambridge: Harvard University Press, 1982). Contrast the sketch with John Gray's four defining features of liberalism: (a) moral or normative individualism, (b) universalism, (c) meliorism, and (d) egalitarianism (as he maps these four features into the characteristics of civil society). In *Post-Liberalism: Studies in Political Thought.*

here is that although the state may be provided with much of its identity by its constitutive communities, it cannot simply be the set of these communities. It is an institution or practice with distinct means and purposes.

A separate political sphere is the natural product of religious and capitalistic demands. Religious communities have insisted (at various historical times) on separations between church and state in order to ensure religious freedoms and to resist the corruptions of the secular world. Capitalism is thought to require markets independent of the state on theories of mutual hostility between state and economy (except of course for those caretaking functions that the state has always performed for markets, such as guaranteeing property rights and security of exchanges). Liberal partitions also are generated by the restricted epistemology required of the state when members disagree at foundational levels. A variety of plausible claims to truth prohibits the liberal state from endorsing any single overriding truth. The political domain in this way is distinct from its member communities, any of which can subscribe to universal truths.

One additional criterion frequently offered in liberal theory to demarcate the state from other institutions is force: a preponderance of coercion or power as the defining means of the state. All of the major contract theorists define the state in terms of an authority created by consent, and some form of physical force as the implementing device to ensure this authority. Hobbes regarded the threat of violent death as the only credible guarantee of reciprocity in human societies. For Max Weber the state was that social unit possessing a monopoly of physical force in a given territory. Recent definitions of the state or political system have stressed state functions, for example the authoritative allocation of values for the larger society, or state structures that are authoritative for individual and group actions. In all of these theories the state is the directive or controlling power in society, the most authoritative power, the most general power, and always the state is characterized by the ownership and use of dominant physical force.[32]

Third, the individual person is liberal theory is the source of meaning

32. The relevant citations for these statements on the concept of the modern state include Max Weber, *Political Writings* (Cambridge: Cambridge University Press, 1994); David Easton, *The Political System: An Inquiry into the State of Political Science* (New York: Knopf, 1953); Harry Eckstein, "Authority Patterns: A Structural Basis for Political Inquiry," *American Political Science Review* 67 (1973): 1142–1161; and my own (more skeptical) "The Structure of 'Politics,'" *American Political Science Review* 72 (September 1978): 859–870. William Galston suggests that the liberal state is characterized (in part) by the reluctance to use moral coercion in *Liberal Purposes* (Cambridge: Cambridge University Press, 1991); 298. I remain the skeptic here. My reading of liberal theory and recent history provides neither theoretical arguments nor empirical evidence to support this proposal. The adversarial dimensions of the political are drawn up (too strongly, I think) in terms of enmity among collectives by Carl

and value in human experience. In both classical and medieval political thought the group is the primary unit of analysis. Individuals are residual categories, usually granted no independent status, and are often no more than artificial derivatives from collective nouns. In the contract theories of the seventeenth and eighteenth centuries, and in the utilitarian theories of the nineteenth and twentieth centuries, the individual has primacy as the rational origin of governing rules and principles. These individuals may be no more than subjects once the transfer of authority is effected (as was the case in Hobbes's theories in *Leviathan*, and arguably is the case in the current political system in Britain). But the political order is still regarded as a derivative of individuals, largely by means of the vehicle of consent, and communities in general are regarded as collections of individuals from whom social predicates are derived.[33]

Fourth, and arguably the crucial feature of a liberal state, is the restrained impartiality that follows a toleration of legitimate diversity. The historical ground of this assignment has been undermined by scholars who have effectively argued that the starting versions of liberalism, in particular the social contract, were partial to white males who owned property and to the versions of the good that represented the interests of this group. These arguments are valid, supported by historical data.[34] But biased origins obviously do not preclude later objectivity. It is one of the serendipitous virtues of liberal dialogues that they extend powerfully to groups and ways of life not originally included in the political and moral framework. It is because of the absence of natural closure for liberal categories that intellectual disputes occur over the possibilities of a neutral state and the scope of the social contract in the modern world.

Liberalism, like all political philosophies, has values and purposes. It stresses individual primacy and calculative rationality, the importance of peace and order over violence and chaos, the political advantages of liberty and equality, and a set of primary goods that express both the solitary and communal status of individual experiences. But the liberal state cannot govern on strong or constraining moral goods if it is to respect pluralism in

---

Schmidt in, for example, *The Concept of the Political*, translated by George Schwab (Chicago: University of Chicago Press, 1996).

33. It is appropriate that one of the true champions of methodological individualism as a foundation for understanding wholes also wrote the definitive ideological tract against the holistic political society: Karl Popper, *The Open Society and Its Enemies* (Princeton, N.J.: Princeton University Press, 1950).

34. For example, Carol Pateman, *The Sexual Contract* (Stanford, Calif.: Stanford University Press, 1988).

moral and religious practices. The state, in the once fashionable phrase, must be a reasonably empty political vessel in order to allow disputes over the good to enter public space. In some ways this understanding of a state without a dominant moral purpose is similar to a conception of a minimal state on free market needs. Both sets of arguments maintain that the practices in question (moral and religious as well as economic) can flourish only in the absence of a state that enforces a strong and particular point of view.

It is helpful to segregate five critiques of liberalism that address parts of this sketch. One is concerned to document the bias of liberal constructions (like Rawls's "original position") by pointing out distortions. This first line of criticism usually offers a reconstruction of impartiality that corrects for flaws and omissions.[35] The second critique stresses the importance of difference over sameness, with the result that the core liberal axiom of treating like cases alike gives way to the more practical rule of treating unlike cases in unlike fashion. The conversations here follow some acceptance of liberal rules and principles, and typically address which groups and grievances are to be taken seriously and which of the serious claims are to be given priority, where membership criteria are to be fixed, and the strategies (e.g., affirmative action policies) that best meet the needs of different groups. Impartiality in this critical perspective is abandoned in favor of a modulated partiality.[36]

The third critique, one that might be labeled undermining, dismisses the terms that define liberalism by giving priority to group or collective nouns. This critique replaces liberalism with holistic forms of social organization.[37] The fourth critique (loosely defined) asserts that liberalism is contradictory at more or less basic levels because its guiding languages rely on categories in politics that cannot be packaged consistently. The modern classic here of course is Arrow's theorem. The most interesting recent entries are proposals that (a) separate distributive and identity politics, and (b) maintain that justice in the former may be inconsistent with justice in the latter. In the simplest sense, a just redistribution of goods may require the denial of distinctions that are vital to the recognition of groups.[38]

The fifth critique elaborates the general liberal program with additional

35. Susan Okin, for example, lists the items in Rawls's OP that reinforce inequality for women in *Justice, Gender and the Family* (New York: Basic Books, 1989).

36. Iris Young develops this critique in *Justice and the Politics of Difference* (Princeton, N.J.: Princeton University Press, 1990).

37. Will Kymlicka begins along this road (but only for a short distance) with his versions of collective rights in *Liberalism, Community and Culture* (Oxford: Oxford University Press, 1989).

38. Kymlicka also offers thoughtful arguments in *Multicultural Citizenship* (New York: Clarendon Press, 1995). See also the essays in Ian Shapiro and Will Kymlicka, eds., *Ethnicity*

content and structure. Michael Sandel, initiator of the most influential version of communitarianism, distinguishes "procedural liberalism" from "formative republicanism." He assigns many of the contestable features of liberalism to the former, including the neutral standing of the state over the menu of choices for the good life. Formative republicanism certifies a state that nurtures norms and ideals required for liberal democracy.[39] Other republican theories introduce elaborate institutional machinery to the liberal mission.[40] This line of criticism is constructive and meliorative (in the best traditions of dictionary versions of liberalism), accepting the basic moral conditions of liberal thought while amending its provisions to more workable forms. The work here is in the spirit if not the palpable form of this fifth approach to liberal practices, using the minimal sketch of liberalism as scaffolding for revisions that alter our understandings of liberal governance.

7

No location found within the basic orientations of liberalism can employ an alternative (sixth) critique. Elaborate traditions of realist philosophy and social thought reject liberalism on the grounds that it ignores the fixed and universal reality that provides truth in public (and sometimes private) life. Appeals to these more basic accounts of experience, however, are not available to manage rival interpretations of governing languages. A satisfactory account of "reality" can start with the rudiments of experience, but also must include at some point the range over which individuals may differ on the scope and content of the real.

The failure of ontology to provide a text to order or merge radical differences in beliefs, or adjudicate the disagreements that sometimes follow them, is demonstrated in any mapping of cognitive foundations.[41] The first

---

and Group Rights (New York: New York University Press, 1997). See also Nancy Fraser, *Unruly Practices: Power, Discourse and Gender in Contemporary Social Theory* (Minneapolis: University of Minnesota Press, 1989). Seyla Benhabib discusses many of these issues and arguments in *Situating the Self* (New York: Routledge, 1992).

39. *Liberalism and the Limits of Justice* and, for the discussion of procedural liberalism and formative republicanism, *Democracy's Discontent* (Cambridge: Harvard University Press, 1996).

40. See Ian Shapiro, for example, in *Democracy's Place* (Ithaca, N.Y.: Cornell University Press, 1996).

41. Edward M. Hundert summarizes work from Descartes through Piaget (and even more recent cognitive psychology and neuroscience) that persuasively draws up such a view of ordinary reality. In *Philosophy, Psychiatry, and Neuroscience* (Oxford: Clarendon Press, 1989).

entry in such a map is the thought that individuals are in some way distinct from the world they experience. Abundant empirical evidence exists to suggest that individuals acquire identity early in childhood by experiencing an objective world that resists their intentions. It is a curious and melancholy fact of human experience that psychokinesis seems real for loved infants for a time, inasmuch as their wants are usually gratified in the having of them. But it is crucial for the development of a self that the infant discover the resistance of the world. If physical reality were not substantially indifferent to mental states, it is doubtful that individual selves would develop. The existence of objects is reasonable to suppose, in that "having a concept of a thing is dependent upon things."[42] But of more importance, the distinct and intelligible self is formed in reaction to a reality that is not entirely egocentric.

The second thought is that individual selves require an intersubjective world in order to develop and function. Again, widespread evidence (generally accepted) demonstrates that infants who do not receive affection from some care givers (other subjects) will die from the inattention even when provided with adequate physical nourishment. Throughout life individuals require connections to others for emotional and cognitive development, and for the concepts that allow successful negotiation through human experience. A purely self-contained individual is impossible on emotional and cognitive grounds. The ability to distinguish between fantasy and reality (of any sort), to acquire logical and empirical concepts, and even to have adequate understanding of the world, depends on the existence of other knowers in one's experience. Human experience is *social*, and the evidence is compelling that other subjects constitute that experience.

The third thought is that the character (form and content) of human experience is strongly conditioned by concepts. The evidence once more is persuasive and distributed across several disciplines. Numerous experiences have demonstrated that subjects "see" what they anticipate they will see. The early Bruner-Postman experiences in which subjects were asked to identify anomalous playing cards (red spades, black diamonds, etc.) and repeatedly "saw" the cards in terms of their expectations (correct or nonanomalous cards) have been extended successfully.[43] The work of Amos

42. F. L. Will, "Thoughts and Things," *Proceedings and Addresses of the American Philosophical Association* vol. 42 (1968–69): 51–69. The quote in the text here is on page 63. The phrase is quoted by Hundert in *Philosophy, Psychiatry, and Neuroscience* as part of a general examination of the role of objects in concept formation. Hundert's quotation of Will is on page 111 of his book.

43. Jerome S. Bruner and Lee Postman, "On the Perception of Incongruity: A Paradigm." *Journal of Personality* 18 (1949): 206–223.

Tversky and Daniel Kahneman documents the widespread use of heuristics (narrative categories that order and simplify data),[44] and studies in biology and neuroscience suggest that the use of types and categories to order inductive experience is probably the result of biological adaptation. Influential studies of science itself have reported on the inertia of established theories in constructing empirical reality. Even the demonstrations of illusions and hallucinations indicate the power of the brain to influence experience. The conclusion is irresistible. An objective reality may be needed to form a self, but the character of this reality is also dependent on the active mental categories of the knowing subject.

These three broad statements set forth a kind of minimal account of human experience that yet has profound implications. If accepted, both extreme subjectivity (e.g., solipsism) and realism (the belief that an independent objective world tests our knowledge claims) are incomplete accounts of experience. Any theory is corrigible. But the burden is on the dissenters to provide a rival account that accords with the last century of contributions in social and physical science, and the philosophical implications of these contributions.

Within these three categories, additional statements about the self and reality seem reasonable.

1. Consciousness (whatever it is) is local. Selves occupy (or are) bodies located in time and space. Put briefly, persons have facticity of a special sort. Each of us exists here and now in history, and, while we can move modestly about in space, we cannot move freely in time. One result of such facticity is that the world is always seen from a point of view. No one can be everywhere at once. Synoptic knowing is therefore impossible on a direct or firsthand basis. Partly as a consequence of this limitation, knowledge develops through the extension of abstractions to events that cannot be experienced directly (e.g., subatomic particles and black holes).

2. Ordinary experience is organized by at least two principles. One is time's arrow. Events succeed one another in what often appear to be lawlike patterns, but which are certainly governed by precedence in occurrence. Causality (which is learned through experience and

44. Amos Tversky and Daniel Kahneman, *Judgment Under Uncertainty: Heuristics and Biases* (Cambridge: Cambridge University Press, 1982). For more on the distinctions between rational and psychological choices, see Robert Abelson and Ariel Levi, "Decision Making and Decision Theory," in Gardner Lindzey and Elliot Aronson, eds., *Handbook of Social Psychology* (New York: Random House, 1985).

seems to be the application of biological categories) states this succession. Antecedent events affect future events, while the future does not affect the past. A second principle is that objects in human experience are reasonably fixed and occupy positions in space. Items are arranged or distributed in spatial dimensions, and have mass (or extension).

3. For a variety of reasons none of which is entirely clear (the elasticity of language, the heterogeneity of experience, the complexity and recursive nature of brain functions), there are multiple variations on reality in human experience. What is called (here and elsewhere) ordinary reality exhibits its own complex nature in allowing distinctions between real and unreal experiences, true and false claims, mistaken and correct perspectives. One can speculate on what a world would be like that permitted only clean and precise fits between knowing and experience. (It certainly would not be a human world.) But in addition to such complexity there are multiple ordinary realities where boundaries between the real and the imagined, the material and spiritual, the inventory of selves and objects, and much more, are items of considerable disagreement.

The acceptance of multiple realities cannot be pressed beyond certain limits. Sanity, or mental competence, requires something like this minimal account of ordinary reality. Psychotic intersubjectivity can produce a coherent world so long as consensus on (aberrant) reality occurs. But the clinical data suggest problems with the coherent structure of such worlds. To believe that one is the only person in existence, or that reality is simply an extension of one's thoughts, or that people (including the self) are objects, or that objects appear and disappear without cause, or that the future can determine the past—a list of such dissenting beliefs describes mental disorders that typically include other dysfunctions. Simple coherence has limits, in other words, as an intelligible and effective map for human experiences.

But the range of idiosyncratic beliefs is both wide and interesting. It is not psychotic to entertain imaginative hypotheses about the source of ordinary reality, or the inventory of items (subjects, objects) included in ordinary reality, or where ordinary reality begins and ends. There are levels of human experience that can demand radical reinterpretation of the mundane. The shift from a Ptolemaic to a Copernican world view permanently altered common and widespread beliefs in the ontological location of human experience. Current abstractions provide both quantum and relativity theories of subatomic and cosmic reality. How such understandings extend to ordinary reality is an uncertain matter. But such multiple levels of reality, even if consistent with each other (which they are not), provide ample intellectual resources for radical views on being and its origins.

People who are sane by all reasonable standards believe that existence is populated by spirits that intervene in human affairs, and that ordinary reality is a limited sector in a larger theater constructed by God. Other equally competent individuals see an existence bound by the physical parameters of a narrow materialism. But the robust scope of such beliefs does not require the abandonment of the minimal account of reality. Nothing about the beliefs falsifies or undermines concepts of a separate self, other subjects, and a material reality characterized by time's arrow, objects in space, and a capacity to yield multiple variations on its core structure. That radically different beliefs can lead to conflicting moral and political claims is, however, obvious and the place to begin understanding the deep pluralism occasionally found in liberal political settings.

2 Pluralism and Boundaries

The main burden of public reason in the liberal state is to reconcile claims originating in political differences among persons who may have nothing in common except membership in the political system. One of the more prominent exemplars for such reasoning is a supreme court in a constitutional regime with judicial review.[1] It is easy to see why. Deliberation is the preeminent mode of rational dialogue in a legal forum. Claims enter legal domains thick with reasons, justifications, descriptions, and in general with attachments that encourage reflections and judgments within a framework of accepted rules of inference, evidence, and argument. Even though all citizens in a democracy must be prepared to use reason in public matters, judicial forums seem more effective in modeling basic expectations for reasoning in liberal settings. These expectations include the thought that the state can be reasonably independent of partisan or divisive values. Public reasoning in its judicial mode is expected to produce impartial conclusions and to achieve the political reconciliations needed for consensual governing in liberal democracies by relying on values that everyone would reasonably endorse.

1. John Rawls, *Political Liberalism* (New York: Columbia University Press, 1993), Lecture VI, for the supreme court exemplar. Rawls has always emphasized the structural orientation of public reason, preferring to assign such reasoning to the basic institutions of society rather than to particular disputes that arise once the basic structure is in place. But one way the basic structure in any constitutional democracy is tested and defined is by applying relevant dimensions of it to actual issues and problems. The U.S. Supreme Court, for example, always interprets the Constitution by ruling on particular cases, not by hypothetical exegeses of the original text. Also, whether a political question is a constitutional issue must be decided by the Supreme Court as a matter of *judgment* within what Hart labels secondary rules (of interpretation). In H. L. A. Hart, *The Concept of Law* (Oxford: Clarendon Press, 1961). But see also the discussion in Samuel Freeman, "Original Meaning, Democratic Interpretation and the Constitution," *Philosophy and Public Affairs* 21 no. 1 (Winter 1992): 3–42.

The tasks required of public reason in realizing these expectations can be demanding. Suppose the radical starting fact of political liberalism: Members of disparate communities must find a way to govern their relations with one another even though their values are hostile or incompatible. If the reasoning of each community under this condition yields mutual opposition, not accord, then rational compatibility must be sought in resources outside community dialogue. Public reasoning is designed to provide these resources. A fully visible set of political rules and principles is to extend across the pluralism anticipated, and even celebrated, in liberalism. The liberal state governs on the expectations that persons have incompatible beliefs and that a shared form of reasoning can adjudicate the disputes that follow differences in beliefs.

The immediate difficulties of this program of governance are evident in any survey of the stages of deliberation. It is an axiom of decision theory that one must be rational in at least two ways: in selecting and in using the appropriate decision rules. The exercise of public reason must shield both of these areas of reflection and choice from the simple dominance of community beliefs if governing languages are to be impartial, stable and generalizable. But the choice and use of decision rules, controlled by inclinations toward risk and the schedule of goods at issue, are notoriously open to particular and even idiosyncratic beliefs. Conditions of risk and uncertainty permit the signature conclusion of contemporary decision theory: One can be both rational and wrong.[2] The influence of a variety of values on the stages of reasoning also invites the more severe restriction: A set of persons can all be rational and right, and still be in a rational dispute with one another because of the heterogeneity of evaluative criteria. This possibility introduces the prospect of a limiting condition: Public reason may have to reconcile differences among communities when communities may be able to control the uses of reason.[3]

2. Remember that there are no rational sanctions assignable to either risk-averse or risk-favorable inclinations. Note also that I am using the standard demarcations among conditions of certainty, risk, and uncertainty, where *certainty* is marked by a probability of 1 between an alternative and an outcome, *risk* by a probability between 0 and 1, and *uncertainty* by an absence of known probabilities. One might ask why the use of formal decision rules is to count as rational. One might answer that formal systems provide a coherence to both preferences and actions, as does a narrative (although in other ways). J. David Velleman draws this analogy in "The Story of Rational Action," *Philosophical Topics* 21 no. 1 (Spring 1993): 229–254.

3. The predictable move here is to credit the culture of ancient Greece with a solution to multiple rationalities. Classical Greece's versions of rationality, developed in a restricted and stable world, are taken to represent the belief that the human intellect can discover fixed and universal structures independent of convention. The state is rational in this program of dis-

This chapter examines the reconciling powers of a merit form of public reason, by which is meant reasoning concerned with claims entered in a deliberative space shielded from historical or political influences. This type of reasoning is revered in all liberal traditions and is found in many liberal practices and institutions. The sequestering of juries, life tenure for justices, and legal rules of evidence are examples. Liberal settings are generously endowed with designs that aim to insulate deliberations from considerations outside the merits of issues and problems. These efforts to secure judgments that are blind to more general contexts are attempts in liberal traditions to satisfy objectivity and impartiality. One goal of this discussion is to demonstrate, or at least persuade, that this version of public reasoning is unintelligible in conditions of what I call deep pluralism, and that the model of reasoning more appropriate to these conditions is one that allows deliberations to be affected by the political settings in which claims are formed and presented.

The effects of this type of discussion extend beyond the confines of pure theory. Any theory of public reason has obvious implications for institutions. A merit version of public reason yields those tiered arrangements that seem to be required in adjudication: the ideas of claimants, public space, and impartial judges that sketch the institutional framework of political liberalism. Also found in merit arrangements is the expectation that reasoning will lead to convergence, not divergence: The exercise of intuition, common sense, science, and reasonableness will incline members of the political order to support the rules and procedures of the political domain.[4] In this way the state and its member communities occupy separate levels connected by the common thread of public reason. This close relationship of merit to the organization of the political domain suggests that

---

covery because authority is drawn from the resources that reason encounters. I am not enough of a classical scholar to say whether the details of this story are good history, though my readings of Plato and Aristotle reveal many cracks and general complications in this account. But it can hardly be disputed that only a homogeneous society produces a form of governance that represents universal truths. The tendency in classical Greece to extinguish rather than tolerate dissent on the fundamentals must be seen as both an affirmation of some version of objective reality and the epistemological cleansing that closed authority seems to require. Note the interpretation of Greek culture by Leo Strauss in *Natural Right and History* (Chicago: University of Chicago Press, 1953), and the more conventional and elaborate approaches in Ernest Barker, *Greek Political Theory: Plato and His Predecessors* (London: Metheun, 1947), and W. K. C. Guthrie, *A History of Greek Philosophy*, 6 vols. (Cambridge: Cambridge University Press, 1962–81).

4. Rawls, *Political Liberalism*, especially Lecture III.

any impressive changes in theories of public reason will require a reordering of political institutions as well.

The discussion begins with a series of thought experiments on the practical operations of public reason. I argue that it is impossible to reason to impartial or fair conclusions with two types of speakers in political settings, largely because of the scope and depth of the disagreements they represent. I also maintain that incompatible beliefs represent the legitimate pluralism of the liberal state and reproduce in public reason the disputes that the liberal state must manage. I further argue that the divisive outcomes of public reason cannot be mitigated by excluding comprehensive doctrines from public space. The routine connections between moral and political reasoning make it unlikely that the political domain can be independent of moral influence. The task is to identify those forms of public reasoning that combine moral and political considerations. The model of public reasoning which succeeds in this assignment is a noncomputational reasoning that allows collective terms to dominate simple merit adjudication. These terms require a survey of considerations beyond the merits of the case at hand, and they open public reason to the more general needs of the political society.

2

One way to approach the indeterminacy of political languages is to recognize and define the type of speaker who interprets the vocabularies of public reason. The most benign interpreter is a native speaker who employs the principle of sincerity in stating what terms mean. Disputes between these types of speakers originate in legitimate differences in interpreting texts. Such disputes can be profound and sometimes are among the more acrimonious in political societies. Abortion disputes, for example, are mainly over the sense and reference of the terms *person* and *harm*. Even when sincerity is conceded to the disputants, the disagreements can continue, for the languages central to the dispute may admit rival and reasonable interpretations among native speakers.

In many ways disputes that are produced on common languages and ontologies are the more mysterious in liberal settings, especially when they are intractable. That competent and reasonable persons (those who want to find an agreement) sharing fundamental perspectives can be in an intractable dispute is a more distressing failure for liberalism than are the problems occasioned by radical differences and defections. It suggests a failure of reason on those conditions where it should be more likely to succeed. It also seems to compromise the effectiveness of consent, which is a central term in liberal governance.

A second type of speaker can be labeled a radical. This appellation is offered here as a neutral or nonevaluative designation in a certain range of disputes. Occasionally, disputes can be traced to the fact that persons have neither a common language nor an ontology for negotiating an agreement. Disputes between secular and religious communities, for example, may not be over the meaning of shared terms, but over the appropriate languages to invoke (e.g., whether God is a relevant consideration) and the scope and nature of the real. Radical status in this special sense means that the disputants may not speak the same language or share understandings of reality, even when they are members of the same political system and are all native speakers of the dominant language. The existence of this type of speaker leads to indeterminacy of translations and good-faith efforts at communication across disparate communities.[5]

A third type of speaker is one who has defected from the political dialogue that negotiates disputes. Such speakers may have a common language and ontology. They may even agree on the sense and references of governing terms, but one or more of them has opted out of the cooperative game. Defection is addressed primarily with some combination of logic and fairness. In moral philosophy the proposed resolutions have usually amounted to appeals to defectors to reenter the cooperative game. Various sameness rules, for example, invite a defector to consider what would happen if everyone did what she or he is doing, or what it would mean if she or he continued to defect when others who are relevantly similar are members of the game, and so on.[6] Defectors in many ways pose the more traditional and uncomplicated problem of political dialogue, namely, that some speakers who are competent and who share basic perspectives nevertheless choose not to comply with the rules and principles of governance. One example of defection is the "free rider" problem in both politics and economics: An individual who has consented to a collective action decides to consume the products of this action without assisting in the production costs. In cases of defection individuals fail to cooperate even though they are members of the political system and have accepted common understand-

5. W. V. O. Quine, *Ontological Relativity and Other Essays* (New York: Columbia University Press, 1969), 80–82, and *Word and Object* (Cambridge: MIT Press, 1960), 72–79.

6. See, for example, Marcus Singer, *Generalization in Ethics* (London: Eyre and Spottiswoode, 1963), and R. M. Hare, *Freedom and Reason* (New York: Oxford University Press, 1965).

ings of what membership requires. Coercive measures can be selectively applied to such persons once the appeals to them have been exhausted.[7]

Let us imagine an ideal forum in which sincere and radical speakers are in a dispute with adversaries of their same type, and the defector is in a dispute with cooperative players.

Sincere speakers may be in a dispute with one another on any of several grounds, in that a common language and shared political (or even moral) principles are no guarantee of lasting harmony. Abortion disputes illustrate some of the extreme divisions that can occur even among reasonable persons. Any tentative (and incomplete) framework for the many ways in which persons reason on political matters allows that rational persons have clusters of beliefs. These clusters are arranged in different ways on different sets of issues and problems, and the inventory and ordering of beliefs in each cluster vary with changes in circumstances. Some of what we include in sets of rational beliefs must include the ordering principles that arrange clusters and beliefs. At least occasionally an ordering will yield a representative or dominant belief. This yield typically follows reflection on several other considerations and often is a derivative belief. The belief that abortion should be proscribed legally, for example, occurs (when it has rational standing) after a chain of reasoning on other matters, including the biological gestation of life, various legal principles and rules, and the membership criteria for human communities.

In the well-known story, contemporary participants in abortion disputes accept roughly the same set of moral and political principles but disagree over the references of the principles. Both pro-life and pro-choice advocates subscribe to the basic features of the liberal program, which includes an emphasis on individual rights and liberties, the *harm* thesis developed in Mill's libertarian philosophies, and the importance of individual life. Both accept the practical conclusion of charging the state with the protection of life. Both acknowledge the reality of human life from birth to death. Many pro-life advocates, however, extend the protective role of the state to embryonic life from fertilization to birth. Pro-choice assigns partial protection in stages to embryonic life, usually beginning with viability, and resists the full state protection of life until birth. Pro-life demands that the law protect fetal life in early gestation on the grounds that it is in all important moral respects identical to life after birth. Pro-choice, by either denying the human status of

7. Competence is important here. The mental powers needed for *mens rea* must be demonstrated before punishment is justified. Also, the regime must meet at least rudimentary tests of fairness. Richard Dagger, "Playing Fair with Punishment," *Ethics* 103 (April 1993): 473–488. Allowances must also be made for legitimate dissent.

early gestation or granting priority status to a woman's dominion over her body, allows other parts of the liberal program to dominate, in this case the discretionary authority to control one's own body.[8] The practical outcome of each set of interpretations and arguments is familiar: For the pro-life side, no abortions, and for the pro-choice side, freedom of choice on abortions for women in at least the early stages of pregnancy.

What can public reason do to resolve such a dispute? Among the problems in disputes among speakers who share the same moral and political program are selecting and defining the principles to use in negotiating a resolution. In abortion disputes the beliefs of the adversaries determine (in theory) the relevant principles. If the Fourteenth Amendment's requirement of due process were to be used to adjudicate abortion, then the effective result would be to deny one of the two central beliefs in the dispute *before* deliberations begin. If, for example, sexual equality defeats a pro-life view, then one assumes either that the fetus is not human life or is subordinated in importance to a woman's dominion over her body. Neither assumption accepts the preeminence that pro-life advocates attach to early stages of human life.[9] It is also impossible to assimilate abortion to other affiliated principles without compromising pro-life beliefs, the crucial one of which is that *another* is present in the body of the woman during pregnancy. One cannot, on this belief, cede control to the woman to decide on abortion without introducing morally controversial parallels of euthanasia decided by others and homicide. The deliberations of due process turned in other directions would simply order the rival concepts differently. To require legal justifications for abortions in the first trimester is hostile to the pro-choice argument that women have full discretion on whether to continue or terminate a pregnancy. Even to explore reasons for ending fetal life in early abortions is already to concede some of the pro-life agenda. In the-

8. See Judith Jarvis Thomson's arguments here that even granting human standing to the fetus still does not override the right to control one's own body, in "A Defense of Abortion," *Philosophy and Public Affairs* 1 (Fall 1971): 47–66.

9. For versions of due process that turn on sexual equality, see Guido Calabresi, *Ideals, Beliefs, Attitudes and the Law* (Syracuse, N.Y.: Syracuse University Press, 1985), and Lawrence Tribe's elaborations in *American Constitutional Law* (Mineola, N.Y.: Foundation Press, 1988). It is a mistake to think that life always trumps all other principles in liberal democracies. It does not, as the death penalty, justifiable homicide, and war demonstrate. Due process permits a wide assortment of actions that take lives. Of course when due process fails or is irrelevant then other devices become prominent, such as obfuscation—an observation developed by Guido Calabrisi and Philip Bobbitt in *Tragic Choices* (New York: W. W. Norton, 1978). The random loss of life in some practices demands that the loss be concealed. Obscurantism is an unlikely solution, even at a pragmatic level, in abortion practices. The data on gestation and abortion are among the more widely disseminated information packages in Western cultures.

ory, governing principles are authoritative over practices. In this case public reason seems to be a simple product of each practice.

Clarifying the meaning of relevant principles is also not very helpful. Abortion disputes do not turn on definitions of liberty and equality, or even harm. The disputes begin on the concept of *life* itself, in particular when human predicates can be assigned to gestational life. The assignment of the predicates influences the relevance, orderings and interpretations of other principles. Ronald Dworkin has argued that all sides on abortion agree about the sanctity of human life but disagree about the relative moral importance of natural or human dimensions of life. The natural in Dworkin's discussions is more or less biological, the human a notion of (human) investment in life. On these terms the abortion debate is in part over whether the frustration of a biological life is sometimes justified in order to avoid frustrating a human contribution to life or to other person's lives.[10] The key feature of the disputes is that reasonable people can disagree on the meanings and orderings of various understandings of life. No compelling reasons justify either pro-life or pro-choice assignments (even on Dworkin's optimistic expectations for rational dialogue). The moral indeterminacy of the early stages of human gestation and the inherent reasonableness of rival orderings of natural and human dimensions of life preclude any deliberative closure of the dispute. It is not clear how public reason can resolve this kind of dispute. All deliberation on abortion seems to start with an acceptance of either pro-life or pro-choice beliefs, not conclude with them as a reasoned outcome.

Rawls has more recently acknowledged that "disputed questions, such as that of abortion, may lead to a stand-off between different political conceptions, and citizens must simply vote on the question. . . . The outcome of the vote is to be seen as reasonable, provided all citizens of a reasonably just constitutional regime sincerely vote in accordance with the idea of public reason."[11] This may be one way to resolve otherwise intractable disputes, except for the reality of strategic voting (along with the difficulty of specifying "sincere" voting), and the chronic breakdowns in arithmetical composition rules documented in collective choice theory.[12] The use of voting

10. Dworkin, *Life's Dominion* (New York: Knopf, 1993), chapter 3<None>. Would that the practitioners were so nuanced. Maybe I have listened one time too many to the acrimonious exchanges of pro-life and pro-choice, but I see an overriding priority maintained for the woman's discretionary powers among pro-choice people whether or not human life can be claimed for the embryo or fetus.

11. Rawls, *Political Liberalism,* lv–lvi.

12. See the arguments and overviews in William Riker, *Liberalism Against Populism* (San Francisco: W. H. Freeman, 1982). Dissents and qualifications may be found in Donald Green

as a supplement in public reason is complicated in yet another way by the recognition that individuals may be members of different senses of a political system, a prospect more likely in strong pluralism.[13] The possibility of multiple political contexts in the "same" political society undermines the notion that all citizens in a liberal democracy subscribe to the same understanding of voting, no matter how minimal this understanding may be. Voting in these disjointed conditions is hardly in any kind of accordance with the shared deliberative standards of public reason.

The disputes between pro-life and pro-choice advocates affect even the role of information in rational decisions. Abortion counseling illustrates this influence. Pro-choice has consistently opposed pro-life counseling of women contemplating abortion on the grounds that such counseling unduly influences women to forgo abortion (even given that the need to ensure informed consent might require pro-life information), an opposition accepted by the U.S. Supreme Court in *Thornburgh* (1986). For years pro-life groups were successful in eliminating federal funds for family planning clinics that counseled pregnant women on abortion as an alternative to carrying to term. The dispute over the type and scope of information provided in counseling can be traced back to metatheories of morality. Pro-life wants detailed (perhaps moral) material on gestation included in the counseling package on the ground that any complete description of abortion must include such facts, while pro-choice wants only minimal (perhaps nonmoral) data provided to women on the assumption that the woman deciding whether to have an abortion assigns moral features to the act. Each proposition forces us to reconsider traditional views on the relationship of information and rationality.

3

Disputes between radical speakers extend the range of indeterminacy. To see these difficulties, think of a disagreement between a secular physician and a Christian Scientist over medical care for the latter's infants. To a Christian Scientist there is no therapy, no cure, because there is no illness. All that is real must be good. Illness, as an apparent and even obvious bad, must be illusory. Prayer and meditation will extinguish the illusion by bringing one's beliefs into accord with the real, which is God's creation. For

---

and Ian Shapiro, *Pathologies of Rational Choice* (New Haven, Conn.: Yale University Press, 1994).

13. Indicated by George Tsebelis in *Nested Games: Rational Choice in Comparative Politics* (Berkeley: University of California Press, 1990).

a secular practitioner of contemporary medicine, illness is real. It is a condition of the person resulting from a variety of causes, including viruses, bacteria, malnutrition, trauma, genetic breakdowns, and other factors. Illness can respond to therapy, sometimes dramatically, at other times slowly and only marginally, and sometimes not at all. The medical practitioner uses physical and mental means to restore health and prolong life. The Christian Science practitioner prays and meditates to change attitudes toward purported illness.[14]

Christian Science and secular medicine contain beliefs that are adjacent and so may seem to overlap. Physicians are more readily inclined to accept effects between beliefs and health, so that exclusive preoccupations with the body (as a physical unit) are not so prominent in therapy today. But this shift in attitudes is only a parallel belief. Christian Science begins with a rejection of "mental" cures and the acceptance of a reality that does not contain illness. Beliefs cannot affect that which does not exist. The core differences between Christian Science and secular medicine are ontological. Each practice derives from an understanding of reality that in all vital matters excludes the rival ontology.

The differences between these types of radical speakers affect concepts of reason. All empirical versions of reasoning, which are prominent in medical practices, use information that is falsifiable and the exclusive ground for deliberations. On the first point, metaphysical knowledge, understood as knowledge that exceeds the boundaries of naturalism, is excluded from reasoning. Only naturalistic knowledge is allowed, though the expressions of knowledge are various and include descriptions, mathematical formulations, speculative hypotheses, and natural laws. On the second point, the reasoning that leads to conclusions (directives and explanations mainly) is confined to the domain of what can be known, however the known is defined. Conclusions justified by reference to what cannot be known are illicit. This secular version of reason is at odds with the spiritual (almost Platonist) approach to reasoning by a Christian Scientist, who relies on perspectives that may be known only by God and accepts a control-

14. The conflict scenario has real-world correlates. The case of David and Ginger Twitchell in Boston—a couple who "treated" their four-year-old son with meditation and prayer while he died of a bowel obstruction—was exactly an issue of Christian Science vs. secular medicine. In 1990 the Twitchells were convicted in Massachusetts of involuntary manslaughter for their actions. I discuss this case in my *Healing Powers* (Chicago: University of Chicago Press, 1992), 251–258. The standard references on Christian Science are (obviously) Mary Baker Eddy, *Science and Health with Key to the Scriptures* (Boston: First Church of Christ, Scientist, 1971), and Robert Peel, *Health and Medicine in the Christian Science Tradition* (New York: Crossroad, 1988).

ling status for the unknown, in the sense that reason depends more strongly on what is not known (by humans) than what is known.

Naturalistic and spiritual accounts of human experience often rely on common assumptions and employ similar research methods. That we must test descriptive statements with evidence drawn from only partial knowledge of our environment, for example, is a working premise endorsed by both skeptics and believers. Inductive statistics are often the preferred methods for those subscribing to this premise. But even shared research programs can still address different realities and produce radically different conclusions. The existence of God and the appearance of God's handiwork on earth are empirical claims in religious dialogues, as are beliefs in at least partial knowledge of higher plans and the presence of various types of spiritual figures, sometimes including God. The naturalist describes and explains, and sometimes expands, an empirical world that has been emptied of extraordinary individual powers and spiritual presences. These differences can also produce divergent research programs. Consider the languages that are relevant to the dispute over therapy. Foundational concepts of health, life, and illness, terms such as cause and effect, and even the scope of experience have different meanings in each ontology. These differences, formed prior to the entry of claims into the forum of public reason, suggest a slight but vital change in Hume's observation: Reason is not the slave of the passions but of ontologies that use reason as an instrument to mandate outcomes.

Such rival ontologies as Christian Science and secular medicine are difficult to reconcile or manage with any form of reasoning. Imagine the members of each introducing claims to the public space of the ideal forum. Collateral principles are often used to resolve disputes of this type. In this case the minor (and hence incompetent) standing of infants can be used by both communities to impose a form of treatment, on the ground that children cannot give informed consent. But what is the treatment to be? Identification of the most effective treatment differs radically as one moves across the ontologies. The state must select and enforce one of the rival ontologies, for public reason will not produce an outcome from a deliberative inspection of evidence and argument.

Imposing one ontology over another is not a call for grieving. Courts routinely select and enforce some claims against others. The logic of a forum does not guarantee that reason will find the consensual outcome that will satisfy all claimants. Also, outcomes can, and probably have to be, nonneutral in their effects. But the enforcement of one point of view in a dispute is legally and morally authoritative only if the procedures of deliberation are in some way not reducible to the languages and interpretations that identify the rival claims. The scope of the problem is indicated by the concession that even neutrality may not be renderable in neutral terms because what it means to be neutral is itself disputable.[15] Principles may be *regarded* as neutral, and general, as they are accepted by the citizens of a state and as they are accepted as neutral. But this pragmatic sense of neutrality, and generality, cannot be sustained in the type of pluralism at issue here; and if deliberation is dependent on partisan interpretations that precede reasoning, then even the pragmatic test is lost: Public reason is no longer grounded in an overlapping consensus but in those values that are exclusively identified with factions. The problem is that rival ontologies can dominate public reason by swallowing all the vocabularies marking off public space.

The communities housing each set of beliefs, the Christian Science religion and secular medical practice, are within the political system in the thought experiment. But an agreement to abide by the outcomes of public reasoning also contains expectations that a set of political principles will produce a decision on independent criteria of fairness. It is not evident that an independent and relevant set of principles can be found for adjudicating claims emerging from rival ontologies. What counts as evidence will differ between the two communities, and rules of inference and argument will be influenced by the competing understandings of reality.

Political liberalism is different from comprehensive versions of liberalism that insist on liberal thought throughout the society.[16] A political liberal can tolerate nonliberal values so long as citizens subscribe to the principles of governance that mark off the political domain and accept the practices needed to sustain the political order. But the principles must be independent in directing or guiding those who are responsible for adjudicating disputes. Public reason depends in part on the capacity of the political domain to address and resolve community disputes from a distance that satisfies impartiality.

Impartiality is crippled by the first two types of dispute. In the case of sincere speakers, the vocabularies of governance are empty without the meanings assigned to them by the disputants. The dispute is in effect re-

15. I make this statement secure in the knowledge that tests of neutrality are numerous and controversial. Consider: Neutrality can easily mean treating events the same way, treating claims in different ways after evaluating their merits, remaining indifferent to actions, refusing to make judgments, refusing to act, acting in such a way as to restore some earlier equilibrium, and so on. Discussed in the collection of readings in Robert Goodin and Andrew Reeve, eds., *Liberal Neutrality* (New York: Routledge, Chapman and Hall, 1990).

16. This is a point made throughout *Political Liberalism*.

produced in the political domain. In the case of radical speakers, the governing language has no power to resolve the dispute. The rival beliefs can so completely absorb the vocabulary of reason that nothing is left as a *public* dialogue. Reason itself is a contentious topic in disputes among speakers of the second type. Disputes must be resolved by other approaches.[17]

The third type of speaker produces the least complicated dispute. A person who defects from a cooperative effort presents a classic problem of compliance. Imagine now a person who is competent, understands and has accepted the authority of the political domain, and consents to the principles that govern the relations she or he has with other members of the political system. Now suppose that this individual fails to comply with legally constituted rules of the system. If appeals emerging from the exercise of public reason do not succeed in ensuring compliance, then the use of coercion is justified on rational grounds. It sometimes seems that this direct and simple type of dispute is the paradigmatic case on which liberal governance develops its concepts and working logic. Failure of any part of the conditions of this dispute—such as competence or consent—yields modifications and extensions of the liberal program. But the case is too easy in its reliance on common understandings in liberalism. The pluralism on which liberalism is predicated can also extend to the meanings and relevance of governing vocabularies in public reason, as the first two types of dispute demonstrate.

4

It helps in framing and addressing these breakdowns of public reasoning to know that a social order can be pluralist in several ways. One is the dimension of scope. Sincere speakers, exemplified here by the disputes over abortion, share a considerable property in a single conceptual scheme. They may have common beliefs on a wide range of events, relationships, and theories, and they generally accept a set of democratic rules and principles. But they diverge dramatically on the meaning and scope of *life*. Radical speakers do not have strong overlapping views. For example, Christian

17. Again, these observations accept the political reality that nonneutral effects are inevitable in liberal governing. The observations instead question the impartial or generalizable languages of governing that are used to justify nonneutral effects. The contentious standing of reason has of course been elaborated in Alasdair MacIntyre's *After Virtue* (Notre Dame, Ind.: University of Notre Dame Press, 1981) and *Whose Justice? Which Rationality?* (Notre Dame, Ind.: University of Notre Dame Press, 1988). My statement of the problems of public reasoning is consistent with the main parts of this work, but the proposals to introduce collective arrangements to deliberations is not a part of MacIntyre's work.

Scientists differ from secular medical practitioners on foundational views of human experience. Each has a conceptual scheme that is mainly separate from the other. The scope of disagreement is comprehensive.

A second dimension is depth. One can disagree about truth, or the concept of truth. Two persons, for example, can disagree on whether the more effective treatment for meningitis is meditation or antibiotics. This is a disagreement on truth. They can also disagree on what it is that makes the two propositions true. This a disagreement on the concept of truth. The depth of a disagreement can be extended or contracted. Abortion partisans disagree on the concept of truth, but the dispute can occur even when the conceptual dispute is confined to the comparatively narrow vocabulary of abortion issues. The dispute over healing that the second type of speaker represents is a disagreement over the concept of truth that generates two exclusive and comprehensive conceptual schemes.

Still another dimension is represented by differences that occur even when all individuals agree on the meaning and interpretation of governing languages. The defector produces a dispute within a common conceptual scheme. There is no disagreement here on truth, the concept of truth, or any important issues of scope. The dispute can be due to material or moral differences, or to defects of various types, including failure of will, flawed character, simple greed, miscalculation, or any of numerous conditions that lead persons to disputes within a shared conceptual scheme. But whatever the sources, these disputes are neither complex nor elusive for public reason.

The first two dimensions, however, can introduce a pluralism outside the scope of public reason. The dimension of depth offers the more recalcitrant problems, and increasingly so as it extends to mutually exclusive conceptual schemes. Contrasts between realist and epistemic conceptions of truth represent these problems. The most direct expression of realism is Tarski's truth schema, which states that the proposition that "p" is true iff p.[18] The establishment of "p" varies with different theoretical perspectives. A moral realism grounded on linguistic versions of the schema might hold only that there are moral facts in experience.[19] Or one might say (less cautiously) that moral properties have the kind of retentive power of rigid designators (in the sense provided by Saul Kripke).[20] Neither of these accounts requires a re-

18. The T-schema refers to Tarski's truth conditions. Alfred Tarski, "The Semantic Conception of Truth," *Philosophy and Phenomenological Research* 4 (1944): 341–375.

19. A variation on this view is developed by Sabina Lovibond, *Realism and Imagination in Ethics* (Oxford: Basil Blackwell, 1983).

20. Saul Kripke, *Naming and Necessity* (Cambridge: Harvard University Press, 1980). This view is discussed in moral philosophy by Geoffrey Sayre-McCord, *Essays in Moral Realism*

ality independent of human experience. But many forms of moral realism extend the T-schema by ignoring certain distinctions and redefining terms. Both Aristotle and Bradley collapse important distinctions between knower and known (in Aristotle the object impresses itself upon the intellect in the act of knowing), which prohibits modern differences between language and reality, and both Plato and Strauss develop an ontological holism in which the real is a whole beyond the range of the human senses.[21] Epistemic theories of truth, by contrast, are based on various forms of justification. These forms include ideal truth conditions, omniscient observers, special devices of consensus (like Rawls's original position), instrumental pragmatism, and more.[22] In all cases of epistemic truth a proposition is true if and only if it meets certain standards for warranted belief.

Dispute management is especially difficult when political differences are informed by these different understandings of human experience simply because each side must view the other as wrong on both method and conclusion. The pluralism that results from these differences is deep, meaning more than one incompatible conceptual scheme represents the "same" social and perhaps physical reality. Each proponent of realist and epistemic truth rejects as a social practice that which defines the other. Yet, each philosophy can and does enter claims into the public space that represents political liberalism.

The problems described here occur in what may be called the conceptual center of the liberal program. Liberal perspectives on truth require the absence of a unique interpretation of language and experience. From this requirement follows the pluralism of belief characterizing liberal regimes. Beliefs may also differ, however, on the sense and reference of governing concepts and principles. This secondary extension of pluralism to the central areas of political authority can reduce the governing languages of the liberal state to partisan interests. The expectations of objectivity and impartiality that historically have characterized theories of the rational state are difficult to maintain if governing vocabularies can be appropriated for

(Ithaca, N.Y.: Cornell University Press, 1989), especially in "Moral Theory and Explanatory Impotence."

21. These hit-and-run points are explored at rewarding length by William P. Alston, *A Realist Conception of Truth* (Ithaca, N.Y.: Cornell University Press, 1996). The views of Strauss mentioned here can be found in his *Natural Right and History*.

22. Rawls ignores truth in favor of reasonableness in *Political Liberalism*, but the OP is still an epistemic device to justify certain governing principles. The ideal speech situation developed by Habermas is one well-known source for epistemic truth. In *The Theory of Communicative Action* (Boston: Beacon Press, 1984).

partisan use in politics. In yet another version of the self-reflective (e.g., liar) paradox, the liberal state originates in a pluralism that can turn on itself and in doing so compromise the authority of the state to govern differences. Stated bluntly, a state that originates in the acceptance of parochial over generalizable truths loses its distinct and independent standing if it cannot manage the extension of disputes over truth and the concept of truth to its governing languages.

5

Several measures have been proposed in liberal theory to stabilize authority when political pluralism affects the capacity of the state to govern. These measures usually address religious beliefs, but the general points hold for any divisive doctrine. The most direct measure is to bracket divisive beliefs and claims.[23] This proposal appears in strongest form in theories of political liberalism in large part because bracketing simultaneously ensures both effective governance in divisive conditions and separations between communities and the political domain. The liberal state, as an artifact created by member communities with rival comprehensive doctrines, must be free to some degree of community values if it is to govern. The difficulty of reconciling diverse moral beliefs in the absence of authority is the occasion for the formation of the state in liberal theory. Obviously the full introduction of incompatible moral doctrines into the political domain recreates the disputes and differences that the state is to manage; and doctrinal views that absorb political vocabularies also compromise the separation between state and community. Bracketing these moral views and using political principles to manage disputes is one way to avoid these problems.[24]

23. Discussed In *Political Liberalism* as the "exclusive view," pp. 247–254.

24. Rawls's definition of justice as a political conception requires that moral values be subordinated to the greater values of the political domain, and that community morals enter public reason only "in ways that strengthen the ideal of public reason itself." Rawls, *Political Liberalism*, Lecture VI, especially pp. 240–254. If the moral values are intractably divisive, they must be suspended for the political process to work successfully. This requirement is nothing more than a restatement of the initial agreement in *any* version of the social contract to be bound by the terms of the agreement. A moral realist may see this suspension as a distortion of realism. In chapter two of *Natural Right and History* Strauss argues that objectivity is jeopardized when value judgments are suspended. Distinctions between genuine and spurious instances of a concept cannot be recognized; and the noncognitivism informing a value-free inquiry cannot accommodate the claims of those who believe that values are truth functional. In Strauss's words, "The historian who takes it for granted that objective value judgments are impossible cannot take very seriously that thought of the past which was based on the assumption that objective value judgments are possible" (pp. 61–62).

A second approach is developed in later work by Rawls. In *Political Liberalism* claims and appeals formed on comprehensive doctrines are allowed into public space if they strengthen public reason. The usual examples offered to elaborate this view are drawn from times of political and moral crisis, such as the abolitionist and civil rights movements. These more inclusive versions of public reason are still stringent, however. They may require believers to shape their doctrines to accommodate political needs, and in any case are little more than bracketing with more explicit conditions for entry. Now, in what Rawls calls the wide view of public reason, a third proposal has emerged. Certain types of comprehensive views may be politically acceptable if they are consistent with liberal principles, and the political claims that follow from them are supported by the values and principles of political liberalism.[25] These are the threshold tests found even in the wide view of public reason. They tell us that the political domain is still to function as a gatekeeper for community values and to remain as the dominant set of governing practices in society.

It can be helpful to remember certain history lessons in evaluating political theories that rely on distinctions between political and moral languages, in particular those famous exercises that instruct us on the failures of partitions between facts and values. Intimate relationships between descriptive and value statements are legion and include the occasional deductive relationship, various overlaps of descriptive and evaluative languages in several social practices, and the strong normative influences of social structures on what may appear to be neutral descriptive languages.[26] But the predictable observation that bracketing any dimension of language is exceedingly difficult, especially when the language is on the normative order of morality, misses the opportunity to elaborate on the many nuanced relationships between moral and political domains that help craft a logic of public reason.

The close etymology of moral and political/legal languages hardly needs mentioning. Both are normative and expressed in forms of practical reason that aim to govern relations among persons and groups in human commu-

25. Rawls has elaborated these views in symposiums at the University of Michigan (March 1995) and the Harvard Divinity School. The latter discussion was published in *Religion and Values in Public Life* (Summer 1995).

26. Holding divisive moral disputes out of the political machinery is a peculiar suggestion on any grounds. The upshot of the proposal is that the state is proportionately reluctant to adjudicate issues as they become more obvious candidates for adjudication. This seems to be the inverse of the proper ordering of state action and political need. The relevant citations here on moral philosophy are John Searle, "How to Derive 'Ought' from 'Is,'" and Philippa Foot, "Moral Beliefs," both in W. D. Hudson, ed., *The Is-Ought Question* (New York: St. Martin's Press, 1969).

nities. Morality is usually concerned with the protection and provision of a set of prudential goods that includes life, health, integrity, and truth and that typically extends concerns for realizing these goods to others as well as the self. Both autonomy and liberty are necessary conditions in moral actions. Politics is a concept that decomposes into such terms as freedom, obligation, legitimacy, and authority. Coercion is one method for directing actions in political settings. Most of the modern vocabularies in morality and politics seem reasonably distinct from (though often dependent on) theoretical terms such as explanation, causality, and even understanding that lead to statements about the way the world is.

Various definitions of morality can be found in contemporary philosophy, which provides at least three plausible models of moral reasoning: deduction, induction, and coherence. These models are more or less useful in different settings, though even a cursory reading of this chapter will display the affinities of the arguments here for a coherence model (also favored by Rawls). The relevant point is that both political and moral reasoning are represented by these three models, and there is no reason to think that the formal expressions of reasoning can demarcate morality and politics.[27] It is also improbable that the state can be insulated from the peculiar form of morality Rawls labels a comprehensive doctrine,[28] or that such doctrines are hostile to the political deliberations of public reasoning.

The state is clearly a kind of moral undertaking.[29] But its distinctive moral

27. Because I am denying sharp distinctions between moral and political reasoning, my arguments can be spared efforts to provide a full definition of either morality or politics. For an unusually clear summary of these three models of moral reasoning, see Tom L. Beauchamp and James E. Childress, *Principles of Biomedical Ethics* (New York: Oxford University Press, 1994), chapter 1. Any number of texts and anthologies in moral philosophy elaborate the relationships of truth to moral thinking, including the standard books by W. D. Hudson, *Modern Moral Philosophy* (New York: Doubleday, 1970) and Hector-Neri Castaneda and George Nakhnikian, eds., *Morality and the Language of Conduct* (Detroit, Mich.: Wayne State University Press, 1965). See also my "The Structure of 'Politics,'" *American Political Science Review* 72 no. 3 (September 1978): 859–870, for a discussion of the concept of politics.

28. Rawls 1996, 13, 175.

29. The political conception can be a moral truth so long as the truth is assigned to the public domain of basic institutions. Rawls properly says that the political domain is not a *modus vivendi*. It is a consensus that "is moral in both its object and its content" (*Political Liberalism*, p. 126 for quote and pp. 147–151 for discussion). But long-standing liberal views restrict the state from making moral judgments on doctrinal truth. Even false beliefs have standing in the liberal political arena or, better, the liberal state is not in the business of adjudicating the truth or falsity of beliefs. The moral standing of the political domain rests on its use of the principles of constitutional democracy. In an aside Rawls muses that if one moral doctrine in the political domain is true, and this doctrine endorses the political system, then all other doctrines yield the right political concepts by default but for the wrong reasons. (In *Political Liberalism*, pp. 126–128.) This aside is puzzling. Because all truth is local on the con-

framework is also influenced by the moral beliefs and practices of its constituent communities, which are among the main resources for defining political issues and resolutions. Even the strongest advocates for a separation between political and moral reasoning acknowledge the type of broad influence represented by the abolitionist and civil rights movements in the United States. These movements, inspired by the morality of religious beliefs, were critical in expanding the criteria for membership in the political system. More generally, moral beliefs can affect modern political societies by defining and redefining the languages of politics. Principles are given a different scope, perhaps also a different sense, as the result of moral influences. Morality can also reshape the dimensions of public space, changing the standards for political effectiveness and the rules of inclusion and exclusion for issues. These moral effects are not just found in times of crisis. They are perennial features of political life. Many originate in beliefs comprehensive enough to raise the suspicions of a political liberal, but still they seem to have beneficent effects in restructuring the scope and logic of public reasoning.

One explanation for the congenial associations of comprehensive doctrines and public reasoning is the obvious distinction between comprehensiveness and divisiveness. Some doctrines are not only comprehensive but also inclusive and even conciliatory. Buddhism is an example. Contrast this encompassing philosophy with current views on abortion, many of which are only partial cuts into human experience but exceedingly harsh toward opponents. That doctrines are comprehensive, roughly meaning that they provide a complete articulation of all values and virtues for the moral life, is not a relevant consideration. Nor is the observation that a doctrine is a form of community morality. Divisiveness is the relevant consideration in public reasoning, and it is also the main issue in the conditions of pluralism described here.

The effects of moral reasoning on political languages are sometimes overriding. Consider, again, the thought experiments on abortion issues and medical therapy. These disputes close the separation between moral and political languages that liberalism establishes. Political terms in these disputes do not have an independent sense and reference. Their meanings originate in the communities that form the political domain and are relevant as they bear on political issues and problems. The abortion and therapy disputes are about the protection of life and the right to exercise discretionary authority over one's body and the health of one's children. It is hard

---

ditions of liberal governance, how can one say that any moral doctrine is true in terms sufficiently generalizable to authenticate the political domain?

to see where the moral and political can be demarcated as these matters enter public space. Bracketing moral beliefs in these cases seems to remove the political dimensions also. Holding divisive moral disputes out of the political machinery is a peculiar suggestion on any grounds. The upshot of the proposal is that the state is proportionately reluctant to adjudicate issues as they become more obvious candidates for adjudication. This seems to be the inverse of the proper ordering of state action and political need.

Even those arguments that establish political dominance over morality do not break all ties between the two practices. The most direct form of political dominance is state adjudication of intractable moral disputes. The abortion dispute cannot be resolved by the disputants. It must be managed by the state, which legitimately does so on the basis of needs in the political domain. But it is fatuous to think that any resolution, even one that temporizes by maintaining the status quo, can be independent of the moral views of the rival doctrines. Any imposed or negotiated solution will represent portions, perhaps wholes, of the pro-life and pro-choice positions. The same observation can be made of the therapy dispute example. Shielding Christian Science from regulation implicitly endorses a meditative approach to healing, or at least the political value of tolerance over the maintenance of life for children. Invading the religious community with imposed medical therapy amounts to a rejection of prayer as a form of healing. In any construction of the state's role there is complicity in a moral point of view, typically (though not necessarily) including a moral belief drawn from one of the disputing communities. Even a political dominance of morality justified by extreme conditions, say, the survival of the society, is still dependent on moral views. In this case survival would have to be morally weighed against the values that would be sacrificed by maintaining the political community. Not all social orders may be worth maintaining from a moral point of view.[30]

The intimacies of moral and political reasoning are nowhere so explicit as in the plea for reasonableness that characterizes liberal regimes. The threshold test for membership in liberal political systems is a willingness to accept the reality of opposing views and the mutual advantages of a system of adjudication for the disputes that follow pluralism. The practical result of the acceptance is that individuals subscribe to a social order in which all moral doctrines must be minimally governed to secure the general advantages of social cooperation. That may require the denial or contraction of any particular moral claims. An individual who is not reasonable in this

30. This is an observation offered long ago by H. L. A. Hart, in *Law, Liberty and Morality* (New York: Vintage Books, 1963).

minimal sense obviously is not a member of a liberal political system. This condition is found in all contractual agreements.

But what it means to be reasonable is still complex. Both slavery and abortion are disputes in which there is asymmetry at basic levels. Unlike a disagreement over the role of the state in the economy that rests on common economic frameworks and variables, these two disputes are traceable in substantial part to radically different definitions of the human person. Whether one can be reasonable is a function of these deep considerations. If one believes that slavery and abortion are (respectively) denials of humanity and murder, reasonableness is not an opportunity, even if one an accepts the advantages of general adjudication. In the phrase of the day, moral reasoning will occasionally require zero tolerance for certain actions and practices by compelling a political view. In Pope John Paul II's bull *Evangelium Vitae* (1995), for example, the inviolability of human life assigned to the first hours after conception requires a political opposition to legalized abortion. Put more generally, morality affects politics by requiring that allegiances to the state be always conditional, never absolute. The practical effect is that whether one can be reasonable on any particular set of political issues and problems is influenced by moral values. The deep pluralism expected in liberal conditions can also be expected to produce rival understandings of reality and moral principles. This extended pluralism will give different interpretations or weights to the sense of reasonableness in different parts of the political domain.

Public reason may be more accurately understood not as a check on morals at the entry points to politics but as a device to introduce morality into political domains. The language of the forum is sometimes decisively invested with community values, and these languages cannot be generalized among communities if the conceptual distance among them is too great. The state is a moral player in closing these spatial differences among community languages and in introducing moral perspectives to political needs. Public space may then be seen as a negotiated space that varies with moral and political issues and with types of speakers. The authoritative role for public reason may be as a kind of filter and monitor of generic moralities as they enter political deliberations and of political domains shaped in part by the influence of moral reasoning.

6

Theories of public reason that bracket divisive views are continuous with the basic liberal impulse to partition human experience. The demarcations among state, society, and individual that mark the historical transitions to classical liberalism establish the grounds for concepts of public space and impartial deliberations removed from divisive influences. But if the insulation between state and community is porous, then an adequate theory of public reason must accommodate the extension of pluralism to governing languages without sliding into political chaos or moral nihilism.

The arguments here indicate that fortifying the partitions between state and community with a more refined political language is a gatekeeper exercise in futility. Nor can it be worthwhile to thicken the liberal program with additional values or interpretations of extant principles as a condition for playing the liberal game. Some recent contributions have padded the liberal program in remarkably strong ways. The liberal state is now regarded by many distinguished theorists as a community with overriding values and substantive goals (they include the good as well as the right) that must be accepted by citizens if they are to be members of the liberal political system.[31] But if language is open to rival meanings, then thicker brackets and additional layers of values and interpretations are also proper targets for redefinition and partisan use. The halting problem can be expected to supervene on the linguistic padding. Language does not escape its elastic foundations by making terms more explicit or elaborate or by adding normative content (such as virtues). That exercise is roughly equivalent to increasing the volume of one's voice in talking to those who do not understand one's language. Shouting usually does not work.

A more effective approach to public reasoning than bracketing divisive beliefs or imposing gateway interpretations on political vocabularies is to recognize exactly what *form* of reasoning can be maintained when governing languages yield multiple interpretations. One first step in this recognition is to identify what must be rejected once language is accepted as chronically open to interpretation. The form that will not work is computational reason, in all of its forms. At its formal extreme, computational

31. This "tough love" version of liberalism is developed (in different ways) by, among others, Steven Macedo in *Liberal Virtues* (Oxford: Clarendon Press, 1990), William Galston in *Liberal Purposes* (Cambridge: Cambridge University Press, 1991), and John Rawls in *Political Liberalism*, and it provides neat and quick solutions to many problems that have been widely viewed as dilemmas for liberal theories. Note, for example, Rawls's easy judgment that of course dissident resistance to standard educational curricula must give way to the needs of democratic citizens for a secular education, pp. 199–200. All of the agonized reflections in, for example, *Wisconsin v. Yoder* (1972), are presumably just misunderstandings of the thickness of the liberal program and the scope of the political domain in ensuring the skills needed for public reason.

thinking is top-down reasoning, meaning that first-order rules and principles are applied to particular cases in step-by-step procedures. This serial type of reasoning resembles a Turing machine as it decides the fit between general and particular levels of a system within the provinces of the system itself.[32]

A computational system has a finite and listed set of transition rules that, when applied to any state of the system, provide for the deduction of a subsequent state. The requirements for such a system are easy to specify: The system is closed in the sense that all the variables affecting the it are abstract components of state descriptions and the transition rules, which means that the formal structures of the system are its states and the set of dependency relations found in the transition rules. No other exogenous variables intervene. Certain physical systems, perhaps only in a laboratory setting, can meet these requirements. A controlled experiment that limits variables to their causal laws and sequential states represents computational reasoning. John Searle's Chinese room experiment qualifies as an imaginative computational system, if the simulator managing inputs and outputs exhausts the mechanisms of the system *and* the system lacks consciousness.[33]

A local and homogeneous political community, one in which the primary values and transition rules are understood without qualifications, may be able to use algorithms to produce subsequent states from previous states. But we are reminded of H. L. A. Hart's caveats on systems of law without rules of recognition: They cannot address unanticipated cases nor disputes over the scope and meaning of primary rules.[34] These limitations are flaws that make computational systems unlikely models for public reasoning. That authorities typically cannot actually compute in mechanistic fashion is one of the points in the thought experiments elaborated here. Contemporary theories of language also concede the limitations and perhaps impossibility of computational reasoning. It may be that computation devolves to coercion to shield political structures from the natural inquiries

32. The original Turing machine was an ideal computer (though imagined with tape and *yes-no* stops). In A. M. Turing, "Computing Machinery and Intelligence," *Mind* 59 (1950): 433–460. I mean simply any computing device based on an algorithm. The halting problem is now elaborated in computer programs that contain representations of Gödel's proof, for example LISP.

33. Of course, Searle's major critics *do* assign consciousness, or at least (in the case of Daniel Dennett) understanding, to the system of inputs and outputs. See Dennett's *Consciousness Explained* (Boston: Little, Brown, 1991), 435–440. For the original description of the thought experiment, see John Searle, "Minds, Brains, and Programs," *Behavioral and Brain Sciences* (1980): 417–457.

34. H. L. A. Hart, *The Concept of Law* (Oxford: Clarendon Press, 1961), 89–96.

of citizens. But the point is that the stability and even possibilities of computational political systems depend on an acceptance of the properties of the system either spontaneously or coercively maintained. Unlike physical systems, a human community must introduce dissenting powers in order to complete the range of variables producing the computations.

In the strong pluralism introduced by radical speakers, noncomputational reasoning must dominate, on the assumption that a reduction of governing languages to partisan disputes leaves all precepts open. An unrestricted and continuing dialogue is a version of noncomputational reasoning that suffices in public domains. When successful, it is a group form of parallel processing: multiple and simultaneous explorations of proposals with many kinds of techniques. Listen to a good conversation. Narratives and linear modes of reasoning compete and complement one another in the movement of expressed thoughts. The goal of the conversation is mutual understanding of alternatives and resolutions and, finally, an acknowledgment of the best or just outcome. The logic is bottom-up in the sense that first-order rules and principles do not dominate but only guide. Procedures (at best) are in place to yield a solution that is not specified in advance. The system of reasoning is creative, not algorithmic. Persons who reason in this system must be open to unanticipated possibilities. Computational reasoning is to be controlled by an acknowledged text. Imperatives and prescriptions for action follow (within a narrow range) the acceptance of acknowledged rules and principles. Noncomputational reasoning can have no controlling text. The text (if there is one) is produced from deliberations as a crafted and open instrument of dialogue. The familiar model of an *open* conversation is the natural form of public reasoning when governing languages are subject to rival and reasonable interpretations.

The self-reflective powers of a conversation collapse venerable distinctions between political and philosophical dialogue.[35] The defining style of political talk is to take anything relevant to the issues at hand into the discussion. A lively political argument on abortion, for example, will easily move among and between distinctions in species of dialogue almost from moment to moment, including those between theoretical and argumentative talk. Discussions on the proper regulation of abortion are impossible

35. For arguments supporting a distinctive type of political talk see Benjamin Barber, *Strong Democracy* (Berkeley: University of California Press, 1984), chapter 8. If talk is seen as a form of currency, then political languages are different currencies that are mutually convertible rather than a single currency generalizable to a variety of human experiences. The term *noncomputation* simply represents the open set of convertible devices for the common currency.

without references to the origin and meaning of life, the standing of the fetus (or unborn child), a woman's rights to control her own body, and, in general, the sense and scope of pro-life and pro-choice languages. But all the distinctions are open to movement, including that between speaker and hearer (which typically can barely be recognized in the heat *and* light of good conversation). A noncomputational version of public reason is dialectical, and it has an unremitting scrutiny that makes all communication transitional and provisional and all items (including organizational frameworks) part of the material for discussion.

7

The capacity of political terms to yield rival interpretations is a variation on more general features of languages. All evaluative languages (at least) seem to be self-reflective, capable of evaluating themselves. G. E. Moore labeled as the "naturalistic fallacy" all efforts to define "good" in terms of properties "belonging to all things which are good." Such definitions cannot satisfy the term "good" because the definition in itself signifies that good and the properties offered as a definition are not synonymous. "There is no meaning in saying that pleasure is good," Moore points out, "unless good is something different from pleasure." Moore goes on to frame the open question argument. Any definition of "good" can itself be subject to inquiries about its goodness. In a typical infinite regress, Moore notes that designating A as "good" indicates that "A is one of the things which we desire to desire." But than we can always ask, "Is it good to desire to desire A?" Like all sound infinite regresses there is no stopping the chain of questions once started, for an affirmative answer to any question raises another in the chain: for example, "Is it good to desire to desire to desire A?", and so on. For Moore these exercises prove that "good" refers to a unique property of things that cannot be defined, or even described, in terms of other properties.[36]

Parallels between the "open question" argument and Gödel's proof are instructive. In one of his theorems Gödel proves that, for any recursive consistent class of formulas, the sentential formula stating that the class is consistent is not provable within the class. In ordinary terms, a theorem cannot be both consistent and complete. Suppose the formula $a \rightarrow b$. To accept this formula requires that an entailment rule establishing $a \rightarrow b$ be accepted.

36. G. E. Moore, "Goodness As A Unique Indefinable Quality," in *Principia Ethica* (Cambridge: Cambridge University Press, 1903), 5–21.

The rule is not a part of $a \rightarrow b$, but presupposes it. This more primordial endorsement renders the formula consistent, but only from a conceptual domain not addressed by the formula. If the endorsement of the entailment rule is brought into the system, then another rule outside the system of formulas and rules must be introduced to state the consistency between formula and entailment rule. The regress is (again) infinite. In each case the system generates a statement that guarantees its own incompleteness once consistency is purchased. Statements about the system are needed to establish relationships within the system.[37]

Moore describes the evaluative powers of "good" as the source of its resistance to naturalistic definitions. "Good" is a tiered concept, accepting empirical content so long as that content is understood to be incapable of filling the term up, of removing its evaluative powers to scrutinize all properties, including those served up to define it. Gödel's proof is a formal demonstration of the contradictions that occur between completeness and consistency in theorems. Yet note the similarities of the presentations. In both cases a term, or set of terms, cannot consistently find a point of closure. Both the "open question" argument and Gödel's proof demonstrate a self-reflective mechanism shared by some terms. This mechanism ensures the impossibility of any completeness within the logic or rules of at least some areas of language.

The elasticity of political terms seem to be a variant on self-reflective mechanisms. Any meaning assigned to terms can be scrutinized and evaluated by the terms themselves, or assigned to an internal domain that is the reflective focus of an external statement. Dispute on the content of such terms may be endless because each linguistic challenge can be framed on one step of an infinite regress. If this understanding of elasticity is accepted, than political reasoning cannot produce conclusive statements. A successful logic of political languages must allow multiple interpretations of terms.

37. Gödel's theorem is presented in accessible ways in Jean van Heijenoort, ed., *Frege and Gödel: Two Fundamental Texts in Mathematical Logic* (Cambridge: Harvard University Press, 1970), and in the first part of Roger Penrose's *Shadows of the Mind* (New York: Oxford University Press, 1994), where it is developed in terms of Turing's halting problem. See also the presentation of Penrose's Gödel by John Searle at the end of his review of books on consciousness, "The Mystery of Consciousness," *New York Review of Books* (November 2, 1995), and the regression examples and intriguing loops in Douglas Hofstadter's *Gödel, Escher, Bach* (New York: Basic Books, 1979). Reiner Grundmann and Christos Mantziaris recognize a version of Gödel's paradox in liberal theory in attempts to provide a conception of justice *for* society that must be situated *within* society. They regard attempts to define the right over the good without some commitment to the good as a self-contradiction in these terms. In "Fundamentalist Intolerance or Civil Disobedience?" *Political Theory* 19 no. 4 (November 1991): 572–605.

The open character of political languages may also be explained by two tendencies in recent political thought. One is the use of terms that force initial propositions to open internal calculations to external considerations. As example: Bayesian decision rules are computational. In all variations on these rules the expected values of outcomes are combined with probabilities to yield a utility value for each alternative. Once the numerical weights are assigned (a noncomputational exercise) the rational agent can mechanically produce an ordering of actions. Suppose, however, that one of the values in a Bayesian equation cannot be confined to the mathematical parameters of the calculation. *Identity* is such an entry. It is a term used to maintain the rationality of political activity when efficacy fails. Solidary commitments, for example, allow the reasoning agent to regard the group as the self (or, in the weaker sense of Kurt Lewin's phrase, see the "interdependence of fate"), and in this way fulfill efficacy as a collective rather than an individual action. A person can also identify with a group to such a degree that the identification functions as a heuristic to interpret and organize experience. But if the solidary value serves as a filter for the calculations of rational agents it is external to the Bayesian equation. The collective undertaking on which efficacy is measured enters on the causal side of the equation, redefining the antecedent terms and specifying value for all other entries in the equation. The self just *is* the group on which an effect is to be made, which provides different meanings for the efficacy that is to be tested. Solidary values are values in a calculation (rational agents can certainly identify with collectives) that exceed the limits of the calculation, and in doing so undermine the (closed) algorithm of the calculation by collapsing distinctions between antecedent and dependent variables.[38]

Levels of knowledge represent another tendency. All rational thinking accepts boundaries between domains of accessible and inaccessible knowledge. The latter is often created by exclusions that restrict knowledge by

38. Gavan Duffy develops solidary values as a way around efficacy failure, in Duffy and Nathalie J. Frensley, "Community Conflict Processes: Mobilizations and Demobilizations in Northern Ireland," in James W. Lamare, ed., *International Crisis and Domestic Politics: Major Political Conflicts in the 1980s* (New York: Praeger, 1991). The growing emphasis on group identification as a heuristic is found in especially interesting form in recent amendments of party identification with the use of stereotypes and prototypes, which provide (for both researcher and actor) a wider range for interpreting political action than the earlier party ID variables did. Jim Josefson discusses this shift in his 1997 dissertation *The Changing Construction of Partisan Identity: Party Stereotypes in American National Elections, 1952–94* (Political Science Department, Syracuse University). The Kurt Lewin quote is in *Resolving Social Conflicts: Selected Papers on Group Dynamics* (New York: Harper, 1948), 184.

type and range. Bounded forms of practical reasoning, by abandoning perfect information, craft a domain of knowledge unknown to the rational agent. The case is persuasive. Any number of reflections and studies have demonstrated that complete information is outside the range of the individual intellect. Also, the notion of complete knowledge may be impossible even in principle. Knowledge seems always to be located within the framework of theory, and theory may provide multiple perspectives that cannot be ranked on truth-functional criteria. One cannot know everything, nor ever close accounts of knowledge, if knowledge is always from a perspective.[39] The effects of inaccessible knowledge on rational judgments are constraining. If there is a domain of knowledge beyond the rational grasp of the reasoning agent, then all rational judgments must be tentative or provisional. Simply put, the inaccessible domain might render the judgments wrong or inadequate. There is no reason to think that the meanings of terms are shielded from this uncertainty. The self-reflective powers of languages may be an artifact of domains acknowledged as limited by the concession that other, inaccessible domains exist. Models of bounded rationality provide conditions for a noncomputational reasoning that restates the analyses of Moore and Gödel.

Here is the intermediate conclusion. Given the noncomputational standing of political terms, we have intellectual and prudential obligations to track, record, accept, and mediate the implications of open-textured terms on political practices and, in particular here, on our understanding of public reason. A plausible account of public reason must accept interpretive discretion while avoiding its critical effects. In the more direct manner in which Moore and Gödel fashion the problem, public reasoning must be capable of self-reflection without a contradiction. It must manage the pernicious effects of the open-question argument, and the abrasive relations demonstrated between completeness and consistency.

8

The halting problem illuminates the open reasoning of computation. Mathematics contains both determinate and indeterminate functions, meaning that there are procedures that do and do not terminate, and in some cases one knows this in advance. For example, an effective procedure

---

39. Herbert Simon, *Models of Bounded Rationality* (Cambridge: MIT Press, 1982). The perspectival view of knowledge is the basis of sociology of knowledge claims.

can be written to determine if a number is prime. This procedure terminates. One can also write a procedure to determine the largest prime number. This latter procedure, however, does not terminate. It describes an algorithm that transforms input sets into outcomes, but not in a finite set of operations. This kind of regress can be demonstrated with the rules of mathematics. Nonmathematical, though still infinite, regresses are widely represented in political and moral philosophy. For example, any particular agreement seems to depend on a general agreement to keep agreements. But if there must be an agreement to keep agreements, then of course there must be an agreement to keep the initial prior agreement, and so on, literally ad infinitum.

Other procedures may or may not terminate. Suppose that we write a procedure for an algorithm (when $x \neq 1$) that requires a repeated halving of x when x is even, or adding of $(3x + 1)$ when x is odd, until $x = 1$. All uses of positive integers have halted this program, but no one can prove that the function terminates for all positive integers. Mathematicians may yet solve this problem with a proof demonstrating that the function must terminate for all positive integers, or does not terminate for a range of these integers. But it cannot now be determined in mathematics whether this particular function terminates. In computer science the termination of a computable function is sometimes undecidable with a given input, meaning that one cannot say that the function will halt or continue.

The halting problem is expressed in a proof of indeterminacy general to all computation. The proof demonstrates that there is no computational machine that can say whether functions terminate. One assumption and two questions must be kept distinct in stating the halting problem. The assumption is a factual proposition that all functions either halt or continue. The first question is whether we can determine if any given function halts or continues. We can determine this for some functions (as in the example of prime numbers above) and not for others (as in the example of the algorithm above). We simply do not know whether the algebraic procedure above halts or continues. A second question is whether there is any *general* program that will answer the first question. The halting problem is a proof that there is no general program that can determine whether any given function will halt or continue. The effort to compute the factual outcome (the function either halts or continues) instead produces a contradiction.[40]

40. Like all proofs, the demonstration of the halting problem can in principle be overturned. But it is a fundamental theory at this time on the logic of computation. See Richard

The indeterminacy of languages in political domains makes the rational outcomes of all disputes uncertain. But public reason does not offer any proof of a halting problem (though I actually have a truly marvelous proof, one, of course, which this margin is too narrow to contain).[41] I am using a halting indeterminacy in public reasoning to refer informally to those disputes that occur in public space when a political text is used as an instrument of the disputes it is designed to govern. When this happens a continuation is produced that may or may not be halted, and one cannot say which outcome will occur. A continuing dispute is typically settled with the use of a text that is outside the boundaries of the initial text, and so exceeds the conditions of the initial occurrence of the dispute.[42] The problem in public reasoning is that governing vocabularies present an open text that can be read differently by reasonable citizens, and the only possibility of deciding whether the regresses of interpretation will stop is by exiting the chain of textual interpretation (stepping outside the logic that creates the indeterminacy, as in stopping the regress on promising by acknowledging a generalizable convention to keep promises). The halting problem would raise the stakes for regresses and their stopping devices by showing us that

---

Jeffrey, *Formal Logic: Its Scope and Limits* (New York: McGraw-Hill, 1991), chapter 7, especially 105–108, and David Harel, *The Science of Computing* (Reading, Mass.: Addison Wesley, 1989), especially 180–188. The programming example is from Harel, 180–182.

41. To the reader: forgive. This spoof proviso (which I am sure everyone caught immediately) is from Fermat's famous comment on his missing Last Theorem. The full and very famous quote, one that haunted mathematicians for centuries until Andrew Wiles provided a proof for the theorem in 1993, and a corrected version in 1995, followed Fermat's claim that there is no whole number that satisfies the Pythagorean equation $x^n + y^n = z^n$ for $n > 2$. Fermat then wrote: "I have a truly marvelous demonstration of this proposition which this margin is too narrow to contain." An engrossing account of the story of the theorem is Simon Singh's *Fermat's Enigma* (New York: Walker, 1997).

42. H. A. Prichard, "The Obligation To Keep a Promise," in *Moral Obligation* (Oxford: Clarendon Press, 1949), 169–179, rejects the possibility that justifying promises leads to an infinite regress. He sees promising *not* as depending on an obligation to keep agreements, which would depend on a general agreement to keep agreements (and thus create an infinite regress), but on "an agreement to do what is ordinarily called keeping our agreements, i.e., not to make a certain noise in connexion with the phrase for some action without going on to do the action." (The quote is on page 173.) Prichard offers an account of promising that transfers the problem of grounding a promise to something else, and it is the transfer that avoids the regress. I see this as very much like those moves to a text outside a line of argument that halt infinite regresses in political discourses. See also Prichard's discussion of intuitionism in "Does Moral Philosophy Rest on a Mistake?," the first essay in the same collection. Infinite regresses are solved in a special way by intuitive approaches: because the primary mark of intuitionism is an admittance that there are no criteria to rank order first principles, one must simply assert an ordering by some special insight that cannot (by definition) be challenged or appealed. A regress never begins.

there is no general procedure to determine whether a function ever halts. At the moment we simply have a long line of continuing disputes inspired by rival interpretations of texts that remind us of the chronic possibilities of regresses. One cannot say currently that any regress will continue or halt even when external texts are introduced.[43]

The difficulties in public reasoning represented by regresses create a kind of linguistic devolution. The governing languages of the liberal state do not fully determine the judgments made in the adjudication forum that represents liberal governance, even as claimants try sincerely to reach rational closure in managing their disputes (they do not know in advance that closure is impossible). The result is that both petitioners and judges are required to employ additional languages outside the political texts of governing principles. These collateral languages have the power to collapse public space into community beliefs. In extreme cases the state is reduced to a truly empty vessel that cannot fix the meanings and values of claims, and thus their merits, in ways that allow adjudication to be independent of those beliefs it is to order. This general pluralism yields a public space that is not fixed but variable with distinctions among rival (and partisan) points of view. There is no obvious rational closure to this process.

The open powers of reasoning extend to methods as well as conclusions. One consequence of indeterminacy in governing languages is that all disagreements and divisions have the seeds, or latent properties, to become ontological disputes. But also basic distinctions among forms of governing, and argumentative categories, are targets for critical inspection and redefinition. Even the distinctions between contested and contestable, accidental and essential, cannot be maintained within the boundaries of languages once governing terms are regarded as indeterminate. The distinctions must be seen as functions of variable conditions. Every outcome, principle and concept in public reasoning must be accepted as defeasible by an open set of arguments, and dependent on corrigible arrangements, once the closure powers of language are abandoned.

Infinite regresses and the halting problem describe formal aspects of computational reasoning. Regresses often lead to arguments that a device must replace a text simpliciter in deliberations. Something (it is often as-

43. I am grateful to James Bennett for reminding me of the powers of mathematics to discriminate between functions that do and do not halt, as well as other helpful comments on this section. Also, my thanks to my younger daughter, Christina Frohock, for finally making me see (when no one else could succeed) that the halting problem is consistent with both determinate and indeterminate functions in mathematics, and to Nadeem Hussain for introducing some distinctions in my description of the halting problem that have clarified this part of the text.

sumed or argued) must set the foundations for reasoning. For Turing this was the "oracle," a hypothetical machine that provisionally solves the halting problem with a definite *yes* or *no*.[44] For Wittgenstein a regress in interpretation is stopped by conventions, by the way that things *are*, with no further questions possible about the conventions.[45] In many religious practices the stopping function is provided by God on the basis of a higher and privileged knowledge.

Much of political philosophy is designed to stop regresses with a foundation or baseline for reasoning. Hobbes refuses to allow a contract between the sovereign and the people on the grounds that some authority will then be needed to interpret and enforce this contract. The sovereign is vested with the authority to halt the regresses of interpretation by possessing a power to resolve disputes that is not subject to higher appeal. Rawls offers the original position as a solution to regresses. It is a thought experiment that justifies certain principles by tracking them to the conditions of fairness that define the OP. Consent for the principles is generated from their selection by OP persons. The original position is the stopping point for the regress of justification: fairness simply is the ultimate appeal or final authority for governing principles. Habermas argues for an ideal speech situation, and this model locates and fixes the standards for actual reasoning and discourses.[46]

Foundational devices are sometimes boundaries that set limits. Plato's highest form, for example, simply ends the regress of justifications: as the ultimate intuitive truth it just is the starting point for dialogue. Other types of these devices are thresholds: we can argue for or against them, and if they are accepted we argue with them as premises. But the arguments are different whether they are about the devices or presuppose them. Rawls's original position is this type of device. The devices also differ as to form: some are rules (Hart's rule of recognition), others are types of rational agents (original position people). But in all cases these foundational items are circuit breakers, the stable stopping *and* starting points for reasoned discussions of political authority.

The thought experiments discussed here suggest a contrary possibility: that all foundations, all original or ideal positions, and governing princi-

44. A. M. Turing, "Systems of Logic Based on Ordinals," *Proceedings of the London Mathematics Society* 45 (1939): 161–228.

45. Ludwig Wittgenstein, *Philosophical Investigations* (New York: Macmillan, 1953.

46. Thomas Hobbes, *Leviathan*; Rawls, *A Theory of Justice* (Cambridge: Harvard University Press, 1971), chapters 1 and 3; Jürgen Habermas, "Toward a Communicative Concept of Rational Collective Will-Formation: A Thought Experiment," *RatioJuris* 2 (1980): 149, and *The Theory of Communicative Action* (Boston: Beacon Press, 1984).

ples, are open to rival and reasonable interpretations. My arguments support the reality of infinite regresses in the use of political terms. The concept of public reason developed here is based on an acceptance of the powers of rational persons to define and redefine the languages that are traditionally used to reach closure in reasoning. The task in public reason is identifying an appropriate halting device that accepts these powers of critical interpretation.

9

Public reason is the centerpiece in theories of the liberal state. It is the visible and transparent device that reconciles claims originating in political differences. Its expectations are marvelously immodest. Citizens are required to tolerate beliefs which they do not believe, may regard as false and even harmful, and occasionally can barely understand. This expectation follows the political acceptance of multiple truths in liberalism. The burdens of partitioning are heavy in this vision: among communities and social practices, between the state and its constituent communities, and within a self that must extend allegiance to both the community and the political system.

Some communities will regard the liberal vision of public reason as pure fantasy. Any political system that invites persons to suspend the imperatives of community beliefs for whatever reason can expect the occasional note of regret. The levels of discourse required in the liberal state are also unwelcome reminders of the role of truth in liberal governance. True statements may be introduced to public reason by members of communities. These truths may also be regarded as general, and even universal, within the framework of communal reasoning. But from the perspective of the political system *claims* to truth are entered into the political domain, inasmuch as the liberal state must avoid a commitment to any of the rival truths of community beliefs. One consequence of this restriction is that the truths on which claims are based must be regarded as local on the conditions of political discourse. The localization of truths regarded as general or universal cannot be a welcome prospect for believers in truth.

The prize that is to replace truth in liberalism is a semantic model that translates community claims into political languages. If political domains are spatially arranged, then liberal governance is a tiered arrangement in which communities resolve or manage their disputes by invoking the third language of the state. Even if communities do not fully understand or communicate with each other, they are expected to master and accept the governing languages of the state, and to use these languages to settle those differences that cannot be resolved without the authority of the state. Public reason is the procedure or practice that is to govern the subjective claims of communities, and produce within a common political language judgments that are coercively enforced by the state.

The problem is that the semantic model yields multiple and rival political languages. I have argued that one consequence of this linguistic plurality is a shift in the conceptual arrangements of liberal governance: not tiers or distinct domains, but filters that modify beliefs and claims through discourse, and a system of governance so fluid at categorical levels that moral and political reasoning are constituent parts of public reason. Even the working distinctions between the political domain and member communities may be opened to interpretation. One powerful device to filter community and political languages is morality, which indemnifies the state (as Rawls sees) but also has three other functions in a complete account of public reason: the interpretation of political principles, the identification of thresholds for acting reasonably (or civilly), and the assignment of importance to other beliefs and their arrangements. In these ways community morals can be ordering devices for the languages of public reason, and the distance between state and community is narrowed. Moral discourse may even be the most decisive filter for public reason in the practical organization of the liberal state.

These conclusions modify understandings of the liberal state. Abandoning an independent language of governance acknowledges that state adjudication is little more than an unreasoned dominance of some communities over others. On these concessions the liberal program effectively succeeds only as a series of fragile equilibriums in which community and individual liberties are measured against the needs of state regulation. Negotiating and setting the equilibrium points involve complex judgments on regulation, exemption, and exclusion on criteria that might be politically charged. The requirement for every liberal state in these judgments is to find and use the collective languages of public reason that permit rational closure for disputes that cannot be governed successfully by primary rules and principles.

The theory of noncomputational public reasoning developed here attempts to integrate three areas. The first and most important (in its powers to organize the two other areas) is mediation, which includes the practice of interpreting texts and translating languages across discourses and practices. The conditions of liberal governance can include communities that may differ from each other on basic understandings of human experience (as we have seen). Political liberalism requires that these communities have an overlapping consensus that includes a common language of governance. But the map that relates community and political languages (of consent, liberty, and authority minimally) is similar to those drawn up by cultural anthropologists attempting to communicate indigenous meanings to those outside the communities studied. The problems in this exercise are well known: maintaining ethnographic methods sensitive to vernacular beliefs and practices; exiting the subject culture with intact knowledge from the resident experience; and finding or developing a metalanguage that translates between internal and external languages without substantial losses of meaning.

The communication forged in this exercise, and the introduction of a text with generalizing powers that connect participant and observer, do not occur spontaneously. The persons conducting an ethnographic study are the primary resources for translating among various communities. They must be able to live and speak in the relevant cultures, and craft appropriate languages of translation. It is inconceivable that anything resembling a social contract based on shared understandings of mutual advantage would occur naturally in these conditions, and little to expect that a set of terms for mutual governance would either be freely produced or accepted as the defining property of a distinct political system. More likely is that a type of person, one who is at least provisionally recognized by the communities as a guide, would be critical to successful coordination. That person is what is meant here by the mediator.

The second area is the role of moral beliefs and practices in public reason. The arguments to follow will maintain that the complex and varied attempts in political liberalism to shield the political domain from various moral doctrines obscure important connections between morality and politics in public reasoning. The history of political theory and social practices is marked by intimate relations between moral and political thinking. Classical and medieval political philosophy routinely expect states to express basic moral considerations of virtue, natural law and the common good. The demarcation of moral and political domains, and the anticipation of antagonisms between these two ways of thinking, may be one of the more remarkable features of the modern world. I argue that some of the difficulties in recent theories of public reasoning can be corrected by introducing a range of moral considerations into the domains of politics.

A third area is marked off by collective arrangements. These arrangements are important as considerations that help demarcate the state from its member communities. The liberal state originates in social partitions, in particular those that separate church and state, and may be usefully viewed as an artifact created by existing communities. But the criteria establishing the distinction between the state and other communities are not always clear. Often these criteria are represented by characteristic purposes and goods. The disputes between the pope and the German states in the late medieval period demarcated church and state according to what we might call their functions, roughly meaning the goods that they seek and provide in human communities. Those who argued a separatist thesis maintained that churches seek salvation for persons after death, while states attempt to secure temporal goods. Recent liberal theory assumes partitions among communities on the basis of distinct goods. Michael Walzer has offered a theory of goods that demarcates social domains: the heterogeneity of contemporary industrial societies represented by different goods sought in different ways. For Walzer these differences underwrite a pluralism that, when maintained, is a protection against tyranny. The nonconvertibility of goods across spheres guarantees the complex equalities of partitioned justice.[47]

The use of characteristic goods has a certain success in demarcating political systems from other communities in modern liberal democracies. Assigning to the state the need to maintain civil order can be tracked from the contract theorists and early libertarian theories of the state to the present time. Certain *generic* (not political) primary goods, in particular the protection of life, are also to be secured even by minimal liberal states. No respectable account of the state has ever denied certain basic functions of the political domain, which must include the installation and maintenance of orderly relations that reasonably guarantee citizens the conditions of security needed to live any civil version of the good life.

But a closer inspection of these functions provides a more succinct account of the state. The state, as guarantor of order and (limited) primary goods in the heterogeneous conditions of liberalism, is unlike any other community in having a concern for the collective arrangements of society. This concern suggests that the state also has a vicarious good in seeing to the success of other systems in the civil society (whether by means of forbearance or intervention). They also indicate that public reason is concerned with the proper arrangements of communal life in ways not duplicated by the reasoning of those communities that constitute the state.

47. Michael Walzer, *Spheres of Justice* (New York: Basic Books, 1983).

3 Narrative Persons

Two of the controlling thoughts in all liberal theories of reasoning are that the individual person is the source of meaning and value in human experience, and that social institutions are in some way derivatives of individual properties. This strong methodological individualism is extended with liberal assignments of both moral powers and powers of reason to persons. Persons in liberal theory are moral agents who are competent and, in complex ways, both rational and reasonable. Without these assignments the liberal program could not begin, for liberalism (whatever its incarnation) is a celebration of the individual person in the production and arrangement of governing rules and principles.

Any theory with such robust individualistic foundations requires a precise and reasonably comprehensive understanding of the person. What is the meaning of "person" in these priority assignments? The liberal effort to establish distinct political domains would seem to favor a minimalist conception of the person rather than one enriched by those community doctrines that the state is to govern or accommodate. It should not be surprising, then, to discover a *political* sense of the person, one unencumbered by philosophical substance, in what is arguably the most prominent current theory of political liberalism. John Rawls has elaborated a view of the person that supports a political domain free of substantial metaphysical foundations, especially for the conception of citizens in a just society. Persons, as "full participants in a fair system of social cooperation" have two moral powers: the power to be just and the power to frame and revise a conception of the good. The second power, when assigned to persons as "self-authenticating sources of valid claims" and "as capable of taking responsibility for their ends," specifies how citizens think of themselves as free. Rawls advances this conception of the person, elaborate by any standards, as political, not metaphysical.[1]

It is never an easy matter to define a metaphysical doctrine. Classical metaphysics is an examination of first principles and perhaps reality. Contemporary metaphysics can be more modest. In the most ordinary sense, metaphysics refers to implicit assumptions in a theory that are outside the primary methodologies generating the theory. At least some assumptions in any theory are continuous with its dominant methods. Copernican theories about planetary motion, for example, rest on explicit assumptions about systems of classification, theories of measurement, definitions of time and motion, and other considerations that can be retrieved and evaluated with roughly the same methods of explanation supporting heliocentric views. But a theory also depends on unexamined assumptions that, when retrieved, seem to require different types of explanation, and sometimes cannot be explained at all. Most correlations accepted as explanatory occur between events regarded as contiguous. Contiguity, however, is usually just part of the general way that experience is organized and understood, not explainable by empirical theories.[2] These latter types of assumptions may be regarded as metaphysical.

Does a political conception of the person rest on this sense of a metaphysical doctrine? The direct answer to this question is the least productive response. Of course it does, for it is inconceivable that any conception would be free of some such assumptions. The interesting question is whether the assumptions influence or control concepts in the theory. A metaphysical doctrine affects a theory in two ways that are worth monitoring in deciphering or understanding the theory. One effect occurs whenever a single doctrine is selectively assigned to theories. Often the single doctrine is so general or elastic that its assignment must be explained with additional considerations. Contiguity, for example, is a broad assumption

1. John Rawls, "Justice As Fairness: Political Not Metaphysical," *Philosophy and Public Affairs* (1985): 223–251, and *Political Liberalism* (New York: Columbia University Press, 1993), 18–20 and 29–35. I neglect several distinctions among *individual*, *agent*, and—in particular—*person* and *self* in this discussion. My defense rests on parsimony. A conjoining of the latter two terms is more than adequate ground for the arguments that follow. Any additional explorations of person vs. self, or individual and agent would be interesting but superfluous in this particular work.

2. Hubert Blalock, *Causal Inferences in Nonexperimental Research* (Chapel Hill: University of North Carolina Press, 1964), for brief though helpful reflections on contiguity. Any distinctions between an empirical theory and its metaphysical assumptions will vary with the particular theory and historical context. I am offering a working definition of a metaphysical assumption with homage to this commonplace observation on variance.

that might be assigned to various correlations, and whether it is assigned or not is probably explainable only with an exploration of cultural or other background variables. Another effect occurs whenever the metaphysical doctrine is one member in a set of well-defined rival doctrines, and the reliance of the theory on one or another entry in the set affects the meanings and arrangements of concepts in the theory. Here a larger understanding of both the effects and the theory is secured by explaining the selection mechanisms that favor one metaphysical doctrine over its rivals. In this second type of effect the mechanisms can be seen more precisely by provisionally extending alternative metaphysical doctrines to the theory. This is an experimental exercise that cannot be conducted with the first kind of effect.[3]

The discussion here will focus on the latter pattern of influence. I will argue that liberal theory depends on two metaphysical conceptions of the person. One is developed in the literature as property dualism. The other is a form of what I call practice dualism. These two conceptions are members of a set containing several rival accounts of the person that each can influence political theory in critical ways. Among the alternative accounts are those elaborated by what I call ontological dualism and the versions of the nondual self found in recent works by John Searle and Daniel Dennett. All of these conceptions are linked to fundamental assumptions on language and social experience, suggesting both the need to retrieve and define the self in political theory and the difficulty of doing this without an exploration of metaphysics. The opening consideration in these discussions is Rawls's conception of the person. But the arguments developed here are not confined to any particular claims or version of liberalism. Metaphysical doctrines of the person are unavoidable assumptions in all liberal theories of the state, and an examination of these assumptions identifies problems in the liberal governance of communities, especially those communities that do not accept dualistic versions of the self. My speculative conclusion is that a narrative account of the self may be more useful in political theory than other conceptions. A narrative account can at least help close the partitions that divide and subdivide the terms of liberal governance, and instruct us on the needs for rational closure within liberal premises. It will

3. It is instructive that Rawls recognizes and denies exactly this sense of metaphysical influence: "If we look at the presentation of justice as fairness and note how it is set up, and note the ideas and conceptions it uses, no particular metaphysical doctrine about the nature of persons, *distinctive and opposed to other metaphysical doctrines* (emphasis added), appears among its premises, or seems required by its argument." In footnote 31 on page 29 in *Political Liberalism*.

also move us further along the journey toward a full development of effective forms of public reasoning by providing an exploration of a concept vital to any complete account of reason.

2

The story of persons in Rawls's theory of justice is generally known. The original position, a formal expression of intuitive (perhaps cultural) ideas of fairness, is adumbrated by a veil of ignorance that denies persons knowledge of contingent facts, including information about individual assets and talents, race and ethnicity, sex and gender, social position, and particular religious, moral, or philosophical comprehensive doctrines. This information is excluded from the original position (OP) on the thought it should not be considered in choosing principles of social justice.[4]

The (by now) standard communitarian critique of the original position is that it requires a metaphysical conception of the person as autonomous, disinterested (a nonpredatory egoist), and prior to its own ends. This empty or at least "unencumbered" self must be antecedent to society and its formative influences. But, so the critique goes, this conception of the self is metaphysically false or untenable. Membership in communities is formative of the self and the normal condition for autonomy. A person denied the information that is excluded from the OP is separated from those conceptions of the good that constitute the cognitive self and introduce those sentiments that make choice possible. Ends help define the person and cannot be seen as the sole product of choice. The identity of persons is inseparable from membership in communities.[5]

Rawls's response to this assignment of metaphysics to the parties in the original position is on the whole effective. He reminds us that the original position is "a device of representation." The veil of ignorance denies information as a thought experiment in which persons are to imagine themselves in certain ways. This hypothetical state of "what if" simply asks participants to conceive of the principles of justice as originating from conditions in which contingent information irrelevant or damaging to fair-

4. *Political Liberalism*, 22–28.

5. One of the more interesting of these views is also among the earliest in a discussion that has filled the airwaves since *A Theory of Justice* (Cambridge: Harvard University Press) was published in 1971. I refer to Michael Sandel's *Liberalism and the Limits of Justice* (Cambridge: Cambridge University Press, 1982). Sandel's more recent arguments against rights-based liberalism and for civic republicanism are in *Democracy's Discontent* (Cambridge: Harvard University Press, 1996).

ness is not considered. Rawls is clear that this mental exercise says nothing about the essential nature of persons (except, presumably, that they have the mental powers to perform the thought experiment): "When, in this way, we simulate being in the original position, our reasoning no more commits us to a particular metaphysical doctrine about the nature of the self than our acting a part in a play, say of Macbeth or Lady Macbeth, commits us to thinking that we are really a king or queen engaged in a desperate struggle for political power."[6]

The original position, in short, is *hypothetical*, not actual, and certainly not dependent on the metaphysical doctrine of the person elaborated in the communitarian critique. Rawls is surely correct here. If metaphysical conceptions of the person are present in his theory, they must be sought elsewhere.

Also, there are good reasons for excluding the communitarian self from the OP thought experiment. Liberalism originates in social pluralism, represented historically and conceptually by the presence of multiple communities with rival beliefs. The "thick" descriptions that fill out and define persons as members of communities risk the introduction of those contentious beliefs that occasion the need for formal selves outside communities. The Rawlsian thought experiment is an attempt (that may or may not succeed) to bracket the communitarian self as a way of adjudicating community disputes. If the empty self of the original position is a metaphysical assumption, it originates in the needs of liberalism to craft principles of justice from a point outside of community beliefs.

3

The oldest accounts of the person express views on the presence or absence of partitions in the self. Plato regarded persons as composed of three parts designated as intellect (*nous*), spirit, and appetite. The well-ordered person is represented by a hierarchical arrangement of these parts in which intellect dominates both spirit and (especially) appetite. Modern philosophy of mind is in part a series of conversations over rival versions of dualism, and theories of dualism competing with various forms of materialism as an account of the person.

The modern doctrine of the person begins with Descartes's substance dualism. Persons are to be understood as minds (or souls) residing in bodies.[7] More recent versions of dualism also bifurcate mind and body. But

6. *Political Liberalism*, p. 27.
7. Descartes, in the Second Meditation ("Of the Nature of the Human Mind, and That It Is More Exactly Known Than the Body"), follows reflections establishing *that* I am with

theories of property dualism generally avoid "mind" language. These theories regard mental properties as not reducible to physical properties without loss of meaning. The stronger versions of property dualism develop mental properties as a necessary condition for consciousness, maintaining that all conceptions of the self require a subjective point of view that cannot be collapsed to physical properties.[8]

There is little doubt that the person in contemporary liberal theory is consistently defined in terms of property dualism. This type of dualism is especially strong in liberal versions of law. Concepts of the self are found at foundational levels in all versions of Western law, where it is widely accepted that the life of the mind is in some important sense distinct from the life of the body. The mental states of individuals are generally shielded from state regulation, a practice justified by the core principle in all liberal traditions that freedom of thought is outside the regulatory powers of the state. Behavior is the appropriate target for the law. This regulatory bifurcation can work only if thought and behavior are distinct and independent domains at least on occasion. If thought and behavior are intimately related or indistinguishable many liberal models of law simply break down, sometimes permanently.

Mental considerations enter law at a variety of points. States of mind are often used to fix the seriousness of behavior. The practice is usually found where rules govern behavior. The game of basketball, for example, distinguishes "routine" from "intentional" fouls, the latter carrying a heavier penalty. Legal infractions are usually graded in seriousness according to the deliberations preceding the behavior. Homicide that is premeditated is a graver offense than unplanned or accidental murder, a scale represented by differences among first-and second-degree homicide and manslaughter. Generally mental antecedents locate responsibility for behavior, and in doing so help establish the culpability of the agent. Sometimes laws will map behavior back into thought in order to assign responsibility. Strict liability law holds individuals responsible for their behavior no matter what their state of knowledge or intentions might be. In this type of law behavior dominates thought. But mental considerations are not extinguished, for the main point to such laws is to sharpen calculations on the possibilities of

thoughts on *what* I am. He proposes that persons are minds in bodies. In the *Meditations*, trans. Laurence J. Lafleur (New York: Macmillan, 1960).

8. For example, Thomas Nagel, *The View from Nowhere* (London: Oxford University Press, 1982). Also the famous views in Frank Jackson, "Epiphenomenal Qualia," *Philosophical Quarterly* 32 no. 127 (April 1982): 127–136, and "What Mary Didn't Know," *Journal of Philosophy* 83, no. 5 (May 1986): 291–296.

punishment in the expectation that the prohibited behavior will be reduced in frequency. Freedom of will is always a vital component in settling legal responsibility, helping to maintain thought and behavior as independent domains.

Mental states also are considerations in settling damages in law, on the assumption that mental harm is a medical reality and that states of mind can affect the human body in both good and bad ways. Laws also locate competence and sanity in the realm of the mental and traditionally have defined the individual in terms of mental powers rather than bodily integrity. The law states and restates distinctions between the legal person as a mental figure and the physical expression of that person in a body and in behavior that are represented in different fashions within the law.

The surface or opening statements in Rawls's theory accept these long-standing liberal views on the nature of the person. The thought that persons have two moral powers, are self-authenticating sources of claims, and are responsible for their ends—these are attributes that require considerable mental powers that in some way are distinct from bodily powers. The conception of the person in Rawls's theory is dense with the vocabularies of autonomy, choice, responsibility, reflection, rationality, and reasonableness that traditionally are the markers for mental properties in property dualism.

These vocabularies range over both the original position and the roles of citizens in the political domain established by the selection of principles of justice. Persons in the original position are mental constructs who engage in their own thought experiments. They are granted the mental powers to survey a reasonably complete menu of governing principles and select a small set of these principles on the prior acceptance of a maximin decision rule that makes the selection a rational choice. It is not clear if the OP persons are disembodied, for appetites must be ceded to these hypothetical persons in order to generate a schedule of alternatives.[9] But the OP is certainly dominated by mental powers that require only minimal statements on body.

Citizens must have mental attributes in order to function in the political system. Many of these attributes are used by Rawls to elaborate a reasonable moral psychology. Persons have a "readiness to propose and abide by fair terms of cooperation," the power to recognize "the burdens of judgment" and affirm "only reasonable comprehensive doctrines." Citizens also

9. Primary social goods, for example, include economic goods, which typically are parts of a rational plan of life that satisfies both physical and mental needs.

want to be "full citizens" by entering and supporting the arrangements of mutual trust and confidence that secure cooperation. This moral psychology is drawn from the political conception of justice as fairness rather than from a psychological theory, and so it is presented as a philosophical thesis. Still, it is a description of a certain sensibility that seems to be required for Rawls's version of liberal justice, and these mental powers extend the liberal understanding of the person as dualistic across mental and physical properties.[10]

4

A more complete conception of the person in liberal theory is found in the dual relationships of citizens to their community and to the political domain. It is helpful to remember that the liberal state was occasioned by the deep pluralism represented by religious disputes. The Reformation is that historical moment when ontological disputes were to be settled with a decisive text, and regarded as an expression of the individual's liberty to reason on essential matters (so long as the disputes remain within defined limits). The state on liberal terms is an artifact created by persons who are deeply embedded in communities that may define (for them) the overall dimensions of human experience. The consent that generates the state covers the political domain, and does not reconcile the divergent views that require the particular principles and concepts of liberal governance. Community views can be maintained in the liberal political system when governing is successful on liberal tests of success.

The separation between communities and the political domain is marked in several ways. In Rawls's terms, communities are represented by comprehensive moral doctrines. These doctrines differ among communities, and may on occasion approach incommensurability. One must be careful here. Whether true incommensurability is ever possible is an open question, because even to make this claim would seem to presuppose a metalanguage that is generalizable to rival communities. Also, as Fodor and Lepore maintain, both semantic holism and atomism are unlikely accounts of language. To understand one of my beliefs it is surely not necessary to understand *all* of my beliefs, which suggests that fragments of meaning can be shared even between radically different communities. Commensurabil-

10. *Political Liberalism*, 81–88. Rawls prepares the section on moral psychology with some remarks on two types of desires: object-dependent and principle-dependent. These remarks add to the sphere of the mental by thickening the discerning and calculative powers of persons.

ity, in short, can be local or partial, thus removing the need to assign incommensurability to rival communities that seem to misunderstand the bulk of what the adversary is saying. But, also, understanding just one of my beliefs is unlikely without understanding *some* of my other beliefs, because it is inconceivable that one could make sense of any belief expressed in the absence of semantic context or background. So if communities understand just one thing about each other it is probable that they understand other things as well, which makes more robust commensurability likely even among radically different communities. The presence of different communities in the same political domain is partial testimony to the existence of a communal language, though one that is probably incomplete in extending across rival communities and also consistent with the deep pluralism found in liberal politics. Remember that moral and political differences can cut down to the boundaries of reality and the nature of the self.[11]

The political domain is represented by a set of public and general principles that are to contain no commitments to any of these doctrines of translation. This domain in principle need not be in a state of conflict with any moral doctrine, and presumably is reasonably consistent with the doctrines of member communities since the state originates in freely given consent. But the differences between communities and the state is profound. Communities are logically antecedent to the formation of the state, provide a framework that may define the foundations of human experience, and are located in social conditions that foster rival comprehensive doctrines. The political domain is "outside" all communities, and governs community relations with a set of generalizable principles that are formed to tolerate and manage the disputes and problems inevitable in conditions of pluralism. Communities are moral in their depiction and organization of human experience. The political domain is a kind of moral conception designed for the "basic structure" of society that yet may be amoral from

11. See Jerry Fodor and Ernest Lepore for a survey of the ways in which these issues are addressed in philosophical linguistics, in *Holism: A Shopper's Guide* (Cambridge, Mass., Blackwell, 1992). The issues spill over (inevitably) into politics. In *Political Liberalism*, Rawls says, "A crucial assumption of liberalism is that equal citizens have different and indeed incommensurable and irreconcilable conceptions of the good" (p. 301). Note also Rawls's discussion of primary goods as resources to mediate among citizens with incommensurable conceptions of the good, in "Social Utility and Primary Goods," in, for example, *Utilitarianism and Beyond*, ed. Amatya Sen and Bernard Williams (Cambridge: Cambridge University Press, 1982), 159–185. For a thoughtful discussion of commensurability and comparability, see Charles Larmore, *The Morals of Modernity* (Cambridge: Cambridge University Press), 152–174.

the perspective of the comprehensive doctrines found in the communities from which the political system is constituted.[12]

The consent that produces the political domain need not be uniform across communities. Persons must agree on a political domain, and agree on the principles that are to govern their relations with one another. (In an older language, persons consent both to authority and to the mechanisms through which authority is exercised.) But persons may not consent for the same reasons. There may not even be an adequate framework for saying whether reasons are the same or different. The reasons for consenting to a political order may be wholly within the religious, philosophical, or moral comprehensive doctrines characterizing each community, not generalizable to other communities. It is in this sense that political consent is not a religious, philosophical, or moral agreement. Agreement on the political domain may rest simply on the more fragile, though less demanding, basis of behavior, expressed by participation in fair arrangements for reasons that might be entirely local to member communities. It is the sign of success on liberal criteria that the state can govern without requiring that mental allegiance—of reasons—required in ordinary moral reasoning. *Why* one consents is of less importance in liberalism than *that* one consents.

One unavoidable implication of any liberal theory of the state is that persons have dual commitments. These dual commitments sometimes are expressed as a conflict between community conscience and public regulation. The conflict is usually negotiated by maintaining commitments within a community while deferring to institutional practices as governing devices among competing communities. A metacommitment to institutional practices achieves rational standing only if compatibility among communities is accepted as a desirable condition. Persons can reject each other's core moral values, but rationally subscribe to procedures of governance. The desirability of governance depends in part on whether community-based conscience can be shielded from public regulation. This bifurcated pattern of reasoning is well known in liberal thinking. It is called the politics of pluralism. Persons must be members of both their community and the political system, even when the demands of each are incompatible as primary commitments.

The working arrangements that ameliorate conflicts between community and political commitments have been explored in painstaking detail by political and legal theorists. Some of the more creative work begins with

12. *Political Liberalism*, 4–15.

the thought that moral and political commitments can lead to dilemmas that escape resolution when the commitments are contrary and on the same moral or conceptual level. Thus Wollheim's problem invites us to accept the reality of simultaneous moral commitments to a collective outcome and to the democratic procedures that produce collective outcomes, and then ponder one's response when the democratic machine produces an outcome contrary to the first (substantive) moral commitment.[13] Wollheim's problem introduces an unusually strong conflict, for the first moral commitment is to a collective outcome that governs all others in the political domain. Conflict between community morality and public obligation is logically weaker when confined to local moral values. But the possibility of opposition remains. A state in need of conscripts for waging war might still oppose a person's resistance to the military draft even when the resistance is drawn from a conviction that is proposed simply for a religious community, and not for the entire political system.

The proposed solutions to Wollheim's problem are informative. Citizens can link the two commitments and regard the value of the outcome as determined in part by the procedure for reaching outcomes in a democratic system. In this spirit the fact that a moral outcome did not receive the numerically decisive support of citizens may be a reason to question its value.[14] Or citizens can make even more pragmatic calculations about the relationships between popular support and efficacy in realizing moral commitments. On this agenda a citizen may rationally order outcomes in such a way that substantive moral values are best realizable in the long run

13. Richard Wollheim, "A Paradox in the Theory of Democracy," in Peter Laslett and W. G. Runciman, eds., *Philosophy, Politics and Society*, second series, (Oxford: Basil Blackwell, 1962), 71–87.

14. Locke makes this connection in stating how one knows that dissent from the government is warranted. In the oft-quoted Chapter XIX of the *Second Treatise* he allows that "every man is judge for himself . . . whether another hath put himself into a state of war with him." (I love this language.) But on controversies between "a prince and some of the people in a matter where the law is silent or doubtful, and the thing be of great consequence, I should think that the proper umpire in such a case should be the body of the people." On page 246 in the Hafner edition, *Two Treatises of Government* (New York: Hafner, 1956), edited by Thomas I. Cook. I suppose we should be grateful for the implied appeal to arithmetical procedures. In *A Letter Concerning Toleration* Locke assigns oversight powers to God. Addressing the issue of a possible dispute over the distinction between temporal and religious matters, Locke poses the question and then provides his generously cited answer: "But what if the Magistrate believe that he has the Right to make such Laws, and that they are for the publick Good; and his subjects believe the contrary? Who shall be judge between them? I answer, God alone. For there is no judge upon earth between the Supreme Magistrate and the People" (Hackett edition, 1983, p. 49).

by supporting democratic procedures.[15] Of course a rational calculation might also conclude that resistance to the democratic outcome, perhaps even violent revolution, is required on one's moral commitment to a particular outcome.

Most of the literature in contract theory pursues more congenial relationships between community and state obligations. Even assuming that the reasons supporting community commitments and those justifying political authority are different, the origin of the liberal state in consent still suggests that community values will be protected and even flourish with the establishment of a political domain. This argument for the state as an artifact to secure general advantage is found throughout the history of contract theory, and includes the especially strong thought experiments in Hobbes's *Leviathan* that attempt to convince us that life itself will be best preserved in those conditions of guaranteed reciprocity established by the liberal state. More recently Rawls has reminded us of the great values of the political domain and has stressed the overriding advantages of political participation for its own sake.[16] Congeniality between community and political domain is amplified with the superior values of the political association. Notice, however, that the bifurcation between community and state is still present even when cooperation dominates. The democratic state typically recognizes the moral reality of dual commitments, and the political reality of possible conflict between community morality and the demands of the state, by accepting the protective shields of minority rights and the occasional exemption from civic obligations.

The theory of the person that informs this expectation of dual commitment can be sketched easily enough. The person in the liberal state has one identity drawn from community allegiances that logically precede the formation of the state, and another identity drawn from the political domain of citizenship. Even in a "well-ordered society" in which these dual commitments are relatively harmonious, the person must satisfy appeals from both domains (and the domains, as we have seen, always represent different values and languages). One indication of these different identities is that changes in the private (or nonpolitical) self that follow radical changes in moral commitments are not expected in liberalism to affect the political self. Public obligations are to remain constant even when persons convert to radically different community beliefs.[17]

15. Donald Weiss, "Wollheim's Paradox," *Political Theory* 1 (May 1973): 154–170.
16. *Political Liberalism*, 201–206.
17. *Political Liberalism*, 30–33.

Identity is one of the more difficult concepts to define and use. To say that persons in the liberal state have partitioned identities is not to advance some complex or bizarre theory, say that mutually exclusive selves coexist in a single body. The expectations are more limited. They closely follow the liberal story. Recall that persons who are formed within communities are to be governed by a state that establishes a public sphere with a separate language and distinct obligations. This establishment requires a sense of person that can meet public responsibilities without abandoning the community self. A public self is created and superimposed on the community self, which is now regarded as private. Persons have a private and a public identity in the liberal state as a consequence of separating the political domain from those communities it is charged with governing.

5

The person in liberal theory is dualistic in two senses. One is a distinction between mental and physical usually designated as property dualism. The second is a partition between community (private) and political (public) self that I have labeled practice dualism. Are these senses of the person metaphysical doctrines that affect the liberal story of governance?

If we look at the two types of dualism in themselves, without reference to theories of politics, it is not certain how matters are clarified by labeling them as metaphysical doctrines. Each is a theory or definition of the person, or at least a rendition that purports to state what it is we mean when we refer to persons. Efforts to explain a range of phenomena connected to the person may also attach to the two types. Choices, intentions, mental phenomena in general may be classified and accounted for with one or both of the types. Perhaps types of neurological activity, or correlations between brain states and action, may be addressed by the two forms of dualism. There may be much that is assumed (and little that is defined or explained) in these two types, but they are certainly within the genre of constructs offered as at least preliminary models to make experience intelligible. In this sense they both seem to fall comfortably within traditions of empiricism, not the brand of metaphysics that resists empirical explanations.

When introduced to liberal theories of the state, however, these two conceptions of the person do acquire metaphysical standing. They are, first, unexamined parts of current liberal programs.[18] The origins of liberalism

18. Polar extremes in elaborating property dualism are common in liberal thought. Hume maintains that we have no knowledge of a unified, irreducible self, that when we think

are replete with attempts to define the person. But the acceptance of a distinction between mental and physical, thought and behavior, is not widely inspected today. Rawls, for example, addresses the prospect that some elaborate concept of the person is assumed in his theory of justice but then denies the proposition. Second, the two conceptions of the person in liberal theory are members of a set that includes rival conceptions of the person. Two of these rival conceptions are outside the assumptions of liberal governance, and would require important revisions in liberalism were they introduced into liberal theories of the state.

The first member of this set is a version of substance, or, as used here, ontological dualism.[19] Persons in spiritual practices are often regarded as physical instantiations of a psychic self or soul. The soul is said to exist in a reality that exceeds the sensory world of human experience. This account of the self is not found in most secular practices today, which are inclined to define the self either as a purely material entity, or as dualistic across a body and a mind that is the locus of thoughts, not a power with access to alternative realities. This version of dualism is indisputably different from either of the dualisms of self found in current liberal theory.

Ontological dualism is an underexplained theory, and perhaps closer to standard understandings of metaphysics. The neurological or cognitive processes of spiritual beliefs are simply not understood. Such beliefs seem to be part of the complex puzzles of consciousness itself. An objec-

---

of the self we think always of perceptions—heat, light, cold, pain—and that empirical knowledge is possible without the concept of a well-defined, integrated self. He regards the self as nothing more than a collection of perceptions. Kant describes a self that has the power to structure sensations, to order them as it renders experience intelligible. The self in Kant's philosophy is the mental apparatus that supplies categories to organize data and so cannot be reducible to sensations. The dominant efforts in liberal theory formation at this time in history are directed toward the separation of persons from a stratified society (and rearranging the society). Liberalism even in its early stages, however, occasionally collapses the person back into society. T. H. Green assigns to the individual person moral powers to endorse the common good as a private good. These capacities lead Green to those positive rights that fuse individual rights to the social good. In Green, *Lectures on the Principles of Political Obligation* (New York: Cambridge University Press, 1986). Then there are Rousseau's famous mergers of self with collective in the General Will. Is Rousseau a theorist in modern liberalism? I think so, though he has strange (and fascistic?) views on individual liberties in *The Government of Poland*, trans. Willmoore Kendall (Indianapolis, Ind.: Hackett, 1985). But if the question can be raised we have even more complicated historical origins for liberal thought. Conceded. And an explanation for why I rely on argument and general explorations of concepts rather than historical research for my case on the nature of the self in liberal political theory.

19. Ontological dualism seems a better term to capture not just the presence of a soul in persons, but the claim that persons have a kind of dual residence—in the conventional empirical world, and in a world that exceeds the conventional limits set by naturalism.

tive brain able to generate subjective states is said to be able also to conjure openings to alternative realities regarded as a source for understandings of the self. But even though inadequately explained, this core thesis of a self located in two realities, found in many religions, has implications for conceptions of human reasoning, and for languages of morality and power.

One of the more important of these implications is that the unknown cannot be a token for incomplete knowledge. For example, if information is not complete but could be on the same search rules that produce that which is known, then well-known decision rules can be used. Among these are utility maximization in conditions of certainty, a combination of probabilities and expected values in conditions of risk, and (among others) maximax and maximin rules in conditions of uncertainty. But suppose that the information set cannot reach conclusions even in principle *and* that (a) the information not acquirable may be governed by different laws than those that make the information at hand intelligible, and (b) the incomplete part of the information set is more important than that which is known. Then other strategies must be devised to address the unknown.

One such strategy relies on external guidance, which manifests itself in one way through faith. A second is a search for patterns in experience that can indicate connections between conventional and alternative realities, and can render human experience intelligible as an entry in a larger scheme extending across multiple realities. A third uses deciphering, not defining, as the critical linguistic exercise, meaning that language must be inspected for levels of significance, for patterns of intelligibility that might display symbols that exceed both meaning and use within human conventions. Because expressions from an external perspective may always contain references outside of their conventional meanings, the direct scrutiny of language is incomplete on its face. Language must also be considered as a puzzle or game that might enlighten some segment of an alternative reality. These three strategies are common features of religious thinking and must be accounted for in any complete theory of a state that governs spiritual beliefs.

The effects of ontological dualism on individual identity are sometimes decisive. For example, one consequence of defining the self in terms of an external reality is that the traditional voluntary foundations of spiritual commitment are modified and perhaps supplanted by the compelling energies of conscience. A person whose identity is drawn from a reality outside the scope of human experience is governed by higher powers. Obligation replaces freedom, and the connection between thought and behavior, mind and body, is one of entailment forged on the risk of losing one's identity. The fusion of higher and physical selves is often a combination of relief and ecstasy, but it typically does not countenance the freedom between thinking and doing that is taken for granted in secular forms of dualism.

The shift in concepts affects the political domain also, primarily in requiring the state to govern a community belief that denies the partitioned self of liberal practices. One way in which the state attempts to meet these requirements (in, for example, the U.S. legal system) is to grant religious practices occasional exemptions from legal obligations on the grounds that religious beliefs are more compelling than secular beliefs. One practical test requires that laws regulating religious practices represent a compelling state interest and be the least restrictive means of regulation. The philosophical effects are more important. In granting exemptions the liberal state must abandon property dualism in accepting a necessary relationship between mental and physical properties. Some religious actions, it is effectively conceded, seem to be logical extensions of beliefs.[20] A second approach is to reject the unity of self found in so many spiritual communities by requiring individuals to bracket religious beliefs in fulfilling civic obligations. In this approach property dualism trumps ontological dualism. In neither case is there a doctrine of the person shared by spiritual communities and state.

The second conception of the self that is at odds with liberalism redefines the core terms of mind and body by denying any distinctions between them. Two recent contributions to explanations of consciousness abandon dualism in favor of selves more or less integrated on the biological terms of the human brain. One, developed by John Searle, identifies mental states with physical properties of the brain. These properties are the subjective qualities of human experience and are as real as any other neurological property. Subjective states, on Searle's theories, are ontological facts of consciousness. Objective states exist also and are best seen as conceptions of the world that meet certain epistemic tests, in the modern sense those tests that generate truths free of special interests. For Searle it follows that there is no distinction between mental and physical, mind and body, because

20. Secular dualisms of thought and behavior are often used in the law even when they have not been examined and cannot be found in the social practices that law regulates. In *Reynolds v. United States* (1879) the U.S. Supreme Court ruled that individuals have unlimited rights to religious beliefs, but the right to act on these beliefs can be regulated by the state. Reynolds, a Mormon convicted of polygamy, was granted the freedom of his religious beliefs but not the actions based on these beliefs. Put another way, a thought-behavior distinction consistent with property dualism was assigned to a religious belief too closely bound to behavior to accept the Court's measured tolerance.

consciousness is a natural (evolutionary) property emerging from the biological facts of human neurology.[21]

A second explanation is offered by Daniel Dennett. In Dennett's view consciousness is a property of the whole brain, a power that has evolved through adaptation and the operation of biological laws. Evolution does not produce organisms that meet all obvious tests of parsimony or efficiency. The brain has long been understood as a layered organism, with more recent additions to the cortex superimposed on earlier levels. One consequence of evolutionary additions is a brain with redundancies and avoidance mechanisms that may permit successful coping, but which may not meet the needs of otherwise persuasive philosophies of consciousness. Research into the brain indicates that the organism performs what are called sensing and thinking operations in a variety of "places," and that there are no privileged observers or audiences in consciousness. Mental activity is a complex set of parallel processing of stimuli that involves multiple revisions in collation and interpretation.

Dennett (in *Consciousness Explained*) represents consciousness as a kind of serial virtual machine, a set of rules imposed on a brain that has been structured by genetic evolution, phenotypic plasticity, and meme evolution. Memes are units of cultural transmission, of imitation, such as ideas, fashions, musical scores, normative concepts. Dennett once argued (but no longer does) that meme evolution has been the decisive effect on the design of human consciousness, structuring a brain that is receptive to, but not designed for, cultural units. Human consciousness may be a self-reflective architecture produced by the effects of experiences on the complex and overlapping hardware of the brain.[22]

Searle does not develop a concept of a self in any detail, though his well-known views on the intentionality of mental states suggest that consciousness generates a self able to ascribe and discover meanings and knowingly follow rules. Such a self, in Searle's philosophy, depends on the biology of the brain and cannot be found in computers. Dennett's concept of a self is more complicated. In his explanation the multiple processes of consciousness, and the emergence of consciousness from various influences, have produced a self that allows a narrative form of construction. Dennett has observed that humans present themselves to others in terms of stories, and tell stories about each other. Narratives are attempts to offer a unified self, a "center of narrative gravity" that makes the self intelligible. Stories, with

21. John Searle, *The Rediscovery of the Mind* (Cambridge: MIT Press, 1994).
22. Daniel Dennett, *Consciousness Explained* (Boston: Little, Brown, 1991).

their linear forms and subjective powers, can be the organizing devices that express the self.[23]

Linkages between the self and a narrative structure seem to depend on an isomorphism of narrative with life itself. Oliver Sacks has suggested that the continuity of narratives provides identity and purpose for individuals.[24] Jerome Bruner has pointed out that narratives accord with the natural development of a life, with a beginning, a middle, and an end.[25] Guy Widdershoven argues that life and story are internally related, that "the meaning of life cannot be determined outside of the stories told about it."[26] This close fit between stories and human lives suggests that narratives have an advantage over more formal models of explanation, which may not so closely accord with the logic of human experiences.

Three consequences follow a systemic account of the self expressed in narrative structures. One, assignable to both Searle and Dennett, is that the self must be understood as graded. If the self is a narrative byproduct of levels of consciousness that emerge from a set of neurological functions, a reduction or enhancement of consciousness must affect the self. Like the computer HAL in the film *2001*, the self may be on a slope from full consciousness to the absence of consciousness. The slope may be nonmonotonic, with lumpy areas and discontinuities, but there cannot be exclusive categories of self and nonself. Instead there are levels of neurological activity and consciousness in which it may not be possible to say whether a self exists or not. The second consequence, widely accepted, is that the narrative of the self must be the product of social and individual influences. Others define us even as we define ourselves. Third, the Cartesian assumption that someone is in charge, that a single integrated self is typically found in individuals, must be either abandoned or expressed in languages that have different functions than those assigned to the languages that represent liberal practices.

Notice that in neither theory of the self—Searle's nor Dennett's—is there either version of the dualism found in liberal theories of the state. The rejection of dualism has profound implications for all dimensions of

23. *Consciousness Explained*, 412–455.

24. Oliver Sacks, *The Man Who Mistook His Wife for a Hat* (New York: Harper & Row, 1987).

25. Jerome Bruner, "Life as Narrative," *Social Research* 54 no. 1 (Spring 1987): 11–32, and "Two Modes of Thought," in *Actual Minds, Possible Worlds* (Cambridge: Harvard University Press, 1986).

26. Guy Widdershoven, "The Story of Life: Hermeneutic Perspectives on the Relation Between Narrative and Life History," in Ruthellen Josselson and Amia Lieblich, eds., *The Narrative Study of Lives* (Newbury Park, Calif.: Sage Publications, 1993):1–19.

liberal theory. These implications are more difficult to describe, however, than the effects of any form of dualism on liberal theory. The reasons are easy to state. First, the modern traditions of the liberal state assume at the most enduring levels both types of dualism described here. Tracking the effects of the bifurcated self on liberal languages is a little like observing the effects of the moon's gravity on tides. The causal effects are both obvious and long-standing. But the collapse of distinctions between mental and physical dimensions of the self in recent work relies on empirical work in neurology and computer simulations. Both are rapidly changing fields of study, with unclear boundaries. It is not certain yet how one can map such radical changes in understandings of the self into the canons of political philosophy. Second, however, any speculation on the effects of a unified self on liberalism suggests a transformation of liberal political philosophy into currently unrecognizable forms. The effects of dualism are so pervasive on the vocabularies of liberalism that introducing a nonbinary self to political theory may alter all concepts and theoretical configurations of the liberal program. The possibilities seem endless. The nonbinary self might be indistinguishable from the practices the state is to regulate or ignore.[27] One result might be a concentration on interests or needs rather than individual preferences, with compromising effects on populist democracy. Or the self might be so embedded in communities that the separation between community and state may be distorted. Premeditation, culpability, insanity defenses, competence—all of these staple concepts in law (and in all theories of jurisprudence) would have to be reexamined, not necessarily abandoned but certainly redefined to some degree. Critical reconstruction may have an open season on an extensive menu of political vocabularies if property dualism and the partitioned self are replaced with a conception of the nonbinary self.

6

Any theory of the state should minimally identify the metaphysical doctrines that are required for the theory's main ideas and the effects of these and alternative doctrines on the theory. It is not certain how the selective mechanisms that favor one metaphysical doctrine over another operate in political theory, but they seem to originate in two conceptual areas. One is

27. Perhaps Derek Parfit's reductionist self reappears here, with the expected theoretical emphasis on larger sets of considerations than are found in individual expressions. In *Reasons and Persons* (Oxford: Clarendon Press, 1984), 345–347.

formed by the background factors that influence the meanings and arrangements of concepts in a theory. The cultural variables that explain the uses of contiguity in correlations are examples of such background factors. Another conceptual area is marked off by the needs of a theory. Liberal political theory requires a particular type of person for its characteristic vocabulary. The selective mechanisms for property and practice dualism are at least partially within the theory of liberalism. This discussion has concentrated on internal mechanisms.

The effectiveness of examining internal mechanisms is clearest in recognizing and tracking the effects of property and practice dualism on liberal governance. Generally, the assumption of a dualist self in liberal theory indicates that the neutrality and general distance of the liberal state from many of its member communities is not possible in any important way. The liberal state is a secular and *liberal* artifact. It must represent those modern understandings of the person as a binary self, and this conception is contrary to many moral and religious convictions and philosophical concepts. Religious or spiritual communities will reject property dualism. Any community that confers primary identities on its members will resist practice dualism. In both cases the liberal state is hostile to the very definition of the person that defines and animates communities. This nonneutral framework is not a function of governance, but of the conceptual needs of the state for a particular metaphysical conception of the person in order to carry out its defining functions. Each of these observations also suggests a conclusion unwelcome for the main body of liberal political theory: dualism may be a fragile basis for developing a theory of politics.

The difficulties in confining selective mechanisms for metaphysical doctrines of the *person* to internal considerations are considerable, however. Conceptions of the person are among the more fundamental understandings in social theory, folding naturally into comprehensive theories of human experience. The connections of the self to larger concerns are illustrated in two rival theories of language and community. In one, an Austinian model—developed on the famous demarcations among locutionary, illocutionary, and perlocutionary utterances—language and behavior can be independent.[28] The speech acts represented by illocutionary utterances and the situation-altering speech of perlocutionary utterances are distinct from the locutionary expressions of thoughts. Speech can be an expression of thought without being a form of behavior except in the innocuous sense that locutions are utterances. This model recapitulates liberal distinctions

28. John Austin, *How to Do Things with Words* (Oxford: Oxford University Press, 1962).

between thought and behavior, and informs legal shields for freedom of speech. If utterances harm no one, and if thought can be confined helpfully to the domain of the mental without affecting behavior, then the state has no warrant to regulate speech. Freedom of expression is assimilated to freedom of thought. And since the thought police is anathema on liberal agendas, free expression follows the assimilation. Liberal dualisms separating mental and physical exclude locutionary utterances from the domain of the political while focusing state regulation on behavior.

In a second model, drawn from Michel Foucault's work, language is always a form of behavior.[29] Even seemingly innocuous expressions, like the locutions of Austin's schema, are unavoidably exercises of power. Language is an instrument of control, but mainly it is the domain in which conflict occurs. To express a thought is to appropriate and use a pattern of words that orders the world in certain ways. It is also to engage in a selective process that favors some interests over others, and finally allows some individuals to dominate others. In a sense, all expressions are speech acts for Foucault, and all speech acts are exercises of power. These patterns of power, however, are not the results of the intentions of individuals. Power is embedded in language itself, not in the attempts of speakers to bring about intended effects. Or, put in the frame supplied by Austin, perlocutionary force is a feature of practices and not a causal path opened by individual intentions.

Any theory that presents language as conflict anticipates state regulation of all speech, for speech itself is regarded as a form of behavior and a natural target of state intervention. Liberal justifications of free speech are impossible because utterances are never innocuous expressions of thought (Austin's locutions). The differences in the two models cut even deeper. Neither mind and body, nor mental and physical, are plausible distinctions in Foucault's account. If thought must be expressed in language to be intelligible, a supposition that is accepted in both analytic and continental traditions in philosophy, then all thought in Foucault's framework must be found in the domain of body as a kind of behavior. Nothing can be shielded on standard liberal arguments from the regulatory powers of the modern state if Foucault's model of language is accepted.

The implications of Foucault's model for politics accelerate the collapse of mental to physical. Human experience, on Foucault's understanding, is driven by impulses to order and master. Among these impulses is the will to

29. The material here on Foucault is drawn primarily from "The Discourse on Language," in *The Archaeology of Knowledge*, trans. A. M. Sheridan Smith, (New York: Pantheon, 1972).

truth, which is concerned to distinguish true from false speech and exclude the latter. Another is to divide and subdivide populations with the use of sane and insane categories. Only the former is officially meaningful as discourse. It is evident how conflict is the natural state of affairs in human communities inspired by such impulses. On liberal terms the state would be the impartial arbitrator and conciliator hovering over these conflicts like an umpire regulating competitive games. But for Foucault the state is the primary representation of these impulses. The state, in his account of human affairs, stages violence, especially to the body. It is therefore neither surprising nor a problem in Foucault's model to say that free expression is not shielded from state regulation. Language, after all, is behavior, and no institution escapes the forces of conflict that define human communities.

We can say that two deeper understandings of persons and human communities control the Austinian and Foucaultian models. One, found in Austin, is the standard liberal expectation that persons are discrete figures who can be bifurcated into mental and physical. This binary self represents the belief that thought and behavior are distinct realms at least on occasion. The other, central to Foucault, is that persons are figures embedded in wider contexts and manipulated by general forces toward social change and maintenance. The conception of a person in Foucault's theories fuses liberal distinctions between mental and physical. These differences in accounts of the person are considerable, so much so that the selective mechanisms for metaphysical doctrines of the self may themselves be traceable to rival models of society that define individuals and wholes in human communities.

If understandings of the self are deep features of rival theories of language and community organization, then a neutral or general account of the person is an unlikely success story. A definition will be regulative in some ways, inasmuch as disagreement over persons is linked to different comprehensive views on social experiences. But this admission makes it even more important that conceptions of the self not be purely stipulative. They must be attentive to the metaphysical doctrines attached to all accounts of the person and grounded in some plausible theory of consciousness.

7

The oldest efforts at rational closure in the exercise of state authority are located within claims for human identity. The story of classical philosophy identifies humans by their considerable reflective powers, and these powers are to reveal (at least on occasion) correct or true conclusions. One cannot imagine a more elegant beginning for the narratives of fusion between reason and concepts of the self or person in Western history. The original story represents an understanding that the proper use of reason will lead to a convergence of both identity and beliefs: persons are like each other in their reasoning powers, and these powers will generate shared conclusions. Even the modern abandonment of these expectations is not a dismissal of the assignment of reason to organized and self-guiding forms of life. The rational self, past and present, is an arranged self, one consisting of regulating powers that are ordered and sometimes fused. Reason, in all variations of the person, is expressed in terms of languages that represent an integrated and reflective self capable of settling on conclusions to direct actions.

Reason itself may be a power that depends on the entire arrangement of the person however defined. The modern distinctions between binary and nonbinary persons may simply bifurcate reason along yet other forms of arranged selves. The fundamental distinction, however, is between organized and unorganized selves.[30] In the former category are found singular and complex selves. A singular self is one-dimensional. Individuals who are identified with a cause, for example, may be primarily defined by ideas. Zealots are sometimes no more than their causes. But selves are usually more complex. The thought that individuals contain multiple dimensions, and even selves, has been suggested and argued throughout history in one form or another. Plato asked how an individual can be in two or more volitional states at the same time. His explanation requires the development of a tiered version of the self, with reason dominating spirit and appetite. The self in Christianity is a psychic landscape on which good and evil spirits do battle with one another. The whole (and rational) individual is one who has sought, and found, external help in dominating unwelcome visitors. Freud developed an ordering of conscious and unconscious levels of the self, with each dimension governed by its own defining rules.[31] Derek Parfit has suggested that individuals may be more like groups than singular units, with parts arranged in different ways according to different rules.[32] In all of these accounts the various parts and dimensions of the self can be orga-

30. Examining various types of aggregates is a way of recognizing possible organizations of the self (on the Platonic assumptions that studying the whole is initially more manageable than studying the self and that lessons for the self can be drawn from parallels between collectives and selves). Various organizational forms are described in Peter French, "Types of Collectives and Blame," *Personalist* 56 (1975), Virginia Held, *The Public Interest and Individual Interest* (New York: Basic Books, 1970), and in Allen Barton, *Organizational Measurement* (New York: College Entrance Examination Board, 1961).

31. Browse through *The Standard Edition of the Complete Psychological Works of Sigmund Freud*, 24 volumes, trans. James Strachey (London: Hogarth Press, 1953–1974).

32. Derek Parfit, *Reasons and Persons* (Oxford: Clarendon Press, 1984).

nized as a kind of system, and in most accounts certain types of organization express a rational or balanced individual.

Individuals can also be unorganized selves. The most dramatic example is multiple personality disorder.[33] Here several selves seem to occupy the same individual with no organizing principle to order or arrange the serial presentations. But nonpathological accounts of the multiple self also are found in various literatures. Serial selves seem to have an identity at one time and quite another at a later period. Criminals incarcerated on death row for extended periods of time sometimes claim, with some legitimacy, that intense reflections on impending death and the time to read widely have produced a psychic conversion, in effect a new self related to the violent youth of the early years only by temporal continuity. Individuals also can be selves fragmented across spatial domains, which seems to happen when circumstances dominate identity. The individual whose states of mind vary with shifts of context, who appropriates the fundamental outlooks of various settings simply because she or he is present in the setting, may have surrendered identity to localities. She or he may be a type of self distributed across social practices, lacking any internal organization. In all cases of an unorganized self the critical dimensions are not integrated by any rule or principle that can make the self whole.

All models of reasoning seem to require some type of an organized self. The diffuse or distributed self typically fails even rudimentary tests of reason or rationality. Even disjoined reasoning requires a self with an identity that is consistent over time. (Otherwise the person could not extend reasoning across the various segments leading to a conclusion.) But also the particular organization of the self is often a byproduct of requirements advanced for other purposes. Aristotle's definition of humans as rational animals describes the binary self of classical theory, one consisting of a hierarchical arrangement of thinking or reflective senses of the person and that sense of the person as a biological creature. The Cartesian self in charge of information is largely a creation of social practices that can be managed only with a self integrated on different principles. The main traditions of the liberal state ensure liberty of thought for this version of the self by assigning property dualism to it. In this and other practices the self is specified and elaborated without any significant reference to the human brain or to theories of identity supported with empirical work in consciousness or intelligence. It is the social theory that produces the conception of the person, rather than the reverse.

33. A fine study of this disorder and its social implications is by James Glass, *Shattered Selves* (Ithaca, N.Y.: Cornell University Press, 1993).

Narratives, and a narrative account of the self, however, can be viewed from another starting point. Narratives have the power to create and reconstitute the self. In Don DeLillo's *Libra*, a fictional account of the assassination of President John F. Kennedy, there are several versions of Oswald. There is Lee Oswald, Lee Harvey Oswald, and several pseudo Oswalds who parade through the underground world of New Orleans and Dallas. DeLillo uses fictional techniques to take the reader through the exercise of "extended sympathy," reconstructing or creating personalities and motives for Oswald. But the novelist also has extended ambitions. A theory of personal identity is advanced and developed. Oswald is undefined even with the imputations of perceptions, actions, incentives. He acquires his identity with the assassination.

A theory of self is proposed by DeLillo by means of the narrative of Oswald's comings and goings. We are given the private and fragmented Oswald who migrates to Russia, then drifts back to the United States. Slowly we witness this isolated and even atomistic self-link to larger movements. Oswald's private self is extinguished as he merges with the assassination plot. The plot's inertia carries him to his identity as assassin. A telescoped social practice or decisive event fixes meaning on the individual.

Now one can *say* all of these things in a psychological or sociological theory, and gather data empirically to support the theory. The power of the novel is in the speculative elaboration of the themes. The coherence among the several dimensions of identity can be forged in complicated ways that a fidelity to data may not permit. We *see* the emergence of Oswald, the historical assassin, through the imaginative rendition of the fictional Oswalds. More: The anomalous identity of Oswald in history is conveyed by the shadowy presence of alternative Oswalds in the novel. Ambiguity of fact is more easily negotiated by works that are not tightly bound to facts.

The harmony between narrative and self originates in the ordering effects that stories have on human life. There is a powerful isomorphism between lives as lived, and lives as told. A story of a person is a compilation and synthesis of actions and events found both in and outside of the person's conscious landscape. But the narrative in many ways *is* the person, which gives stories the power to define selves in nonbinary terms, or as protagonists who are integrated subjects within the rules of the narrative. Narrative conceptions of the self can also provide stories that summon common human experiences, and these stories may mediate the strong pluralism of liberal settings.

Three implications for the self follow an acceptance of the logic of narratives. One is that the interesting relationships between narratives and data provide a wide range of flexibility for defining and redefining the self. It may be that narratives foreclose any possibility of identifying a definitive self. Selves expressed as narratives may be infinitely malleable on any of several rival dimensions. Second, the self as narrative may be integrated, but the organizing device—stories—are diffuse and multiple commodities in social practices. Narratives may be able to do that which appears to be exceedingly unlikely: define and interpret an organized self that may yet be distributed across social practices. Third, the natural sympathy of narratives for metaphysical claims makes stories congenial devices for representing mental or spiritual senses of the self.

The domains of political authority are also shifted with an acceptance of narratives as expressions of consciousness. The state is more accurately understood as the representative and legislator of stories, not of individuals or actions. A state oriented to the dominant and subordinate narratives of its time and place may still fulfill the requirements of liberal governance. But a theory of state developed on the adjudication of narratives has accepted a more holistic conception of the person. That understanding so vital to both classical and modern political theory, the *rational person*, is no longer an expression of those versions of dualism that have animated so many liberal political philosophies.

8

Narratives are complex items. They are certainly too complex to say that a narrative *is* any one thing. Any discussion of narratives and their roles in public reason must examine broad domains, those that are governed by the most general of rules. Begin with the thought that stories can be used as devices to communicate truth and disclose realities. The simplest is an example, a story that represents a more literal truth. Leo Strauss, in *Natural Right and History*, defines justice as "the habit of benefiting others." He offers as an example the story of "the big boy who has a small coat and the small boy who has a big coat. The big boy is the lawful owner of the small coat because he, or his father, has bought it. But it is not good for him; it does not fit him. The wise ruler will therefore take the big coat away from the small boy and give it to the big boy without any regard to legal ownership."[34] Alas, we are not told if the small boy also gets the small coat. But the point is clear. The story illustrates how fulfilling this particular definition of justice (benefiting others) requires at least on occasion ignoring or overrid-

34. Leo Strauss, *Natural Right and History* (Chicago: University of Chicago Press, 1953), 147.

ing property rights. The example restates and amplifies, with persuasive force, what justice means.

A story can also elaborate experience as a kind of surrogate theory. Heuristic devices to manage information and guide decisions are often stories that render the world intelligible with common sense reductions of complex events. Politics is especially congenial to the telling of stories that "explain" the exercise of power and distribution of goods. Ronald Reagan's famous story of the welfare cheater, Martin Luther King's skillful use of stories about oppressed black children—stories about politics are so effective in depicting the political order that they are also natural instruments of persuasion.

The best stories, meaning those that are complex or puzzling, seem to have connecting powers. They can be taken to a different forms of reasoning by way of interpretation. Sometimes the connections are to more literal ways of thinking. Plato's allegory of the cave is easily extended to a graphic representation in which lines divide empirical from geometrical and metaphysical forms, and separate physical references from their forms. But other stories, parables in particular, seem to connect to forms of thought that can only be glimpsed, not known. They suggest, and are sometimes inspired by, possible realities seen as independent of subjective experience. Stories such as these have porous contours. They imply and partially illuminate those external conditions which the parable is about.

Consider the parable of the wedding feast. In this story a king finds that no one has come to his daughter's wedding. He instructs his servants to go out into the countryside and bring to the feast anyone they can find. They do so. Then, during the festivities, the king wanders among the guests and sees a man who has no wedding garment. The king asks the man why he is not properly dressed. The man does not answer. The king orders his servants to expel the man: "Bind his hands and feet, and cast him into the exterior darkness: there shall be weeping and gnashing of teeth." The concluding line of the parable follows as a moral: "For many are called, but few are chosen."

Parables are usually presented as simple stories that illustrate moral or religious lessons. Many are no more than that. The parable of the Pharisee and the publican is a clear lesson in piety and humility. No one hearing it can doubt that pride in following the moral law undermines good acts. But other parables are more complex. The parable of the wedding feast has several levels. It is an admonition to heed invitations to the moral life. But it also contains a puzzling and hard judgment in the conclusion of the story. The parable seems to be pointing to a reality with laws not fully comprehensible on the terms of human sentiments.

A successful parable will elicit from the audience generalizable convictions about human experience that may be at intuitive levels of thought. A parable is always located in some particular setting, but its context is a liberating rather than a limiting device. The particular situation introduces the familiar in such a way that tacit beliefs are to be summoned in order to disclose general understandings. These understandings may not readily surface. Parables are sometimes mysterious, not transparent, and the audience may have to work at interpreting the story. But a successful interpretation will always conclude with a moral lesson from a point of view that yet is accepted as universal.

One of the more significant strengths of narratives is that they can simultaneously contain rival ideas in a single framework. Consistency attained in a single conceptual domain is an obvious virtue in serial reasoning. But narratives, unlike objective reasoning, can entertain multiple domains (as various points of view in character and plot) without a contradiction, mainly by viewing beliefs as provisional devices to frame and mediate experiences. The virtue of the more generous narrative version of consistency is in the scope of presentation. A full treatment of many perspectives can illuminate the distance among claims, and the links between ideas and their underlying ontologies. One source of this capacity is the tolerance and even enthusiasm of narratives for what might be called controlled obscurity, for deflected or ambiguous meaning. An empirical theory that is unclear is flawed. But a story may be purposely loose or turgid to invite the reader to interpret the text by discovering meaning. It is this resonant quality of narratives that can accommodate metaphysical (counterfactual, speculative, spiritual) claims, and both affirmation and dissent in political forums without contradiction. The harder commitment to truth found in serial reasoning is logically bound to present more conflict and contradiction in addressing diverse political beliefs.

The rational powers of narratives are often expressed through shared understandings, often by appeals to conscience. Sometimes an appeal to conscience is divisive. All stories rely on certain linguistic conditions (minimally, a speaker, language, and audience) amidst a stock of scripts, ontologies, tacit knowledge, foretellings—in general, the full range of human artifacts that make language possible for intact individuals in human communities. Reality, including the full inventory of subjects and objects as conventionally understood, may even be constituted by narratives. But in any pluralistic society rival discourses will provide different realities. Spiritual discourses, for example, often accept alternative (higher) realities, the supremacy of God over law, the subordination of life to religious values, the dominance of religion over community, and a concept of the person elaborated by ontological dualism. Secular world stories in liberal democracies usually rely on multiple social realities, the supremacy of reason in law, the protection and celebration of life, community dominating religion, and a definition of persons in terms of property dualism. These differences are among the more divisive in political life.

The abortion dispute originates in fundamental views on human life. Both pro-life and pro-choice regard human life as sacred. But human life is sacred as a natural gift for those in the pro-life movement, independent of what persons make of it. Pro-choice emphasizes the human construction of life, the dimensions of achievement and assigned meanings, over the more nearly natural dimension of life.[35] These are *stories* of human life, depictions of experience that organize material in acceptable ways. No ameliorative rules or principles can quite manage the divergent effects of these narratives.

The intractability of narratives is sometimes addressed successfully with the oblique functions of stories. One is that of avoidance mechanism. In *Roe v. Wade* human gestation is partitioned into trimesters. It is clear to anyone with even introductory knowledge of biology that gestation is a continuum. Yet trimesters are useful fictions in negotiating some of the intractable problems in abortion disputes. They offer a convenient set of demarcations under which moral and legal judgments can be housed. Abandoning trimesters while maintaining viability can require intrusive examinations of particular women (see *Webster*). The crucial matter is not that the "truth" of trimesters is irrelevant. It is that there is no happy method for saying that they are anything other than fictions. The demarcations are vital to law as fictions that help resolve or manage disputes by avoiding them.[36] Such fictions are also important in reaching settlements in mediation sessions so long as the disputants regard the fictions as convenient for their own needs.

But some narratives—meta, mythical—have unifying powers. They can bind persons with the use of references that are outside the boundaries of more formal or direct types of reasoning. They summon persons to more holistic forms of reasoning, and to those moral and political areas where shared understandings dominate partitions. The unifying powers of stories originate in the standing of the person. In all narratives the self is embedded in stories, not distinct as a separate Cartesian individual. One of the enduring myths of modern thought may be that the self is a prelinguistic

35. Distinctions introduced and elaborated by Ronald Dworkin in *Life's Dominion* (New York: Alfred E. Knopf, 1993).
36. *Webster v. Reproductive Health Services* 492 U.S. 490 (1990).

datum, an "I" that is the source and monitor of consciousness rather than an implicate in language. If, however, we regard the self as a neurological arrangement whose defining expression is language, then the self as a subject of thought and action must be produced in language. In this sense narratives are both the vehicles for expressing the self and a form of expression that provides for collective experiences. Stories can unfold events in a sequence that fits the natural chronicle of lived experience. There may be no distinction between lived experience and experience as told in stories. Then the self becomes a kind of story, and, no matter how the story goes, the self is situated in the particular form of language we call narratives.[37] Rawls, Austin, and Foucault are alike in failing to engage what may be most distinctive about human experience—its capacity to be expressed in narratives that can present the self as a unified story. One consequence of this placement is that the discrete individual of modern thought is replaced with a self extended in languages that must be both common and public.

The unifying powers of stories are important in communication across cultures, which presents in especially difficult terms some of the incommensurable differences that occur among disputants in political conditions. In these conditions many of the distinctions of liberal theory must be abandoned because they have no generalizing force. These include polarities between mental and material dimensions of human experience, as well those between the secular and the religious, all of which can and do vary among cultures. Some deeper foundation of human experience often must be found to reach closure. The great narratives of political experience can forge unity in describing and identifying the roles of persons in a universal political culture. Plato's Allegory of the Cave and Martin Luther King's "I Have A Dream" speech, for example, relax literal truth in favor of metaphor, symbols of various types, myths even.[38] Subjective experience is

37. Anthony Paul Kirby discusses these points in *Narrative and the Self* (Bloomington: Indiana University Press, 1991). See also the linkage between narrative and individual identity forged by Margaret Sommers to overcome certain limitations in both "identity politics" and the concept of narrative. Selves are defined with this nexus as stories with an ontological grounding. In Sommers, "The Narrative Constitution of Identity: A Relational and Network Approach," *Theory and Society* (October 1994): 605–649.

38. Put simply, you have misunderstood the dialogue if you follow King's report that he has seen the promised land with a request to see his stamped passport. The point on King's speech comes from Tom Green's excellent lecture, "Public Speech," The Eighteenth Charles DeGarmo Lecture (Atlanta, Ga.: Caddo Gap Press, 1993). But do not forget that the negative powers of narratives, in this case their powers of exclusion, may be the dark underside of their enlightening powers. Unlike liberal principles narratives may not be fully transparent. This controlled obscurity may be both a strength and a weakness of narrative modes of reasoning.

constituted as the foundation of a common political understanding. Narratives, to put the point bluntly, can occasionally bind *persons* as well as claims, rules and principles, and in doing so invite a unity of belief that serial forms of public reason must leave untouched.

The main observations, however, consist of a set of possibilities for public reasoning. If the dualistic self parallels and fulfills the partitioning needs of liberalism, a reshaping of the person in terms of narratives modifies the consolidating logic of the liberal state.[39] In particular, a renewed attention in public reason to narratives as both claims and instruments of adjudication suggests different understandings of evidence, inference and public space.[40] An acceptance of narratives as expressions of consciousness might lead to a state more accurately understood as a representative and legislator of stories, not of individuals or actions. A metaphysical doctrine of the self may even find an entrance route into those theories of the liberal state that currently occupy the central grounds of political philosophy, and compel a revision of the ways in which persons can be therapeutically absorbed into the collective life of the political system.

9

Relationships between parts and wholes, between the individual and the political society, are shaped in different ways by narratives and the more strictly linear forms of reasoning that are also prominent in liberal theory. Assigning priority standing to discrete individuals favors methodological

39. The main body of rationality theory today complements various senses of the binary self. The calculative rationality of decision theory stresses a "cold" or unemotional weighing of evidence, inference, and argument that amounts to an injunction to be rational by suspending affect. The rational agent is one who has successfully divided cognition and (in an older language) appetite. Also, what it is to be rational is a function of the choice of appropriate decision rules in the right conditions (certainty, risk, uncertainty in standard decision theory), which invites a weak kind of practice dualism. That this body of theory needs close and sustained critical therapy can no longer be doubted. The heuristic needs of reasoning are outlined by Amos Tversky and Daniel Kahneman, in *Judgment Under Uncertainty: Heuristics and Biases* (Cambridge: Cambridge University Press, 1982). Narratives might fulfill heuristic requirements in public reason. Certainly they promise a different understanding of reasoning in presenting the whole story of the person to the liberal public forum. These narrative accounts of the self would be comfortable with the convenient fictions that seem always to be a part of governance, even in law.

40. The failure of legal systems to find and use algorithms in applying principles to cases provides opportunities to demonstrate the alternative methods introduced by narratives in legal decisions. General discussions of narratives in law are in the volume edited by Kim Lane Scheppele, ed., *Michigan Law Review* (August 1989). See also the legislators' narratives of justice presented and discussed in Grant Reeher, *Narratives of Justice* (Ann Arbor: University of Michigan Press, 1996).

individualism in establishing connections between parts and wholes. But the logical or arithmetical composition rules required to combine individual properties in the production of collectives lead to mapping problems: the rules cannot accommodate the emergent properties of collective states. The priority assigned to individuals also underestimates the antecedent influence of social structures in nurturing and defining individuals. Even the distinctions between individual and collective typically accepted in liberal thought seem to miss the important patterns of fusion adequately explained in a variety of collectivist theories. One result of these assumptions is the set of dilemmas and paradoxes of collective choice theory.[41]

Institutions and practices that do not rely on the derivative methods of liberal political theory avoid the rational breakdowns of collective choice theory with different assumptions about self and collective. One of the more persuasive alternatives to causal or numerical theories that are used to *produce* collective levels of human experience from descriptions of individuals is the assertion of a parallel between the structure of the self and the political society. Plato's symmetry between the ordering of the soul and the organization of the polis is one version of this type of connection. In recent studies James Glass has identified parallels between the mental states of persons and forms of collective action. He argues that social forms may reproduce the organization of the inner self, and this symmetry between self and social form represents defining patterns of healthy and pathological mental states.[42]

For example, the characteristic denials of the humanity of some members of the human community, and the ideologies that exclude the perspectives of others, represent in Glass's views a pathology that threads through individual and collective. Democratic politics, by contrast, are extensions of healthy mental states and protection against the tendencies of the

41. Summaries in William Riker, *Liberalism Against Populism*, (San Francisco, CA: W.H. Freeman, 1982), and on thresholds in utilitarianism, David Lyons in *Forms and Limits of Utilitarianism* (Oxford: Clarendon Press, 1965). These mapping problems have inclined some to augment thin (or formal) theories of rationality with various substances. For example: institutions (Robert Grafstein, *Institutional Realism* [New Haven, Conn.: Yale University Press, 1992]), and norms and ideas (discussed by Jon Elster, *The Cement of Society: A Study of Social Order* [Cambridge: Cambridge University Press, 1989]). The transitions from parts to wholes is complicated in yet another way with the recognition that individuals may be members of different senses of wholes. This possibility is elaborated by the proofs developed by George Tsebelis, in *Nested Games: Rational Choice in Comparative Politics* (Berkeley: University of California Press, 1990). And, as I suggested earlier, the possibility of multiple political contexts in the "same" political society also undermines the liberal notion that all citizens subscribe to the same terms of governance, no matter how minimal this set of terms may be.

42. James M. Glass, *Psychosis and Power* (Ithaca, N.Y.: Cornell University Press, 1995).

human psyche toward disintegration. For Glass democracies reduce the likelihood of delusions by controlling rage through the dialectics of civility, and by requiring a respect for the views of others. The structural features of democracies that encourage genuine reciprocity among members of the political society ensure harmony within the self as well as social coopera- tion. The self, in linking with others in social practices, can simultaneously recognize and contain regressive and toxic emotions. Democracy on Glass's account is needed for both public and private well being.[43]

If we accept this theory of political forms we must reject a purely ratio- nal or cognitive approach to politics. There are, first, surface reasons for this rejection. Illusion must play a vital role in any psychological account of political forms, and affect must be an important feature of political experi- ences. Also, the emotive origins of political attachments must be accommo- dated. But there are more basic considerations. A model of political partic- ipation developed on the terms of psychology introduces to political landscapes the unconscious and those psychic realities that signal our iden- tities as mental beings. Political organizations must be regarded as expres- sions of inner states. They are not arrangements derived from rational choices or justified by utilitarian formula. They instead reflect the complex organization of the person, and their moral qualities are symmetrical with the functional states of mental life.

It is an easy matter to collapse individual and political society on the terms of this version of psychology. The two domains—self and collective— are not entirely distinct. There may not even be a continuum between per- son and social form on a narrow reading of the symmetry thesis. Plato be- lieved that the structure of the soul and that of the city state are isomorphic in the sense that observations and conclusions about one could be trans- ferred without important loss of meaning to the other. Glass, however, re- sists the next step, which would be a fusion of one and all in a reduction of symmetry to unity. He uses the totalitarian movements of the twentieth cen- tury to indicate the pathological implications of submerging the individual in the larger society. For Glass the therapeutic possibilities of political life lie in the respect for individual autonomy that keeps harmful emotions below psychotic thresholds. Only as individuals have the kind of mutual liberty guaranteed by negative rights, and the social reciprocity found in civil soci- eties, can the polity realize the needs of persons in social life.

No theory of a symmetry between self and collective succeeds in all re- spects while maintaining a distinction between the two units. Plato cannot

43. Glass, *Psychosis and Power*, especially chapter 10.

quite harmonize the three parts of the self with parallel parts in the state. The artisans, like all individuals, must allow their reason to dominate appetite if they are to meet the terms of justice. Yet appetite is the part of the self that represents the artisans in the just state, and the artisans are dominated by the guardian class in the state. Reason is bifurcated. The public reason of the higher guardians is direct, that of the artisans deferential (an acceptance of the ruling class's rational authority). In a strange way the artisans, the least able of the three classes, are the most complicated: they presumably can reason directly in ordinary matters, and must reason deferentially in matters of state. If irony has a place in the *Republic* the presence of two powers of reasoning in the lower classes may explain why the virtue of the artisans is restraint (temperance) while the virtues of the two other classes are celebratory (wisdom and courage).

The psychological parallels of self and whole are untidy in other ways. The psychotic individual is closed to reasoning, and may have beliefs that are inaccessible. The group, psychotic (if the term can be applied for the sake of these points) or otherwise, must always be able to disclose at least part of its core beliefs in the mobilization of its members. Also, one of the persuasive definitions of a psychosis is that the individual so afflicted has beliefs that prevent him from securing his prudential goods.[44] Groups, by contrast, can organize a psychotic consensus among members that may seem intelligible and even be inordinately effective in securing goods, at least for a time. Then there are the inverse relationships of sanity and psychosis in the moves from self to collective and back again: a psychotic group may be composed at least in part by sane individuals, psychotic individuals may still compose (and be contained by) reasonably sane groups, and psychotic groups may give a kind of eerie solace and even consistency to individuals who are psychotic on different conditions than the pathologies defining the group.[45] Finally, the boundaries between psychotic and sane may be blurred at group levels in ways that are not found among individuals. Political societies that are sane on all conventional standards may carry out psychotic actions,[46] and certain tendencies that are psychotic in individuals may be functional in maintaining groups (such as the establish-

44. Robert Daly, "A Theory of Madness," *Psychiatry* 54 no. 4 (November 1991): 368–385.

45. Look at the chilling home movies of Nazi leaders relaxing at home with their children during the Holocaust. Rudolph Hess supervised the killing of two million people while continuing to be a member of the Catholic church. There is no doubt that the German political system provided assurances that the mass slaughter of humans was an exercise of high sanity.

46. Britain during times in its occupation of India and the United States during the Vietnam War are two recent—and contentious—examples of these possibilities.

ment of rigid boundaries between the group and rival groups, the identification of "enemies," etc.). In these and other ways self and group seem not to be exactly parallel.

10

Charles Taylor has distinguished between ontological and advocacy claims on self and whole. The ontological claims are grouped around atomism and holism. Atomism maintains that the primary unit in human experience is the individual, whereas holism assigns wholes bedrock ontological standing. Advocacy claims are organized by distinctions between individuals and collectives. Individualism is represented by the liberal stress on individual rights and principles, and collectivism assigns a priority status to community goods. Taylor points out that the two-by-two table yielded by this set of distinctions can accommodate a joining on each pole: the common sight of atomism-individualism and holism-collectivism, as well as the uncommon spectacle of atomism-collectivism and holism-individualism.[47]

A model that presents a closer relationship between ontology and advocacy is generated by these (and other) distinctions among parts and wholes in liberal democratic theory. I have argued that the partitions in experiences found in liberal organization of communities impose various types of dualism on the self. The primary forms of such dualism are property and practice. In conditions of pluralism some form of practice dualism is necessary. To see this requires a recognition that the communal self is a reality, but also a product of multiple variables. The facts of human psychology and environment allow for multiple formative influences on the self or person. Identity can be generated not just by some nostalgic sense of the old neighborhood, but also by the harder variables of race and ethnicity, place (in the sense of both geography and culture), and economic structure.[48] In heterogeneous societies one can expect persons to be different in rough accordance with the backgrounds that influence identity. So much is noncontroversial. In the expected pluralism of the liberal state multiple communal selves must engage the political system, and in doing so allow the partitions

47. Taylor, "Cross-Purposes: The Liberal-Communitarian Debate," in Nancy Rosenblum, ed., *Liberalism and the Moral Life* (Cambridge: Harvard University Press, 1989): 159–182. Taylor offers Humboldt as an instance of the atomism-collectivism category, B. F. Skinner as a representative of the holism-individualism category.

48. Speaking of narratives: Toni Morrison does as good a job as anyone (including social scientists) in delineating the multiple sources and conflicts of human identity in her novel *Tar Baby*.

between a political and a communal person that I have called practice dualism. There must be at least this intermittent partition in the self as the community and the political system connect with one another in governance.

Property dualism is less durable. It is difficult to imagine a complete abandonment of all forms of dualism in liberal political frameworks because so much of the liberal state depends on at least an occasional independence of thought and behavior. But, unlike practice dualism, property dualism can give way in some conditions to a unified self. A variety of circumstances permits the self to be absorbed for a time in political dialogue and discourse, where the engaged self can be defined within the process of talk itself. The identifying mark of a complete dialogue or discourse is a type of union between self and procedure, and self and other.

The beginnings of all conversations are movements from the singular to the collective. Taylor construes this as a shift from monologic to dialogic, as a transfer of the matters at hand from *me* and *you* to *us*: "A conversation is not the coordination of actions of different individuals, but a common action in this strong, irreducible sense; it is *our* action."[49] For Taylor the goods associated with this shift are both mediate in the common experiences we share, and convergent in the sense of public goods available to all only through collective action (but which we may not experience together). In Taylor's (and my) understanding of a political society there must be immediate common goods that are shared. Aristotle saw the bonds of the polis as analogous to friendship. In my arguments the solidarity of a liberal state resembles the bonds found in all mediated dialogues and discourses that secure agreeable outcomes.

In many ways the unification of persons by means of process is one version of an experience that is exceedingly common. Persons can be integrated as singular units in an experience that dominates and absorbs identity. A full mystical experience that culminates in the loss of self is unusual even in the literatures that record such experiences, but individuals can identify with phenomena and other persons in a momentary and partial fashion.[50] The intense transitory identifications of fans with teams and ath-

49. Taylor, "Cross-Purposes: The Liberal-Communitarian Debate." (The quote is on page 167.)

50. One set of recent experiments may have located the region of the brain involved in mystical experiences. A research psychologist, Michael Persinger (*Neuropsychological Bases of God Beliefs* [New York: Praeger, 1987]), claims to have induced mystical or religious experiences in subjects by stimulating the temporal lobe with magnetic forces. If this is true, then mystical experiences of a certain type might be replicable in a formal setting.

letes during sporting events is a well-known phenomenon. More enduring identifications are found in allegiances to causes and institutions. Individuals can avoid participation dilemmas by identifying with a larger social arrangement, and in doing so introduce costs and benefits that exceed the egoistic calculus assumed in so much of positive theory. The fact is that persons seem to dissolve and retain the self in numerous ways, so much so that the loss of self described in mystical experiences is probably partially experienced throughout ordinary experiences. That persons can merge with a dialectical process is itself a fairly ordinary expectation. Practice dualism is a defining part of liberal arrangements, which helps explain the depiction of the liberal self as an entity outside communities. But a transitory union of self with experience can recreate the thick communal self at the political level, allowing an internal unity of self across the partitions of a liberal society.

Return now to the distinctions between ontological and advocacy relationships between parts and wholes. Think of a common (or public) space, an area in which differences are managed peacefully, and where individual members of communities come to engage in public reasoning. The text of such a space must contain the different and often rival languages of the communities, for the common space in liberal governance is a kind of community defined by the rules of conversations. Persons submit to this public community as members of the political system, and in doing so can be represented by the procedures of conversational public reason. The powers of narratives to house multiple truths and define persons are especially effective as instruments of communication in this setting. Participants can absorb and communicate with each other and their constituents with stories that cut across cultural differences at the fundamental levels of individual identity.

Ontology and advocacy begin to intertwine in the common space of public reasoning. The considerations in this space are not presented in terms of whether individuals constitute wholes, which is argued in all versions of methodological individualism, nor whether wholes define and realize individuals. Instead we witness individuals entering a kind of talk that is itself a holistic or collective experience. Individual and whole are unified in common space on the terms of certain procedures that yield immediate goods. *This* communal self is then bound by the terms of advocacy set out in the conditions of mediated speech acts. The liberal and communitarian self in this way can be joined in a familiar political community defined by political norms. Ontology begets a type of advocacy.

The norms of a mediated discourse are reasonably anticipated from our understandings of good conversations. Individuals are not mysteriously lost in these processes of public reasoning but are absorbed into the talk that uses and crafts collective arrangements. In this peculiar merger of self and process can be found the kind of truth that is required in public reasoning. It is a truth framed with the use of mediating instruments to guide the conversations of persons concerned with the collective arrangements for their political society.

4 Mediated Closings

The version of public reason meeting the terms of modern political experience must satisfy a set of conditions that represent the loss of the *direct* authoritative and generalizable text. The first is the simultaneous acceptance and management of mechanisms (e.g., Moore's open question argument) that explain the widespread interpretation and reinterpretation of all governing principles. A definition that accommodates these mechanisms will outline a state that resists closure from fixed political principles or unique interpretations of these principles. Second, the state must include the dimensions of human experience represented by subjective (mental, first person) and objective (physical, third person) languages. Subjective perspectives are the resources that decompose objective political terms. This critical power must be recognized in any theory of state that begins with the results of its exercise. But it is also inconceivable that a state can be defined without objective languages. Third, and following closely on the second requirement, the state must successfully connect individual and whole in political terms. A theory of the state would be incomplete without such connections given that they mark the modern transitions from anarchy to the state. Fourth, and finally, an adequate theory of the state must include a reconciliation of liberty and power in conditions of uncertainty.

The easiest, though less direct, way to begin accommodating the list of requirements is through the exclusion of political systems that fail the conditions. Several putative theories of governance can be ruled out immediately. Purely formal systems, which mechanically grind out political outcomes with arithmetical or logical combination rules, cannot bring subjective languages into governmental processes. Nor can the neutral or impartial state of liberalism meet reasonable tests of adequacy. The critical powers of a modern citizenry undermine the "umpire" state of classical liberalism. Also discarded, though in this instance at the formative stages of the modern state, are all states based on theistic or moral truths. A political theory that originates in the acceptance of pluralism at foundational levels is not likely to put its own house in order by restoring discredited traditions that celebrate revealed truth.

The exclusion of formal and simple coercive systems of governing, however, still leaves a rich assortment of alternatives under the rubric of what I have labeled *collateral reasoning*. The absence of path independence between principle and action leads us to a set of devices (there is no better term for these actions) that avoid the problems of rational closure by activating several oblique or "sidebar" approaches to governance. These approaches represent collateral reasoning. They offer versions of public reasoning that meet the terms of modern political experience by abandoning both the thought that rules and principles are decisive resources in governing and the merit forms of reasoning that follow the thought.

It is important to remember that disjunctions between governing terms and actions occur even among persons who are members of the same community, and even when this community is characterized by a strong consensus. If language will not compute, it will not compute in all settings. But open and unstable languages may still be generally acknowledged and used effectively in public reasoning if norms are deeply shared. If the social setting is heterogeneous, however, and especially if the political system is characterized by divisive pluralism, then a more demanding requirement is placed on language. The terms of governance must be translated across the radical differences that signify communities in opposition rather than accord. It is this requirement that is raised by Winch and others, and it takes the critique of objective and universal standards in reasoning, especially as provided by Habermas, to a different and considerably more important level of issues.

A merit form of public reason has obvious affinities with the types of public expression exemplified by modern science. The dismissal of a privileged subject in favor of a disinterested type of thinking accessible to, and binding across, all rational subjects frames closure in terms of modern scientific expectations of objectivity. This objectivity is satisfied through consensus in stipulated conditions. It demarcates reason from subjectivity on a variety of criteria, including accuracy, visibility, accessibility and predictive powers. One consequence of this legacy is that ideographic or subjective modes of thinking are regarded as little more than sources of inspiration to be reframed into visible (shared) knowledge. Rational closure is to be achieved by those objective languages that screen out the subject.

The affinities of merit public reason with science also help us to understand how such reasoning fails in practice. It is widely acknowledged (by Thomas Kuhn, among others) that the rules and principles of scientific inquiry cannot explain in full the judgments that working scientists make on retaining or falsifying theories. Even on the acceptance of criteria for a good scientific theory—accuracy, consistency, broad scope, simplicity, and frameworks that lead to new research—choices among competing theories will vary among scientists. The explanation of this variance offered by Kuhn is that choices depend on both objective or shared factors, and subjective factors like individual biography and personality. The languages of science, like those of politics, underdetermine practical judgments. For Kuhn, and for others, there are no algorithms for theory choices. The open issue in public reasoning is how the undetermined part of judgment or choice is to be accounted for when it cannot be explained by the system of reasoning in which it occurs.[1]

2

Two modern accounts of liberal democracy represent a state unable to govern on computational reasoning. One is the *fallibility* theory of democracy developed in different ways by Charles Peirce, Karl Popper, James Smith, and Thomas Thorson. This theory justifies open practices with an epistemology that rejects any truth that can bring interpretation to a fixed rational closure. The pragmatism of Peirce's "Do not block the way of inquiry" is the elegant rule for later philosophical dismissals of traditional understandings of truth.[2] Popper's empiricism follows Peirce's skepticism and the positivist linkage of the meaning of a statement to its mode of verification. The restriction of verification to empirical and analytic statements in positivism denies the truth status and (as a consequence) the meaning of value statements. All normative political philosophies are reduced to a level playing field, in the pejorative sense that justifications of any political arrangements—democracy, socialism, authoritarianism, and

1. Thomas Kuhn, "Objectivity, Value Judgment, and Theory Choice," in *The Essential Tension* (Chicago: University of Chicago Press, 1977), 320–329, especially 338–339.

2. Charles Peirce, "The Scientific Attitude and Fallibilism," in Justus Buchler, ed., *Philosophical Writings of Peirce* (New York: Dover Publications, 1955), 54. This statement, drawn up on an acceptance of human intellectual limitations that previews this century's development of bounded rationality, is critical to Thorson's brief for democracy. I also endorse its importance in generating open systems of governing.

so on—are little more than expressions of taste or rhetorical devices once value statements are no longer truth functional. Popper's substitution of falsification for verification provides for the normative effect of the program as a social practice. If all scientific theories are no more than hypotheses that have so far resisted disproof, and if no statement can ever be conclusively established as a final truth, then direct justifications of political arrangements can only be as tentative and provisional as scientific hypotheses. Authority gives way to the shifting canons of theory and evidence.

The justification of political forms that emerges from this program enters through the side doors of inquiry. If there is no authoritative truth, and if one consequence of falsification is that no statement or institution has more than tentative standing, then the only form of government with standing is one that is itself open and provisional. The Smith-Thorson thesis is that democracy is the only form of governing that meets this test. In this view the absence of truth-functional statements yields a state that is without commitments to truth, but committed to procedures that maintain the possibility of critical interpretations and dismissals of even the most basic political forms.[3] For Popper the open society follows the epistemology of falsification. Tolerance and encouragement for political freedoms are the natural properties of such a society.[4]

A second account of liberal democracy is crafted on the central standing of *uncoerced discourse*. John Stuart Mill stresses the importance of free speech in Milton's metaphor of a marketplace of ideas. *On Liberty* presents the well-known utilitarian defense of liberty in terms of individual priorities, and the more nearly deontic defense that freedom is essential to human persons. But the use of open debate to identify superior political assertions that cannot be identified in any other way is clearly an endorsement of a social mechanism that is to perform epistemological functions. The absence of a priori truth bids us to use public debate to construct hierarchies among statements.[5] The parallels with Darwinian evolutionary models are striking. Forms are "justified" as they emerge from the selection processes of natural competition, not as they fulfill some *a priori* conception of proper forms.

3. James Ward Smith, *Theme for Reason* (Princeton, N.J.: Princeton University Press, 1957), and Thomas Landon Thorson, *The Logic of Democracy* (New York: Holt, Rinehart and Winston, 1962).

4. Karl Popper, *The Open Society and Its Enemies* (Princeton, N.J.: Princeton University Press, 1963).

5. John Stuart Mill, *On Liberty*, ed. Elizabeth Rapaport (Indianapolis, IN: Hackett, 1978), chapter 2 primarily.

James Fishkin's model of open dialogue assumes that there is no single ideal procedure and no ultimate criterion for justice. Justice, as the product of democratic dialogue, requires a "self-reflective political culture: one that is *significantly self-critical as a result of unmanipulated dialogue.* A political culture is "significantly" self-critical when the social practices defining its regulative institutions are consistently subjected to widespread and conscientious criticism" (p. 146). Fishkin's schema is based on extensive liberty, which he emphasizes by excluding both explicit (the imposition of penalties because of the content of one's conscientious political views) and structural (on communication itself) manipulation (pp. 148–156). The proposed design is to give effective voice across every significant cleavage in society (p. 156). The result for Fishkin is "the collective reasonableness of a political system examining—and accepting—itself through unmanipulated dialogue" (p. 203). In this institutional arrangement the openness of the political society is realized through extensive and unlimited critical scrutiny.[6]

Habermas provides the general framework. He observes that truth can be challenged at a fundamental level. When this occurs three alternatives are opened to speakers. One is to break off communication. Another is to engage in strategic communication, or resort to force. A third is to continue speech at a different level. In this third alternative theoretical discourse replaces ordinary speech by regarding truth claims as problematic and subject to the influence of arguments. We are then in the domain of discourse rather than speech acts in ordinary language. All practical discourse for Habermas must contain the freedom to move from speech to discourse and back again, meaning that discussion must contain the possibility of progressive radicalization. But beyond challenge are the conditions of discourse that make a settlement of disputes over both truth and validity possible: the unrestricted and unconstrained structure of communication. This structure orders the "peculiarly unreal" form of communication known as discourse, where participants submit to the "unforced force of the better argument."[7]

To see these proposals at a manageable level, I ask the reader to imagine a group of individuals with different and rival conceptions of the good drawn from incompatible understandings of human experience. Allow in the thought experiment a principle of futility, which is to mean that no

6. Fishkin regards cultural self-criticism as providing for "limited liberalism" and a "context-dependent" theory of justice. In *The Dialogue of Justice* (New Haven, Conn.: Yale University Press, 1992).

7. Jürgen Habermas, *Knowledge and Human Interests* (Boston: Beacon Press, 1971).

amount of principled governance or adjudication can alter the conceptions or the understandings. Two conditions follow the admission. First, the asymmetric values of the group rule out utilitarianism. The absence of a single-value scale denies all maximizing techniques to reach a collective good. Second, and bearing on rightness or fairness interpretations of justice, the conception of the group situation will vary with individuals.

A *situation* in the modern world originates in some complex way with perspectives. A group can change with the addition and subtraction of members in both the simple additive matter of size and also in the sense that understandings are introduced or taken away with numerical change. Perspectives can be combined or juxtaposed to yield different meanings. Whether a situation is observed by a privileged (innocent, knowledgeable) witness affects meaning. The religious acceptance of an unknowable observer expands and deepens meaning for believers, and the use in science of the impartial or distant spectator defines situations. A group of multiple perspectives is itself multiple and perhaps fluid in all important respects.

The introduction of a social contract and liberal principles to such a group invites contradictions as profound as those generated by additive or logical combination rules. The purposes of liberal contracts and principles are inevitably subverted with incorrigible divisions over meaning and interpretation. Such divisions produce multiple definitions that fragment reason. But the attendant and corollary languages needed to salvage what reason sets out to achieve are also clear. The principle of futility urges a principle of accommodation. If liberalism turns to the objectivity of perspective as a surrogate for classical objectivity, it is also reasonable to locate justice among those devices that accommodate subjective interests with as much freedom as possible.

But now think of a conversation among persons who have just shared a convivial meal. Let a narrative carry our thoughts along, with critical faculties checked for the moment so that the discourse theory of public reason can be inspected in its ideal moments. The guests and hosts are seated in a relaxed and unordered arrangement in the physical space of a home. It is a small dinner party of friends and colleagues (from any professions or crafts). The food and beverages have been consumed, the coffee and tea are on the table with fruit and dessert in front of each guest. The conversation has reached that relaxed and spontaneous moment when reflections are easily transformed into words, ideas enter the flow of talk, the thoughts of each guest are formed and expressed within the rhythms of language that mark the connections occasioned by the fact that persons are gathered for an evening meal.

Now suppose that the conversation is political. This condition is met if the talk centers on the collective properties of events, and considerations of the structure and purpose of group life.[8] Suppose also that the conditions for unrestricted dialogue are present. The members of the dinner party freely advance opinions that are provisional stops in the conversation, entries that are to be critically examined by other members of the party. Occasionally, perhaps frequently, the guests introduce opinions that they do not believe but judge necessary to move the group closer to shared conclusions. These conclusions, when identified, have a more restricting effect on the conversation because they survive the critical powers of the conversation. They are also provisional, though in a more enduring sense. They provide a kind of inertia to the conversation that keeps it from moving too far off the multiple lines of talk that lead to an acknowledgment of a desirable collective outcome.

This political conversation is a flawed but productive metaphor for a type of public reason, and in this sense is like the metaphor of a social contract in providing standards for evaluating political actions. But unlike the conditions and logic of social contract theory the standards of communication found in conversational dialogue must be realized in some form of experience as a condition for their foundational use. Both contract and dialogue theory can yield ideal propositions, core experiences that provide a model to be approximated in political experience. But while contract theory can represent the model as a pure hypothetical, dialogue must occur to produce intelligible standards. The conditions of the conversation are those of a just society: equality among the participants, the absence of external coercion, a common language and shared rational criteria. The logic is patterned: a dialectical scrutiny of proposals to arrive at a governing alternative. But conversational reasoning is not adjudicative. Dialogue versions of public reason produce conclusions from the fluid though controlled use of evidence, argument, and narrative. Outcomes are undefined before they occur and constrained by the properties of collateral reasoning rather than the applications of moral and political principles. It is impossible for such reasoning to be modeled successfully in a purely hypothetical state of affairs in part because so much of its form and outcome are indeterminate.

The inventory of communication devices in a good conversation will

8. Rawls defines reasoning as public when it is (a) the reason of the public, (b) concerned with the good of the public, and (c) conducted open to view. In Rawls, *Political Liberalism* (New York: Columbia University Press, 1993), p. 213. The dinner conversation meets these requirements metaphorically if the guests at the party can be regarded as the citizens of the polis.

not accommodate the comparatively rigid categories of truth-seeking versus strategic communication.[9] The search for a right answer by means of proofs or empirical methods of falsification is not likely to be successful in situations where there are no right answers. But truth is not necessarily abandoned in these conditions. Participants in a conversation are trying to buy a settlement. They simultaneously attempt to establish a truth, and negotiate differences with a colleague or adversary. The overall framework that seems most appropriate for this reasoning is a combination of truth-seeking and strategic communication known as dialectics. An ideal dialectical forum would consist of conditions in which adversaries advance a series of arguments and counterarguments, with rebuttals, refutations, assertions, and the like. A panel of mediators might be present to adjust claims and order presentations. Burdens of proof would be shared by the friendly adversaries in roughly equal fashion.[10] Dialectical exercises have the additional virtue of expanding our moral powers of "extended sympathy" in seeing experience from the point of view of the other.

If the dialectical forum still appears to be a court of law, the appearance should be restructured. When U.S. Supreme Court Chief Justice William Rehnquist concluded his time in the U.S. Senate as chair of the impeachment trial of President Clinton, he said, "I underwent the sort of culture shock that naturally occurs when one moves from the very structured environment of the Supreme Court to what I shall call, for want of a better phrase, the more free-form environment of the Senate." The transition described by Rehnquist between the deliberations of the Supreme Court and the reasoning of the Senate illustrates the differences between legal and political discourses. The formal public deliberations of a court of law are controlled by well-defined rules of interference, evidence, and argument. Discussions in political institutions are less structured—in the words of Rehnquist, "more free-form." In the open disputation of a dialectical forum the stakes are moved even farther away from structure. Within the loose form of speech acts (which do include linguistic rules of grammar and syntax) the participants in a dialectical exercise can engage in role playing and entertain contradictions without a breakdown. Someone may support both p and $\sim p$ as an exercise in dialectics in order to explore on a provisional basis the negation of one's cherished beliefs. The point is to reach that moving equilibrium in which method validates outcomes, and where argu-

9. Or Habermas draws too tight a distinction between these two activities.

10. On the assumption that shifts in the burdens of proof are often strategic moves. But consult Richard H. Gaskins, *The Burdens of Proof in Modern Discourse* (New Haven, Conn.: Yale University Press, 1992).

ments dominate principles. Like the intriguing parallel between intellectual competition and biological evolution suggested in Mill's *On Liberty*, the players in dialectical exercises may be able to accept that last standing argument as the desirable *and* binding alternative in politics.[11] Legislative bodies, in part because their dialogues are less structured, can more nearly realize dialectical talk than can a court of law.

Now suppose that the dialogue is a form of discourse, meaning that the participants have entered a discussion in which every term, criterion, treasured belief—everything is on the table for critical inspection. Suppose also that the members of the dinner party conversation have surrendered to the logic and rhythm of the discourse, meaning that they are willing to accept the outcomes of the discussion as binding. In such a setting the self is subordinated to the process, and may even be fused with the language and logic of the discussion. No anchor holds individuals in the particulars of empirical reality when these moments occur. Individuals and *this* type of process can be indistinguishable as arguments dominate the proceedings.

3

A version of public reason modeled on a conversation is the ideal opening metaphor to explain closure on liberal expectations. It effectively represents the only model that seems to fit a noncomputational form of public reasoning: unconstrained dialogue in the tradition of a discourse. It is also a device that avoids the one effective critique of all ideal dialogues: the problem of specifying which species of discourse defines the ideal. If scientific, moral, religious, and other dialogues compete with one another in rendering experience manageable, and if there is no overarching system that can fuse or order these dialogues, then no single ideal is possible. A conversation is the source for a dialogue structured by the talk itself. Conversational reason also succeeds where texts are unstable, open to rival (and reasonable) interpretations, and even where the text has no meaning until participants assign meaning. The vulnerability of political languages to rival interpretations invites forms of dialogue that produce meaning in the talk itself.

It is unrealistic to expect that liberal principles can be fully maintained in a dialogue form of public reason. Equality is a fugitive presence in dialogue of almost any type. Even if the entire range of background inequalities were somehow neutralized, and the structure and setting of the discus-

11. Nicholas Rescher, *Dialectics* (Albany: State University of New York Press, 1977). The Rehnquist quotation can be found in the New York Times, 13 February 1999, A12.

sion designed to ensure equal access, the distribution of talent in using the instruments of dialogue would be unequal.[12] This is a commonplace phenomenon, one known by dinner party hosts and trial judges. Some argue more effectively than others, are more adept at seeing and controlling evidence, tell better and more compelling stories. Sometimes the simple ownership of the true story is a (warranted) advantage. But whatever the source or reason the expectation that equality of either verbal access or outcome will be realized in any discussion is probably unrealistic.

Liberty, however, does seem to find space for influence and internal constraint in the rational imperatives of dialogue. There is first the reasonable distinction between liberty and license that constrains any conversation. Members of the dinner party are not effectively free to move outside the parameters of a given dialogue by, say, straying from the point, or sharing unintelligible anecdotes, or excessively abusing others with unneeded remonstrations. Those who do these things are censured by the group in formal and informal ways.[13] But, second, there are the constraining effects of dialogue itself. Language, as we all know, has rules. At the most rudimentary are those rules of syntax and semantics that must be followed or recognized in order to speak and write. At another level are those rules that express the logic of language use.

The formal properties of language that do provide rational constraints on freedom are represented in speech acts, which recognize that speakers *act* as well as speak, and often incur obligations and modify both persons and conditions in doing so.[14] The powers of language to affect situations are widely accepted. It is exactly as language is both an expression and a form of action that liberal practices have so much trouble in regulating speech. On one hand language is an expression of thought and so shielded from regulation (thus the championing of free speech in the West). But on the other hand language is a form of action with powers to obligate and capacities to do harm (and thus falling under the regulatory powers even of libertarian states).

12. No one denies this statement. But there is considerable disagreement on whether it is even meaningful to talk about neutralizing background inequalities inasmuch as their sources are so various and extensive in social arrangements.

13. Mill relies (disproportionately, one might say) on social censure as an alternative to state regulation. He seems to regard society as holistic, with many informal methods of coercion, and the political domain as atomistic, with one primary form of coercion. In *On Liberty*.

14. Austin, *How to Do Things with Words* (Oxford: Clarendon Press, 1962). John Searle, "How to Derive 'Ought' from 'Is,'" in W. D. Hudson, ed., *The Is-Ought Question* (New York: St. Martin's Press, 1969), 120–134.

More elaborate rules of dialogue set out the conditions for any successful communication. We might allow, for example, that all dialogue requires the acceptance of a principle of cooperation. One version of this principle stipulates that participants make contributions as required by the accepted purpose or the direction of the verbal exchange in which they are engaged. Several maxims specify the principle in terms of rules for those who are contributing to the dialogue: quality (do not say false or inadequately supported statements), quantity (try to provide complete information, not too little or too much), relevance, and manner (admonishing as to brief, clear and orderly communications). Such rules are generally offered as practice summaries of effectively organized communications.[15] They typically are set against a background of assumptions and knowledge that help define all dialogue.

A stronger restriction of liberty follows the effective use of dialogue in reaching binding conclusions. One point to a political discussion is to produce statements that have rational standing. In Mill the process must permit a critical treatment of every opinion so that the outcomes of dialogue consist of those conclusions that have survived critical scrutiny. But these conclusions, having survived, are settled as the "best" opinions. One no longer has the liberty to criticize them with the same latitude routinely found in the process leading to conclusions. It is the successful survival in disputation that grants such conclusions their action-guiding powers. To be rational at end-game time in this critical system is to be guided by the conclusions of discourse. The sanctions that rationality imposes on persons are not to be cavalierly dismissed. Competence is a close relation of rationality, and competence is the entry ticket into the dialogue. The more complete liberty of process is restricted on this promise of a sanction for journeys into irrational domains.

All conclusions of rational dialogue have constraining effects. Even the skepticism of science produces outcomes that govern research priorities and methods. Hypotheses that have so far resisted disproof can be criticized only with evidence, argument, alternative explanations that are better than those that have produced the resistant strain of hypothesis.[16] In reli-

15. H. Paul Grice, "Logic and Conversation," in Peter Cole and J. L. Morgan, eds., *Syntax and Semantics 3: Speech Acts* (New York: Academic Press, 1975), 41–58.
16. The agony of defeat usually follows the failure of a challenge to a settled opinion or dominant theory. On March 23, 1989, two chemists at the University of Utah, Martin Fleischmann and B. Stanley Pons, made a surprise announcement that they had achieved cold fusion, which means that they had initiated a nuclear fusion reaction at room temperature. The immediate reaction of most physicists was a combination of skepticism and scorn, that of chemists a cautious support. But when the experiment was inspected more closely and diffi-

gious dialogue the conclusions of critical reflection can mandate actions, extinguishing liberty with the compulsions of conscience. The critical dialogue of politics is reconciling, generating conclusions that manage differences with the uses of collective goods. In none of these versions of dialogue is the liberty found in process reproduced at the concluding stage of the discussion. The exercise of liberty in the dialectical setting of contested expression leads when successful to truths that restrict liberty on rational grounds.

The key, as Mill understood, is to install a compatible arrangement among the family concepts and practices of competence or rationality, negative liberty, and uses of information as the starting point to a reconciliation of liberty and coercion. Some attempts at compatibility are obvious but unlikely to accomplish much in political settings. The most prominent entry in this category is the metacommand that coerces *logically* to liberty: "Act freely!" Social practices contain variations on this command, including those that require persons to exercise discretion or simply be themselves. In all instances a coercive imperative is consistent with liberty in requiring persons to exercise liberty. To include such imperatives in the domain of settled opinions is to reconcile liberty and power on rational grounds. But the logic of all states requires substantive constraints on actions, inasmuch as a political system is formed in part to adjudicate the otherwise irreconcilable claims that persons make and the contradictory actions that follow these claims. If political outcomes were always successful with admonitions to act freely, there would be no point to having a state in the first place.

Mill's scheme of compatibility between reasoned constraint and liberty is still best. In *On Liberty* he argues for negative liberties that shield speech and certain types of actions from government regulation. His defense of free speech is developed on both utilitarian and deontic considerations. The free and critical discussion of opinions produces a society governed by better convictions than those produced by a closed society, in part because only a dialectical examination can yield an ordering of opinions on merit. But freedom also has intrinsic value. It is important because it is embedded

culties in replication were experienced, most of the scientific community rejected the claims as nonsense. Though Fleischmann and Pons survived to take positions in a French laboratory generously funded by research money from Japan, and though the possibility of cold fusion continues to fascinate some researchers, the norms of science were quickly used to dismiss the initial claims as bad science. The two chemists had proposed a startling revision of some foundations in physics without the careful experimentation and argument required in science. They struck the king without killing him.

in the human condition, so basic that freedom of expression is necessary to the "mental well-being of mankind."[17] On both justifications the state is limited to the regulation of actions that harm interests or rights. The case for such restrictions is based in part on the assumption that coercion and liberty are antinomies, or in what is now defined as a zero-sum relationship: more of one is proportionately less of the other.

Yet Mill locates more subtle relationships between coercion and liberty in his justifications of freedom of expression. The main body of concepts in *On Liberty* is organized on an understanding of persons as naturally free and truth-seeking creatures. Free speech is necessary to mental well-being *because* it establishes a public debate that subjects opinions to dialectical examination. This dialectical practice is the only way that truth can be found, demarcated from error, and have its salutary effects on persons. The process of critical scrutiny is inseparable from either freedom or the successful pursuit of truth. Freedom of expression is required to discover truth, and is valuable as a means to fulfill our need to know the truth. The dialectical process, moreover, moves to provisional conclusions if it is successful. Disputation can even lead to truths that need no longer be disputed. A set of statements can survive dialectical examination as stable outcomes. These opinions presumably are the received wisdom of the community. Mill regards the absence of critical debate as a loss, but he marks progress as the recognition of settled truths.[18]

The close ties between free expression and truth have interesting effects on freedom at points of rational closure. Two are especially important. One is that a standard justification of freedom in *On Liberty* is both restricted

17. *On Liberty*, p. 50.
18. *On Liberty*, p. 42: "As mankind improves, the number of doctrines which are no longer disputed or doubted will be constantly on the increase; and the well-being of mankind may almost be measured by the number and gravity of the truths which have reached the point of being uncontested." I have always found this, and his following remarks on "the consolidation of opinion," remarkable given all that Mill has to say about the inevitability of refutation. I interpret this passage as referring to a provisional settlement of opinion, in the sense in which scientific laws can sometimes attain a kind of revered standing beyond day-to-day falsification—though always on the understanding that (on Popper's felicitous phrase) these laws are still no more than hypotheses that have so far resisted disproof. I take Mill's settled opinions to have achieved this kind of conditional escape from contestation. The risk in settled opinions is posed by Coleridge's delicious observation: "Truths, of all others the most awful and mysterious, yet being at the same time of universal interest, are too often considered as so true that they lose all the powers of truth, and lie bed-ridden in the dormitories of the soul, side by side with the most despised and exploded errors." In Barbara E. Rooke, ed, *The Collected Works of Samuel Taylor Coleridge*, Essay xv (Princeton, N.J.: Princeton University Press, 1969). I am grateful to Tom Green for calling my attention to this passage in Coleridge.

and (consequently) diminished in importance. If the domain of stable out-comes is inhospitable to free expression, then such freedom is not general-izable. Mill hopes that the practice of open critical discussion will continue after truth is established. But he recognizes that dialectics can be only a kind of mental calisthenics in these conditions in that there is little point to the critical examination of opinion that has the imprimatur of truth. The main rationale for freedom of expression, and its purpose in social prac-tices, are lost in those areas where dispute is irrelevant.[19]

A second effect is on liberty of choice. Mill expects free speech to result in a merit ordering of opinions as critical examination proceeds in the form of open debate. These ranked opinions are action-guiding, for the es-tablishment of warranted statements helps persons negotiate experience successfully. Persons can choose and act rationally. Freedom, recognized by Mill as a natural property of persons, permits idiosyncratic actions—but not in all conditions. The libertarian arrangement of concepts depends on an understanding of persons as rational creatures, as endowed with capaci-ties to use information to identify and act on one's best interests. The per-son who disregards obvious truths and acts on obvious errors risks a forfei-ture of this rational standing. Remember that competence and rationality are conditions for the exercise of freedom. Choices and actions that deviate in large ways from an established ordering of opinions are reasons to re-gard the person so choosing and acting as failing these conditions. Pater-nalism is the famous enemy of liberty in Mill's theories. But those who lack capacities for choice and action are outside the parameters of the libertar-ian game. Children and the mentally deficient, for example, are not candi-dates for freedom even in the most comprehensive versions of libertarian-ism. It *must* follow that settled opinions are coercive. They restrict choices and actions on the sanction of incompetence or irrationality. Put another way, one does not have freedom to select and act on opinions that are graded very low or acknowledged as egregious error without jeopardizing one's standing as the kind of creature who can exercise freedom.[20]

19. Mill calls the substitute dialectic in conditions of uncontested truth "some con-trivance." He still welcomes it as a device for understanding assertions, much in the way (I suppose) that Plato's use of the Socratic dialectic revealed truths that could not be contested. See page 42 and following.

20. The *Thornburg* (1983) ruling is a case study in the recognition of the coercive powers of information. The issue was whether pro-life organizations could legally provide women contemplating abortion with information on fetal development. The Court said no on the grounds that such information, even if morally neutral, would tend to coerce women away from a choice of abortion. It is an easy matter to see that the standard package of concepts in informed consent—competence, rationality, and negative liberty—cannot be held together

The high standing that Mill assigns to truth suggests that information or knowledge, and perhaps rationality, are the dominant entries in his theory of the state, not liberty. Liberty is (a) justified in part as an instrument to establish truth, (b) marginalized in domains of settled opinions, and (c) restricted by the statements it yields when exercised as freedom of expression. The objectivity that successful debate produces in the public realm is coercive in a benign sense, however. It is an internal restriction on choices and actions, and simply states that dialectical examinations of opinions can make us more rational as free creatures. We are rationally constrained by what we discover in the exercise of free inquiry. It is difficult to imagine any form of rational activity that would not produce such an outcome. The coercive powers of the state are more chilling for Mill because they originate in an external source. The state represents the actions of some governing others. For this reason public objectivity must originate in the kind of free debate that produces the only truths that can constrain actions—those that survive unrestricted critical inspection.

The importance of rational constraints is self-evident in the liberal state. Radical and unrestricted interpretation of political vocabularies undermines reasoned governance. Some form of provisional rational closure must be assigned to interpretations if public reason is to bind liberty and coercion in a congenial arrangement. Otherwise the public domain is exactly like Mill's understanding of private experience: the unrestricted liberty of a privately controlled domain of action. Privacy allows persons to assign their own meanings to events and practices, and these assignments are not governable even by the amenable and generalizable constraints occasionally found in the political society.

But a public harmony between reason and liberty is always difficult. We know now that the manner in which opinions are ordered will sometimes (perhaps frequently) encourage liberty of choice and action. The strongest coercive effects of merit-ranked opinions are from those hierarchies in which singular or uniform opinions precisely stated to rule out interpretation are in a cardinal arrangement generalizable to all possible actions. But such an arrangement is not found even in the narrowest type of established science or the strictest of theistic religious orders. Even precise opinions must allow interpretation, cardinal scales are unlikely devices to rank opinions, and hierarchies typically are restricted to some domain of experience no matter how robust their scope might be. In the relaxation of these fea-

---

successfully if information is (a) regarded as necessary for informed (and rational) choices, but (b) an unwarranted restriction of free choice.

tures of merit orderings are found the conceptual interstices of liberty: of interpretation, of weight to assign to different entries in the ordering, and of extension and retraction of opinions to different areas of action. Each contributes to an ongoing and extended harmony between liberty and power on the common uses of rationality.

The main preoccupations of *On Liberty* are with those considerations that allow the state to override negative liberty within a framework granting priority standing to liberty. But the internal coercion of settled opinions affecting persons through the filter of rationality is not a violation of negative liberty, which is ensured so long as other persons or agencies do not regulate one's thoughts, speech, or actions. There is a great and decisive difference in Mill's political philosophy between the coercion of persons and the coercion of arguments. Rational coercion is a form of persuasion or convincing, where the respondents influence one another through the presentation of intellectual and rhetorical appeals. To be coerced by these appeals is to *assent* to an opinion, which by its own logic requires a joining of freedom and rationality.[21] This possibility is the main source of harmony between liberty and coercion in the public sphere.

4

A dialogue version of public reason adjusts liberal theory in several ways. First, the constraints of language and argument restrict liberty in ways consistent with reason and morality. Second, equality of both access and outcome are functions of the discussion, having no independent standing. Third, adjudication gives way to dialectics, with outcomes emerging from the critical examination of alternatives by all participants. (Equality of participation replaces the hierarchical ordering of a court judgment.)

21. Or Locke, for example, with one of his gentle distinctions in *A Letter Concerning Toleration*: "But it is one thing to perswade, another to command; one thing to press with Arguments, another with Penalties." On page 27 of the Hackett edition. Even the coercive powers of the state seem to be more benign when they are exercised on rational grounds. There is a passage in Robert Bolt's play, *A Man for All Seasons*, that illustrates this distinction in an exchange. At one stage in Cromwell's interrogation of More the prelate accuses Cromwell of threatening "like a dockside bully." Cromwell: "How should I threaten?" More: "Like a Minister of State, with justice." Cromwell: "Oh, justice is what you're threatened with." More: "Then I'm not threatened." (I am using the Vintage Books edition of the play for these citations.) For More the *just* powers of the state are coercive in different and acceptable ways because they are thick with reasoned arguments, proofs and vows. More of course believes that his innocence is a shield against this power. (And it would have been in a just state. Refusal to sign an illegally framed oath leads to his incarceration in the Tower, and false testimony brings him to his execution.) No such protection is available against the coercion of the dockside bully, which is unreasoned force and violence. The exchange quoted here is on page 77.

Fourth, narratives and empirical materials coalesce in the free association of alternatives found in any sustained dialogue. Fifth, the self (as participant) is defined by the role that the individual plays in the discussion, and these roles may themselves evolve spontaneously.

But accepting the central placement of discussion in public reasoning leaves much to be settled. Dialogue forms of public reasoning are incomplete, needing additional arrangements to function successfully. There is no assurance that any types of discussion among rational persons will produce the closure that eludes adjudication. The starting proposition in liberal political theory is that the state is formed on the understanding that free and autonomous persons cannot coordinate their actions successfully to ensure peace and stability, and to produce a variety of other public goods that make human communities civil and civilized. There is nothing in the arguments for political authority that follow this proposition to suggest that unrestricted and continuing dialogue among such persons will produce the harmony and cooperation that state-of-nature conditions deny.

It is helpful to recall that the working text of public reason is not clear because it is not written. The words (rules, principles) of governance cannot in themselves be sources of authority. Now one may think and even believe that the uncoerced dialogue of reason wields the conceptual power to extract meaning from the vocabulary of the liberal state. The case that Mill offers is influential in its convictions that the free expression of opinion will eventually—in a linear or staccato process—produce an acknowledged (if provisional) truth that can guide actions *generally*. But there is much to offer against the likelihood of that outcome.

First, the fact that interpretations of texts can deviate so radically from any set of convergent points suggests that critical dialogue might as easily lead to more as less disagreement. There is some empirical evidence to support this prospect.[22] Second, the nature of the disputes over interpretation suggests a more pessimistic outcome for a dialogue of free association. Radical differences in understanding a text may be traceable to different ways of life, and are similar to the puzzlement that occurs among persons who are trying to understand one another when each is speaking a different

22. In *Negroes and the New South* (New York: Harcourt, Brace and World, 1966) Donald Mathews and James Prothro found that increased contact between the races sometimes led to less understanding and more acrimony. This *general* finding, not so astonishing today, is replicated in numerous informal settings. I have found, for example, that more discussion between pro-life and pro-choice on abortion issues in my classes produces more substantial disagreement.

language. The problem is translating one language into another. The approach of political liberalism is to suppose that there is a political language that can act as the translating device for the modest purposes of adjudication and reconciliation. But we have seen that these are not modest purposes, but rather immodest goals, and that the proffered languages are easily bent to partisan purposes when much is at stake in the interpretation. The system of governance is chronically open, and cannot be closed with a text alone. Third, the differential access and control of dialogue that we may reasonably expect in any discussion is unlikely to find its own resolution. Inequalities of verbal skills and intellect are not leveled with the formal constraints of language. One well-known consequence of these inequalities is that some persons will dominate others independent of the arguments and interests being addressed.

Dialogue also seems to require a kind of guidance in maintaining frames of reasoning. One of the primary arguments in social theory currently is that speech acts and even discourses have certain properties that are objective and universal, and that one proof of these properties is that they cannot be denied, discussed, or even addressed without presupposing their existence (in part by necessarily using them). This argument has many attractive implications, among them that it eliminates (thankfully) the need for first choices as a condition for dialogue and discourse to be initiated. There is no need for primordial commitments when speaking already is an occurrence of the conditions of speech and discourse.[23] But critical perspectives, and radical reinterpretation, can also extend to the criteria of talk itself and this transform dialogue into discourse. One consequence of this possibility is that public reason must be carefully defined in particular, and perhaps local or practice, terms, not simply by the objective and universal properties that may seem to be the defining conditions for all dialogue *and* discourse. It is also important to recognize the differential resistance of various criteria to critical reinterpretation.

23. Most prominently in Habermas, *Theory and Practice*. For the record, it is not clear (in spite of my wishes) that the use of discourse settles the issues of moral commitment with a simple representation. Even if it is conceded that persons must be players in a language game if they use language (no prior commitment needed) it is not certain from this fact exactly what game it is that they are playing. Those in the promising game, for example, may be playing their stakes strategically, not truthfully. So Hare might be right in his brief against Searle: one incurs an obligation in a language game only if one makes a first commitment to the rules and principles of the game. See R. M. Hare, "The Promising Game," in W. D. Hudson, ed., *The Is-Ought Question*, 144–156.

5

Language on open types of reasoning is an elastic or ambiguous background that guides without halting the deliberations and dialogue of reasoning. This background can constrain persons when it represents the deep and vague consensus that typically supports the institutions of public reason. But one of the points of the present text is that language cannot specify settlements when it is translated into directives. Instead the translations are noncomputational derivations that yield to the partisan communities found in the liberal state. Because noncomputational reasoning is represented by dialogue, the problem is to identify the devices of closure in what can be called the forensic practices of authority.

I suggest that one practice and one set of considerations can shape political dialogue into useful instruments of closure. The practice is mediation (*broadly* conceived). The considerations are the holistic references that define political deliberations. These two devices work because public reasoning is a form of collective judgment, with the expectation that some persons will be helpful in translating and adapting the terms of authority to the circumstances of politics. We reason together in political practices, and we reason about the collective arrangements that express our relations to one another.[24]

Mediation is the standard term to describe the role of those who assist others to make their own decisions. The term has many complex meanings, and different practices represent mediation. But certain properties are found in all or most forms of mediation. By definition mediation is triadic, with a third party (the mediator) intervening to bring about a settlement among sets of other parties who are adversaries. The mediator is to help alter enough of the conditions (including the beliefs of the disputants) to allow the participants to reach their own settlement. The techniques employed by a mediator to secure such a settlement vary considerably as conditions and mediator styles differ. They include (but are not exhausted by) the identification and modification of the causes of the dispute, attempts to get parties to recognize indisputable facts (when such exist), efforts to mitigate power disparities among participants, and the disclosure (when possible) of the deeper assumptions that may be indigenous to one or more of the communities in the session and how these assumptions may explain the dispute.[25]

24. Benjamin Barber, *The Conquest of Politics*, (Princeton, N.J.: Princeton University Press, 1988), chapter 8, for an effective development of this thought.

25. P. H. Gulliver, *Disputes and Negotiations: A Cross-Cultural Perspective* (New York: Academic Press, 1979), chapter 7.

So much of contemporary political theory acknowledges the role of collectives in forming concepts and regulations (as in Habermas's observation that universality of a norm—contra Kant—can only be settled in the group setting of unrestricted and unconstrained discourses). But the groups typically used as demonstrations in these arguments are lateral, flattened by the equity concerns of liberal democracy. Liberalism originates most importantly in the Reformation, however, and if the direct text elevated to authority by the Reformation can no longer speak directly to the congregation (if it ever did), then some agency must intervene between text and individuals. I am calling this intervening figure a mediator, who introduces the familiar roles of translation and assistance to a group setting that is now very slightly hierarchical, or perhaps just laterally nonuniform in its membership.

The presence of what we might call third parties is one of the most common of human occurrences. We have a vocabulary for the roles: mentor, therapist, shaman, priest, physician, intermediaries in general—those who can and do intervene to provide assistance. These figures recognize alternatives, fuse differences, clarify, make explicit the hidden, and summon the material and psychic resources that make public reasoning successful. Juries and town meetings, for example, may begin on conditions of equality and even sameness but quickly elect or recognize a foreman, a discussion leader, a someone who can help in the reasoning of the group. The only power that attaches to the mediator is that given by the group, and it is not the power to arbitrate. It is the power to find and identify for others the text that will allow a resolution of those difficulties and deficits that make public reasoning necessary.

Formal theory does not accommodate the contextual logic of third-party resolutions. But it is curious that the introduction of an additional person is common in solutions to mathematical problems in social theory, including those represented in game theory. Many of these games represent problems of coordination in the competition for scarce resources. Resolutions of Prisoners' Dilemma games (including the Tragedy of the Commons) can be negotiated easily enough with the use of exogenous incentives (including coercion) supplied by a person outside the game simpliciter.[26] One memorable breakdown is the Dining Philosophers Problem, which describes the eating problems occasioned by one less fork than there are diners. The solution requires a new player called the doorman and

26. Mancur Olson, *The Logic of Collective Action* (Cambridge, MA: Harvard University Press, 1971); Discussions in Brian Barry and Russell Hardin, eds., *Rational Man and Irrational Society* (Beverly Hills, CA: Sage, 1982), 19–69.

the assumption of shared memory. The doorman monitors and herds philosophers who are short a fork and cannot eat successfully without restrictions organized by this third party (who is not dining). (I have a do-not-ask, do-not-tell attitude on why the problem is described with dining philosophers.)[27]

The logic of a mediated form of reasoning is amply illustrated in medical practices, which are currently dominated by mediated dispute resolution. Medicine is a consensual activity (at least since the putative and, one supposes, real shift from beneficence to informed consent as a model of doctor-patient relationships). Occasionally the activity breaks down, usually (not always) as a dispute between patients and their surrogates (typically, families) on one hand and medical staffs on the other hand. The breakdown can be due to a disagreement over therapy, a confusion over alternatives, the absence of needed information, a failure of communication, an anomaly in therapy options, or any of several other items that threaten the cooperative relationships among these individuals. In these instances a member of the hospital ethics committee can be called to mediate. Occasionally the entire ethics committee is called into session to address the issues and/or problems. It is also a common practice to have the full committee review the mediation conducted by any of its members.

Several features help define this type of mediation. One is the composition of the committee, usually a combination of lay persons and medical staffs, sometimes including an attorney from the larger community. Another is the fact that the ethics committee is always a standing committee in medical institutions. This fact eliminates the need to select a mediator, which can be a difficult undertaking in settings where an acknowledged mediation unit does not exist (as in many labor-management settings). But the defining features of such mediation are drawn from the boundaries and purposes of medicine.

In the simplest sense medicine is a profession that aims (in older agendas) at the restoration of health and/or (in a more recent agenda) the maintenance of life. These purposes generate and are influenced by certain boundaries that limit actions. For example, active euthanasia is not an alternative in current medical practices in most Western countries. Passive euthanasia is now a marginal possibility, and is widely discussed in the issues of physician assisted suicide in medicine today. The purposes of medicine and the boundaries in place at a given time help the mediator shape the discussions among participants in mediating sessions. Alternatives

27. David Harel describes this problem in *The Science of Computing* (Reading, Mass.: Addison-Wesley, 1989), 258–260.

must be limited to those that are acceptable in medical practice, and information that is not relevant to the set of acceptable alternatives that can settle an issue or problem must be carefully filtered out of the discussion. The family participant in mediation who wishes, say, to kill the patient for personal gain is simply advised that such alternatives are outside the moral possibilities of medicine, in part due to the settled (nonnegotiable) standing of professional ethics and moral principles that prohibit killing for gain. Boundaries can in this sense demarcate what can be discussed and what must be accepted as background for discussions.[28]

Public reason can be similarly crafted according to the boundaries and purposes of governing. Rawls has consistently maintained that public reasoning must be directed at structural matters, including constitutional questions in a liberal democracy. But (as suggested here) the typical way to negotiate structural matters in a liberal state is by addressing political issues and problems (a practice assiduously pursued by the U.S. Supreme Court), and in any case it is remarkably difficult to demarcate structure and practical politics in thriving democracies. A better way to sharpen our understandings of public reasoning is to see it as shaped by collective arrangements and limited by the need to maintain those arrangements that are harmonious according to the needs of the participants and the moral discourses of a political society.

The background of public reasoning is in part a storage area to hold those values that are outside the immediate realms of discussion. Robert Nozick suggests that goal-oriented actions are morally successful if they are limited by moral side constraints that exclude certain actions from consideration (for example, Kantian prohibitions against using one person as a means to secure the well being of another).[29] Discussions typically must regard certain matters as settled, taken for granted as a condition to negotiate other matters. At times the settled matters can be moral principles that (presumably) originate in a type of discussion but now are not negotiable. These background items are outside the boundaries of public reasoning as moral constraints on deliberation.

The mediated discussions of public reason can in this way be limited to that range of information relevant to a set of means and collective arrangements that exceed certain moral thresholds. The mediator on these conditions has the authority to exclude purely private or morally unacceptable

28. A helpful overview of mediation in medicine (and bioethics) is Nancy Neveloff Dubler and Leonard J. Marcus, *Mediating Bioethical Disputes* (New York: United Hospital Fund of New York, 1994).

29. Robert Nozick, *Anarchy, State, and Utopia* (New York: Basic Books, 1974), 30–33.

considerations, and move the discussions to a concentration that will generate outcomes within the boundaries of the set of acceptable collective possibilities. Consent is not compromised on the exercise of such authority. Like all forms of mediation, public reasoning must be organized according to the relevant items that the participants have occasion to examine and to resolve or manage.

6

Even when only partially realized, a mediated form of dialogue shifts both the sense and reference of several concepts in political practices. One is neutrality. The conceptual reconstruction is welcome on a term that has little support in recent theory. One casualty in noncomputational reasoning is the neutral state of early liberal lore. The history of liberalism is only sparsely populated with neutrality claims. But the story of just governance is represented in depictions of a figure blindfolded and perhaps even blind. The impartial forum that adjudicates disputes is the main image of liberal law. The state fulfills this image by refusing (in the standard narrative of justice) to allow any claims drawn from concepts of the good to contaminate political and legal judgments. Integrity is thought to be met when bias is avoided. The natural expression of a liberal political domain is the state governing impartially. The concept of impartiality is used to demarcate the state from its member communities. Even a restricted impartiality is not a requirement of any other community in the political system.

Neutrality (noted in Chapter 2) is a complex term with different meanings in different linguistic contexts.[30] A state or person can be neutral by (a) maintaining a position between the poles of any set of claims (if poles can be identified); (b) being indifferent to the relevant terms of a dispute; (c) guaranteeing that one's decisions and actions have equal effects; (d) giving equal regard to rival claims; (e) ensuring that there are no effects from one's decisions and actions (as in the neutral gear in an automobile); and, in general, (f) bracketing all attitudes, stances, commitments, and the like. Each

---

30. One is tempted to add the language of "dispassionate" to the state in recognizing the separation between state and society that marks the historical emergence of all versions of liberalism. "Neutrality" is more difficult to maintain once thick liberalism is in place, in that a state dense with values and purposes will compete with communities over concepts of the good life in some areas traditionally shielded from state regulation on thinner versions of liberalism. In William Galston, *Liberal Purposes* (Cambridge: Cambridge University Press, 1991). Also see the discussions of neutrality in Don Herzog's *Happy Slaves* (Chicago: University of Chicago Press, 1989).

of these senses of neutrality (not offered as an exhaustive list) is difficult to realize and may on occasion be at odds with other entries on the list. Equal regard, for example, may require unequal effects.[31]

All states, and all ways of life, introduce limits on conduct drawn up from what are thought to be noncontroversial goals and shared values. Liberalism is distinct in accepting instrumental rationalities and the priority of the individual, and a set of political principles and rules that are designed to allow and encourage individuals to pursue their own versions of the good life within a framework of reasonable order. A state organized according to these values and purposes, interpreted as thick or thin, will obviously oppose a wide range of community actions. The plausible response of champions of liberalism is that once this moral standing of liberalism is accepted the state is to be neutral within limited contexts by not taking sides in disputes over the good life that occur within liberal expectations.

Obviously the liberal state endorses and uses procedures that represent the values of liberalism. Governing by fiat on the divine right of rulers is a procedure that illustrates a failure of liberal tests and so is ruled out. Governance by definition also means ordering and implementing some entries over others, inasmuch as few consolidations can fulfill any version of Pareto. So the outcomes of governance will not be neutral even when the governing methods are neutral in counting, and hearing and ruling on, entries introduced to the consolidation metaphor of liberal thought. But one might still think that the state must be neutral on reasonable conceptions of the good at least when these conceptions are within the parameters set by primary goods and do not undermine civil order. Primary goods help establish the competence of persons, and thus the scope of their freedoms in determining and pursuing versions of the good life. Civil order expresses the terms of social cooperation that allow persons to conceive of and act on versions of the good where others are acting on their own conceptions of the good. The state, in a word, must be fair, meaning in part that it does not unduly favor any conception of the good over its rivals in a set of goods that meet tests of reasonableness.[32]

31. Imagine two persons with unequal needs for a fixed and scarce good. If the rival claims are given an equal regard, the resulting allocation may favor the person with the greater need. Unequal effects are the rational outcomes of equal regard. John Rawls maintains neutrality of aim in justice as fairness while rejecting the more comprehensive neutrality—of both procedure and effect—once so avidly embraced in liberal theories of the just state. Pages 190–195, *Political Liberalism*. But even neutrality of aim may be too much to expect of the just state once liberal partitions are given up.

32. Rawls, *Political Liberalism* for the views on neutrality described in the text.

The difficulty is that social cooperation in real world cases seems to require judgments that thicken the adjudications of the state with moral and other perspectives. The state, for example, must work with an extensive set of primary goods in order to determine the standing of persons and their actions. A person who wishes to cross a ravine by levitating above the earth cannot be taken as a competent person by those who believe in the laws of modern physics. The state reserves competence for those who accept the dominant ontology of the political system. Because the pluralism of the contemporary world includes rival ontologies (including the stark differences between religious and secular communities) the state must favor some conceptions of human experience that define and order the good. This *necessary* nonneutrality is not formed from the need to ensure cooperative arrangements. The need to settle on *competence*, not reasonableness, is the source of this neutrality failure on the good.

Providing for fair social cooperation as a guarantee of neutrality introduces additional limits. Fairness typically means that the state (a) cannot provide resources for one individual to have an unwarranted advantage over the other, and (b) is to ensure that irrelevant factors not affect the outcome of the contests that seem to characterize liberal settings. But these two tasks—on the surface a negative and positive responsibility—require that some variables be held constant on a prior understanding of proportion and relevance. Generally, in Western societies, natural differences judged irrelevant, such as race and ethnicity, are canceled whereas other natural differences regarded as relevant, such as IQ and health, are permitted as competitive resources (though sometimes their rewards are redistributed). The reasons that allow some competitive variables and not others are often moral and sometimes utilitarian. They rest on contestable rankings of natural differences and distinctions between natural and social variables. These reasons are not contained in concepts of fairness. They are rather judgments located in the domain of the good rather than the right. Because fair competition cannot proceed without identifying and controlling such background factors, the good dominates in telling us what fairness means. The formal neutrality of the right is the casualty. The liberal state must be either acquiescent or interventionist on background versions of the good even after guaranteeing civil order and primary goods.

A state that guarantees civil order and primary goods, endorses and uses ontologies to settle competence, and installs and maintains background conditions of fairness, is in more complex relationships with its citizens than any reasonable concepts of neutrality or impartiality can tolerate. These relationships must affect the distance between communities and a state putatively distinguished from the rest of society on neutrality tests. The initial encounters are skirmishes. Because there are obviously no public orders without orderings of values, a state that fulfills its defining charge in transforming anarchy into a political society will inevitably confront and override rival arrangements that meet rival tests of public order. Some interpretations of the right may also favor public order (in any of its forms) more than others. For example, extending free speech to incendiary issues such as race and sex may immediately increase the chances of conflict in certain circumstances. In these cases the right is not independent of public order but intimately connected to it, and may even have to be interpreted in terms of the needs of order. So much can be expected in subscribing even to minimal states, and these relationships between the right and public order can be seen in all political theories.

The right may also be interpreted variously, and interpretations will favor certain conceptions of the good over others even as public order is guaranteed. How individuals understand the good, and which versions of the good life are accepted, vary with different social arrangements. Success rates in achieving any version of the good also vary in different practices. Some of these effects can be understood as byproducts of state efforts to cancel morally arbitrary features of concept and competition. But others are simply the generously documented effects of laws and procedures on how we understand the good life and the chances of succeeding in any of our understandings of the good. Because the admissibility of practices is influenced by the right, the intimate connections between the good and the right are considerable.

The liberal separations of the right and the good, of state and society, are deeply contextual, circumstantial even, once these effects are accepted. An odd circle of influence taxes liberal partitions. Political rules and principles shape practices that affect conceptions and success rates of the good. But much of politics consists of entries into public space of interpretations of the right. Individuals and groups try to maintain and change the dense assortment of political structures and practices that influence their lives and define public space. Political disputes and partisan activities are often about justice as mediated by understandings of the good. The circle undermines distinctions between the right and the good. Just political arrangements condition the good, and the good conditions the public demands and supports for just arrangements. The state is, and must be, a player (not an umpire) in this game of overlap and fusion between state and society.

These observations suggest that neutrality fails in three broad ways. First, the state must find and use criteria of competence in order to recognize legitimate exercises of liberty. These criteria can and do vary among communities and are chronically mixed into conceptions of the good. Second, the state must set background conditions of fairness that make legitimate competition over the good possible. These conditions inevitably favor some conceptions of the good over others. Third, the expectations of liberalism, in particular the moral and intellectual powers extended to persons, influence and order communities. The understanding of persons assumed routinely in liberal theory does not exhaust the range of conceptual possibilities, and in taking some versions of the person as universal the liberal state extends powerfully into disputes among communities that differ over the definition of the person. The result of these failures of neutrality is the spectacle of a state that is very much a part of the social fabric that produces it. Even the metaphor of a neutral state collapses as the roles of claimant and consolidator fail to demarcate citizens and representatives of the state in political practices. It is for these good reasons that neutrality is no longer a viable concept in liberal theory.

Mediation represents a reassignment of neutrality from the mediating figure to the processes and outcomes of the mediating sessions. This shift in the reference of the term provides understandings that are more consistent with recent critiques and definitions of neutrality. The strategy rules of mediation require that the mediator be devoid of ideology, bias, perhaps even affect in the sessions, and also maintain an unbiased relationship with the disputants. One surface meaning of these requirements is that the mediator is to remain equidistant from the participants, assisting each disputant equally in the discussions, especially in the identification and disclosure of interests. But even at the surface equidistance might still require a provisional or temporary partisanship to ensure the symmetry that equidistance represents. Like all dialogue, mediation sessions often reveal differential talents among participants, with some able to dominate others. To ensure equity the mediator may have to assist some disputants more than others. Like the modern liberal state some form of partisan intervention is often needed to bring interests to the table and ensure fairness. The mediator, like the state, uses power selectively in order to be impartial. Neutrality in this kind of activism can only be an attribute distributed among processes and outcomes, and probably only at the end of the sessions. It is not a term that refers to an attribute of the mediator (or state).[33]

33. Sara Cobb and Janet Rifkin, "Practice and Paradox: Deconstructing Neutrality in Mediation," *Law and Social Inquiry* 16 no. 1 (Winter 1991): 35–62; Janet Rifkin, Jonathan Millen, and Sara Cobb, "Toward a New Discourse for Mediation: A Critique of Neutrality," *Mediation Quarterly* 9 (winter 1991): 151–164. Also, for a study of the relationships of bias and disputant power over the mediator, Gary L. Melton and Dean G. Pruitt, "The Mediation Process: The

There is little doubt that the mediator possesses authority. The conclusions of mediation may be the product of the participants, but all mediators have powers assigned to the role. Mediators typically set the rules for discussions, establish times and locations for sessions, and determine the beginning, middle, and end to proceedings. But this power becomes authority through the acceptance of the participants. Like authority in political contexts the authority of the mediator is created by the consent of the governed. Like the authority of the liberal state, the mediator's authority can also be used selectively to cancel bias. Situational bias is well known in mediation. Issues occur over who is to sit at the table, what constitutes a good outcome, and whose discourse is used in the sessions. The sense of neutrality or even impartiality that maintains a distance from these realities simply allows the bias found in all proceedings to work its effects on the outcomes. One of the desirable functions of mediator authority is the active neutralization of bias to establish that deeper sense of impartiality that no passive mediator/state can achieve.[34]

7

A second concept elaborated with mediation is access. One way to begin understanding the full scope of access is to see liberal governance as a form of ethnographic social inquiry. The state must disclose and decipher the internal meanings of social phenomena presented as claims. The requirement is part of the democratic logic of the liberal state. If we accept pluralism as the occasion for the liberal state, and if we allow the arguments made here that nothing can effectively halt diverse and divisive interpretations from going to the center of governing languages, then liberal governance must find arrangements for allowing persons quite unlike one another—perhaps speaking different languages and maintaining beliefs in different realities— to be heard in the exercise of political authority.

The opening reasons for this ethnographic requirement are fairly direct. If a member of a culture or community is governed by a language of rules and principles that are unintelligible to her, or at variance with her interpretations of the language, the claims of such a person could not be negoti-

Effects of Mediator Bias and Disputant Power," *Personality and Social Psychology Bulletin* 13, no. 1 (March 1987): 123–133.

34. Terrell A. Northrup, "The Uneasy Partnership Between Conflict Theory and Feminist Theory," unpublished manuscript; Albie M. Davis and Richard A. Salem, "Dealing with Power Imbalances in the Mediation of Interpersonal Disputes," *Mediation Quarterly* 6 (November 1984): 17–26.

ated successfully in a liberal democracy. Consent is impossible, and governing that is foreign to the internal meanings of claims cannot have grasped the meanings of disputes. The generality expected in law cannot be assumed because the citizen who is subject of the law is excluded from the language of the law. Coercion is proportionately unjustified. A type of recovery is needed: subjective meanings must be retrieved and cast in an objective (or generalizable) language. Put another way, the political system must be both subjective and objective so that the law, and the discourses in which public reason is to occur, can fulfill those minimal expectations of access that allow generality in law.

There are two well-known approaches to translation across radically different communities. One is (at least originally) represented by Peter Winch. In *The Idea of a Social Science* he identifies the task of social inquiry as a grasping of "the *point* or *meaning* of what is being done or said,"[35] to trace "internal relations," not to apply "generalizations and theories to particular instances."[36] In one of the more frequently quoted passages in the book, Winch states that historical (or social) explanation "is like applying one's knowledge of a language in order to understand a conversation rather than like applying one's knowledge of the laws of mechanics to understand the workings of a watch."[37] For Winch there is finally no effective language generalizable across different communities. All translations from one community to another distort and lose meanings. Claims are ultimately indigenous, confined to the particular forms of explanation found in different cultures.

A second approach is more optimistic about the possibilities of translation. Habermas believes that there is a comprehensive rationality that is universal. Communicative competence for Habermas requires an acceptance and use of concepts of truth and rightness. which are not local but transcultural. Habermas offers a developmental ("empirical") theory to support this approach that depends (as so many do) on the structural generalities disclosed by Piaget. A second theory ("systematic") is more intriguing in claiming that a discursive (or argumentative reasoning) style of thinking and talking is logically contained in all cultures even if not used. Habermas argues here that all communication requires claims of some sort, and interior to claims is the possibility of validation. Validation for

35. Peter Winch, *The Idea of a Social Science* (London: Routledge & Kegan Paul, 1958), p. 43.

36. Winch, p. 115.

37. Winch, p. 133. See also Peter Winch, "Understanding a Primitive Society," *American Philosophical Quarterly* I (October 1964):307–324.

Habermas is negotiated through some form of "discursive redemption" in which claims are critically examined and ordered. The generality of claims is produced through the consensual outcomes of collective dialogue, not by means of a monologue conducted by some rational figure.[38]

The dominance of discursive reasoning is unavoidable in conditions of pluralism in a liberal democracy. Even nondemocratic claims must be regarded as entries in a discursive setting. But the convergence to generalizable interests, identified through agreement, is unconvincing. The point is that truth and even agreement are open to critical inspection, and the pluralism of liberal settings can influence all criteria for successful dialogue. Winch is surely correct in thinking that ceding priority to discursive reasoning is ethnocentric. Liberal democracy is local. But even within the terms of liberal democracy the rules and principles of both dialogue and discourse may be indigenous to particular communities. A common condition in liberal democracy is the presence of radical disagreement that extends to the methods for resolving disputes. It is this divisive feature that charges the state with translation responsibilities.

There are extreme and moderate conditions in Winch's program. The strong conditions are those in which communities are largely incommensurable. In these conditions it is logically impossible that the claims introduced to public space in community languages can be contradictory because incommensurable languages share no template on which common sense and reference can be established. The moderate conditions are those in which different communities have common or metalanguages that permit translations across their differences. If indigenous languages are present in the liberal state and must be represented in political terms in some way, and if objective requirements vary with differences among communities and the claims that communities introduce to public space, then liberal political theory requires that strong conditions be transformed into moderate conditions. The language of governance must be shared in some way by the communities that are members of the political system.

But there is no reason to think that the rational forms that bring about and encourage pluralism will produce a consensus on interests, or on outcomes, that will settle differences. The more agreeable solution is third-party assistance. The initial task of this third party, whom I have called a mediator, is to identify and introduce a set of methods that establish a language permitting communication among communities. The task may not be a direct intellectual undertaking. Kuhn describes the transitions from

38. Habermas, "Toward a Theory of Communicative Competence." *Inquiry* 13, no. 4 (1976): 360–76.

what he once labeled as extraordinary science to the conditions of normal science (in which a single paradigm appears) as a combination of scientific demonstration, the normal attrition of opposing scientists, and the more nearly political maneuvers of ongoing acts of persuasion combined with coalition building.[39] We cannot imagine this process without the linguistic exercises of translation, however. The mediator must provide meanings across communities, saying in some nonpartisan manner what members of different and rival communities cannot say to each other because of communication failures.

Establishing methods of communication and conducting translations are the tasks of state building, and they represent a pattern recognized in a variety of practices. Heterogeneous conditions are molded into a single complex and variable system. In the formation of liberal political systems the indigenous languages of communities are incorporated into a language of governance that is both general and tolerant of community differences. The establishment of boundaries between the governing authority of the system and the authority of its members, and an acceptance of mechanisms of dispute management, are the signature properties of the system's existence.

The devices used in mediation to ensure access to proceedings are also the means that can produce conclusive settlements. One of the more difficult disputes to mediate is occasioned exactly by the noncomputational standing of reasoning: participants are in a dispute over the meanings of terms and over which terms are appropriate to depict and resolve their differences. These are disputes over interpretation—what do experiences mean—and typically are framed as stories. The mediator must ensure that the structure of the mediation sessions does not favor some stories over others and that the balance of power among the disputants does not allow one story to control others. Mediation requires that all stories be heard. One more failure of neutrality would be the natural (or uncontrolled) dominance of one party's stories in mediation sessions. Access is the opportunity to tell one's story effectively. But also the means of access provide resolutions to the disputes. Instead of the often disjunctive transmission of information found in linear reasoning, stories offer a frame to make experience intelligible. The adversarial accounting that disputed "facts" can produce gives way to a coherent account of events. If a narrative can be constructed that orders or fuses the various stories into a narrative that

39. Thomas Kuhn, *The Structure of Scientific Revolutions* (Chicago: University of Chicago Press, 1970).

reconstitutes the social reality at issue *to the satisfaction of the participants*, then provisional closure has been achieved.

Dialogue has its own conflicts. The traditional antagonisms generated by principles are replaced with more primary tensions between texts and meanings. Open and variable texts are the materials on which ideographic reasoning works, largely through interpretation of narratives from a critical perspective outside of the story. Critical examination of texts is an important method to render literary practices and outcomes intelligible, and to discover truths that may be only tacitly understood by the author, or not known at all until the literary work is interpreted. In similar fashion the social theorist can inspect and bring to the surface meanings and intentions that participants know only in part (if at all), but which yet can provide deeper understandings of society than beliefs viewed critically. The relationships between text and interpretation are complex, and can lead to well-known strains between understanding and explanation, and belief and justification (inasmuch as there may be reasons for A to believe that P without these reasons being reasons that can be offered either to explain or justify P). But interpretation is an important form of public reason that yields understandings of social landscapes both within and outside of narratives.

The practice of mediation addresses the problems of unequal skills and access among participants, and the divisive effects of intractable interpretations. The skilled mediator engages in translation across disparate languages, shapes interpretations of principles and procedures, and assists in providing equitable access to the process for reaching conclusions. The mediator in the dialectic is the mentor who helps the participants learn each other's languages by introducing vocabularies of reconciliation suitable for the occasion. Note that the halting devices in dialectics are based on levels of knowing. The mediator occupies the higher intellectual ground on which closure originates. Authority in mediation is access to a source of knowledge that is fugitive to the participants in a discussion. What is unknown to the participants can be known by the mediator, and this unknown can move discussions toward a resolution.

8

Public reason in the liberal state is a product of the indeterminacy of judgment that helps shape modern political experience. Arriving at rational closure on these conditions is a little like the current attempts in astronomy to locate the missing dark matter that would explain the shapes and movements of galaxies. In both cases the standing theoretical assumptions are inadequate in accounting for what is observed and deduced, and generally believed about the system in question. The difference is that scientists search with current theory for an invisible mass, while political theorists must admit the chronic limitations of all theories and standing concepts to retrieve the missing domains of politics that would permit a reasoned settlement of political differences. These are nontrivial concessions. Public reason on these conditions must acknowledge the ambiguities of guiding concepts, and seek the openings that allow a consistence among concepts that may be regarded as antinomies.

Unlike many other forms of deliberative reasoning, however, public reason does not always have the options of intellectual temporizing, suspending judgment, or waiting for data to falsify or retain the relevant theory. Like moral reasoning and courts of law, public reason often must come to conclusions without the full intellectual case being completed. But in politics (including law) this deliberative outcome may still have to be enforced with some form of coercion even when it is incomplete on the requirements of pure deliberation.

The intimacy of public reasoning and coercion offers a simple and long-standing solution for problems of closure in public reason. Divergent understandings and linguistic openness can be controlled through coercion. Spinoza's alternative can always be embraced: a dominance of authority that eliminates dissent. Spinoza permits freedom of thought and speech in his theory of the state. He regards them as useful to the maintenance of a peaceful state, and necessary to attaining virtue. But he will not allow thoughts or speech to be seditious. Spinoza, like so many of us, is a realist. He acknowledges that the state cannot regulate thoughts because it does not have the power to do so. But the state can regulate those actions (the "works" of an individual) that follow thoughts. Spinoza maintains that there must be total obedience to the state, on the grounds that the decrees of the state represent the will of all and the pragmatic outcomes of political dissent are worse than the evils of total obedience.[40]

The problems addressed here do not occur in philosophies of the state that embrace coercion at the expense of dissent. If any resource is granted

40. Spinoza allows that if a law is contrary to religious convictions the authority of the state is unaffected. The individual can privately maintain convictions but must passively submit to the commands of the sovereign in the domain of action. Spinoza does admit an exception: an individual receiving divine revelation has a proper exemption from obedience to the state. But even this blessed intervention is left empty by Spinoza as a practical method for dissent. A Theologico-Political Treatise, trans. R. H. M. Elwes, (New York: Dover, 1980), chapters 16–19.

ultimate authority to resolve a disagreement over interpretation it is axiomatic that the dispute can be settled. Binding arbitration must succeed every time by definition. But a dispute resolved coercively without the comforting protections of public reasoning does not reconcile power and liberty. One important source of political freedom is the power of language to resist efforts to set boundaries on criticism. This power is also the source for the problems of closure that have been explored here. How can the binding powers of the state be rendered consistent with reasoning powers that seem to have no natural closure? Or, put more succinctly, what are the conditions on which power and freedom are complements?

Mediated dialogue can be developed on the boundaries of coercive interventions, in two ways. First, if talk has been tried and does not lead to a settlement, then coercion is a more acceptable alternative to public reasoning than in situations where dialogue has not been tried at all. Second, coercion can adjusted to liberty in mediated dialogue by admitting the ambiguities of power as a fulfillment of more profound forms of liberty.

Adult members of the Jehovah's Witnesses occasionally will admit their child to a hospital and, upon receiving the news that surgery is required, signal that a court order mandating a blood transfusion would be welcomed. Only with the court order could the parent avoid the religious strictures against transfusions and accept needed blood for the child. Legal coercion in these cases is needed for the parents to get what they really want but cannot in the context of church pressures. One might say that such individuals are "forced to be free," and have welcomed the coercive intervention. These well-known compatibilities between coercion and liberty are paralleled at the collective level with the generalized coercion, often a result of mutual agreement, that avoids the collective breakdowns documented in game theory. Put in Hobbesian terms, coercion may be the necessary condition (perhaps never applied) that allows individuals to cooperate freely to secure a collective good that will be lost, or only attained suboptimally, in a purely voluntary (noncoercive) group.

Alan Wertheimer has offered a conceptual geography of coercion that distinguishes between nonvolitional coercion (which undermines an agent's capacity to make rational choices) and constrained volition (in which an agent is confronted with unwanted alternatives presented by another). The second part of this distinction is elaborated with a two-pronged theory. The choice prong recognizes that R is coerced when a situation is created that gives R no reasonable alternative but to act in a certain way. This might be called the numerical sense of coercion, because the coercive qualities of an act turn on the expansion or contraction of the number of alternatives made available to R. The proposal prong settles on the rightness or wrongness of the alternatives as a way of determining coercion. These two prongs are important in any elaboration of coercion. The first addresses the will of the respondent, the second concentrates on the morality of the situation.[41]

Lexical definitions of coercion monitor the autonomy or freedom of the respondent in the face of pressure or threat. If the exerted force controls the respondent then we say that the resulting thought or act is coerced. But the nature of the alternatives also bears on coercion. If A creates a situation in which an indigent R has no choice but to accept a tax-free bond of two million dollars without penalty, it is hard to assign coercion to this act even with demonstrable pressure. It is in this second prong that the complications of coercion and consent appear. Suppose that R is coerced to do a moral act that improves R and betters her situation. Or suppose that R is coerced into a higher state of knowledge that then leads to a wider range of alternatives for R. Or (as in the example of the tax free bond) suppose that coercion directly fulfills the immediate and most demanding interests of R.

In each of these scenarios the value of the alternatives enlightens both coercion and liberty. But the influence of morality in elaborating coercion is more fundamental. The numerical sense of coercion turns on whether R's options are increased or decreased by another. Determining this change, however, requires that we have a baseline with which to work.[42] Settling the baseline is a moral undertaking, requiring a description and explanation that will include background and perhaps causal knowledge of R's situation. Moral assessments are unavoidable. Imagine that R is an addictive personality who has suddenly been given the opportunity to buy crack cocaine at bargain prices. Has R's range of alternatives increased or decreased? The answer is less important than the obvious need to engage in moral conversations to settle the issue. It is with this same type of exploration that the voluntary status of actions, and issues of responsibility for actions, is settled. Coercion cannot be opened up for discussion without introducing wider considerations from a variegated family of related concepts, including the unifying effects of a guaranteed coercion that originates in consent and is never used. Dialogue is needed to establish the background variables and practice rules that help settle the meanings and ranges of liberty even as liberty is a condition for having dialogue.

41. See Alan Wertheimer, *Coercion* (Princeton, N.J.: Princeton University Press, 1987), for this distinction, especially p. 172.
42. Wertheimer, *Coercion*, as developed in chapter 9.

9

Liberalism presents a version of public reason that mirrors its own basic inclinations to partition self and society. The image of the forum is a powerful depiction of discrete individuals (and sometimes groups) entering public space with claims that must be adjudicated.[43] They invoke rules and principles that are to fulfill transparency requirements, which is one of the components of *public* reason, and the arguments and deliberations in the forum proceed in steps to a conclusion that *follows* sequential considerations openly examined. At the center of such reasoning is the perennial effort to reconcile the freedom of the claimants with the authority of the state.

Serial reasoning is found throughout modern practices. Its prominent forms are typically linear or sequential, often modular, sometimes formal, but they always proceed in stages that can meet tests of explicitness and consistency. Like the serialization of stories in magazines, serial forms of reasoning are arranged as tasks, and sometimes modules, to be completed in finite periods of time. Any inspection of literatures in economics, moral/political philosophy, and philosophy of science will disclose impressive differences in reasoning. But the sequential use of rules and evidence is maintained with impressive tenacity across disciplines that aspire to the formal and public reasoning of modern science. Reasoning proceeds in a series of steps. Values and principles, descriptions and information, and decision rules and strategies are the materials arranged for the production of explanations, choices, or preferences. Reason, on these models, is an empty device that acts on the arranged set of items in stepwise fashion. The dominant patterns of reasoning are orderly sequences from one component to another.[44]

Seriality in reasoning parallels liberal partitions. If experience is arranged in segments, models of reasoning that proceed in discrete steps are isomorphic with this arrangement. Dualistic selves are complements of

43. The metaphor of an enclosed area into which individual entries are sent is remarkably popular in political theory. At one time David Easton's "black box" was the rage in political science. It consisted of a spatial metaphor drawn from systems theory with the nonrigorous designations of *inputs* on the left side and *outputs* on the right side. At the center of the diagram was the box, which represented the main internal operations of the political system. In Easton, *A Systems Analysis of Political Life* (New York: John Wiley, 1965).

44. The modern ideal for this order may be the deductive nomological explanations revered in positivist philosophy of science. Carl Hempel and Paul Oppenheim, "The Covering Law Analysis of Scientific Explanation," *Philosophy of Science* 15 (1948): 135–174. Ironically, philosophy of science is itself a kind of story. In Joseph Rouse, "The Narrative Reconstruction of Science," *Inquiry* 33 (June 1990): 179–196.

these partitions. The identity of persons in liberal settings extends over the separations of community and political domain, private and public, mental and physical that characterize liberal conceptions of experience. The natural instrument to accommodate these spheres is a type of reasoning dominated by segments rather than wholes. Serial and visible forms of public reason are natural extensions of the pluralism that liberalism encourages and reasonably expects to occur.[45]

The virtues of this form of reasoning are also the sources of its limitations. The liberal state, as a form of governing that occurs across disparate communities, depends for its consensual base on the powers of reason to appeal to principals who may radically disagree on even the scope of reality. The reasoning that meets these needs is not always the formal or explicit types of reasoning characterizing the visible traditions of science. Communities and concepts (of the individual, of the state) that require holistic languages will not be addressed successfully by the ordering rules of segmented reasoning. Public reason in fact must employ other forms of deliberation simply to extend across rival ontologies. Sometimes deliberation gives way to the avoidance mechanisms that states employ when reason breaks down entirely.

Serial models of reasoning produce and sustain the hybrid institutions that govern disparate communities. Law in Western societies is a hybrid. One of the main functions of liberal law is to join communities with rules and principles that govern publicly (that is, visibly) and impartially. In these institutional arrangements are procedures that specify how claims from each community can be ordered in a way that satisfies pragmatic expectations. If each community is a form of intellectual discourse, then the procedures might outline the methods for settling on evidence, inference and argument that can allow for civic (not intellectual) compatibility. Public reasoning succeeds in using these procedures by endorsing only the institutional arrangements, not the community values that are to be coordinated in the legal system.

The obvious question is, Why would members of rival communities accept hybrid institutions? The answer depends in part on a separation between community conscience and public accommodation. One can consis-

45. Linear models of reasoning may be an unacknowledged source for the remarkable persistence of partitions in political arrangements, such as Richard Rorty's suggestion that the creative energies represented by Nietzsche be confined to a private sphere, which would liberate the public domain for the political goals of preventing harm represented in Mill's works. In Rorty, *Contingency, Irony and Solidarity* (New York: Cambridge University Press, 1989). To abandon properly and effectively the false dichotomies of public-private may require, and does require, a different conception of reason.

tently decide to maintain beliefs within a discourse community while deferring to institutional practices as governing devices among competing communities. If the institutional practices can shield, at least on occasion, issues of conscience from institutional regulation, the accommodations are more desirable from a narrow community perspective. Public reason must be exercised in terms of procedures that are generalizable among communities that reject each other's core values. But the acceptance of the procedures is in part a function of the latitude they provide for the moral, religious, and philosophical diversity that is a reasonable expectation of pluralism.

The communal imperative might require that persons privately reason to a schedule of interests. But we are instructed by bounded models of rationality that deliberation is more effective as it relies on information gathered and collated with the help of others. If the other is a mediator who has special access to a range of knowledge not available to the citizen, then full liberty requires a congenial relationship with the mediator. In medical practice the patient's autonomy might depend on the provision of a schedule of alternative therapies by the chair of the ethics committee, or the agreeable and competent physician. The bounded reasoning of the rational person demands the cooperation of those with needed information.

In this scenario the standard hostility between freedom and power, liberty and authority, autonomy and beneficence is muted. A compatibility drawn from the security of ongoing dialogue replaces the opposition expected among these concepts. Mediated talk is effective as it is modeled on a continuing discussion, and a comfortable arrangement of concepts and practices, that mediate the differences among persons and between language and experience. The inertial guidance system of shared thought and experience supplants the adversarial relationships on which liberalism is developed. Continuing discussions are the conditions on which this version of reason is deployed.

The modifications introduced to this model of dialogue by mediation help flesh out public reason. The guiding responsibilities of the mediator in public reasoning include establishing trust and guiding the discussions toward collective arrangements. The state is not equivalent to any of its constituent communities (as we have seen) in its defining purpose, which is to attend to the arrangements of the entire society. This responsibility means that the state can and does overlap with its member communities, but cannot simply be the set of communities. It is more, or at least different, because of its collective concerns. This conceptual holism is the primary frame for public reasoning, and so must be the organizing frame for the mediator. Like all frames it can be brought into the discussion as a topic instead of a condition. But if it is jettisoned in favor of private or particular concerns, and these concerns are recognized as such, then the reasoning being conducted is no longer public reasoning. This is another way of saying that even basic frames can be critically inspected, but not without those possible costs introduced from shifts in the discourse itself.

5 Interstitial Speech Acts

Imagine two political societies A and B. Suppose that A and B have identical governing principles and that these principles meet tests of justice (they originate in fair conditions of consent, they express the primary democratic values of the culture, and so on). On these tests of sameness we might conclude that the two societies are equally just. But of course they may not be. Suppose that society A as a matter of law and practice routinely excludes all residents of a certain skin color and sex on the grounds that these people are not capable of participating in self-governance, whereas society B has no exclusion policies based on race or sex but maintains a high voting age (say thirty years) for full participation. Suppose further that the numerical set of excluded members of the population is equal in the two societies. There is much we may want to improve on in each of these political societies. Why would most theories of justice still regard society B as flawed, but more just than A? And how would a disagreement over the relative justice of A and B be negotiated? The answer is that additional considerations in what I have labeled collateral theories help settle the disagreements, and these theories are requirements in settling on mediated outcomes.

Collateral theories may be seen as concentrations on minor premises, and on amalgams of empirical statements and evaluations. For example, any evaluation of societies A and B would address the relevance of race, sex, and age to political participation. The standard considerations in such discussions include the degree of fit between attributes and role, and the efficiency or usefulness of connections between (a) individual attributes and roles and (b) the more traditional moral criteria of individual and social need, desert, merit, and integrity. Each of these criteria and principles is a mix of empirical and evaluative languages. All are open to rival interpretations, though some interpretations are settled in certain historical periods.

On any understanding of current moral theory race and sex are not relevant to rules of exclusion for political participation. One reason is that these two attributes are thought not to define or affect political competence. Age, by contrast, is seen as relevant at the early stages of life. No Western democracy extends the franchise to young children, for it is generally acknowledged that infant children are not competent no matter how precocious. The reasons for these determinations, however, are drawn from defeasible empirical and moral theory. In Western cultures social and physical sciences instruct us on the natural equalities of individuals, and social norms assign moral and political standing to these differences within a variety of political discourses.

The determinations could be, and have been, otherwise. Biological and moral views that we now (rightly) call racist and sexist were prevalent throughout Western history. Athenian democracy was noted for its narrow franchise, and Aristotle's defense of slavery depended on his empirical theories of a natural inequality among individuals. But in any historical period determinations of relevance are formed on the basis of a web of empirical and moral criteria within which principles of justice are but one entry in settling on just social arrangements.

Three observations are appropriate. One is the theme statement of this work, that the languages, and perhaps discourses, that control public reasoning are not the primary rules and prescriptions that are to yield directives in practical reasoning. Persons can accept the form and logic of practical reasoning, the principles that guide and instruct agents, and still disagree in the most profound ways on courses of action. Descriptions and the collateral theories that help define experience are the (open) considerations in producing directives. The second observation is that public reason must occur among diverse groups and, at least occasionally, the subcultures that make up the pluralism of liberal democracies. A public rendition of collateral reason then must represent the languages crafted to communicate and govern across these differences while maintaining the differences: a language of niches that is yet generalizable. The third observation is a reminder that collective arrangements are what we talk about when we engage in public reasoning.

2

The odd and rewarding union of noncomputation and collective terms in public reasoning can be elaborated by revisiting physician-assisted suicide. Long traditions of medicine regard physicians as healers (in the broadest sense), obligated by common sense interpretations of beneficence and nonmaleficence. Recently these obligations have been reopened in medicine with discussions of physician-assisted suicide. The surface issues in these discussions in the United States are whether the law can or ought to allow terminally ill persons to receive from their physicians the assistance needed to end their lives in a more humane manner than would be the case if they acted without the help of their doctors. In the cases contested before the U.S. Supreme Court, two separate federal courts, in *Washington v. Glucksberg* and *Vacco v. Quill*, had ruled that state prohibitions of physician-assisted suicide were unconstitutional.

The first thing to notice is that a formal legal reading of the issues in this dispute will not cut very deeply into the range of items that must be considered in public reasoning on physician-assisted suicide. The connections among items is wide and profound, and include both conceptual implications and empirical consequences. In *Vacco*, for example, the determination that two sets of persons are similarly situated (those who can legally withdraw from life support and die, and those not on life support and so in need of assistance in dying) depends on collapsing a philosophically troubled but venerable distinction in medicine and moral discourse between killing and letting die. The distinction between killing and letting die cannot always be maintained. Any number of arguments can be offered to show that it is meaningless and even pernicious on moral grounds.[1] The justices in the Second Circuit Appeals Court explicitly dismiss the distinction in their opinion in *Vacco*. But there are also effective uses of the distinction that suggest its staying power in moral reasoning is for good reasons. The New York Attorney General, arguing the state's appeal in *Vacco*, observed that the removal of life support was simply the exercise of a right to be let alone. Those who seek assistance in killing themselves are calling upon a third party to help them actively. Presumably the first set of persons is passive, whereas the second set is active in two ways: in intervening to shorten their own lives and in enlisting others to help them do so (in this case their physicians).

If we trace the distinction between killing and letting die by doing the genealogical studies that Michel Foucault urges on us, we will discover its origins in another distinction: between the natural and the conventional or artificial. In long and distinguished traditions of natural law an intervention in natural processes is wrong on the surface and must be defended with thick and persuasive justifications. This protection of the natural is one

1. James Rachels, *The End of Life: The Morality of Euthanasia* (New York: Oxford University Press, 1986).

source for opposition to abortion, birth control, artificial insemination, artificial means of life support, and so on. On these views letting die is allowing natural laws to dominate, killing is playing God, an arrogant and unwarranted interruption of natural laws. Justice Anthony M. Kennedy remarked during the oral arguments before the U.S. Supreme Court on the Second and Third Circuit cases that active intervention is needed in assisted suicide while withdrawal of equipment was letting "nature take its course."

But of course patients in a medical setting have left nature far behind them, and are eminently interested in those interventions that will stave off natural diseases and death. Laurence Tribe, in his arguments for the plaintiffs in *Vacco*, observed, "None of these patients is in a state of nature." The *essentially* artificial nature of modern medicine helps explain why health care workers tend to dismiss most distinctions between killing and letting die. They often believe that, for example, committing a respirator and withdrawing a respirator are logically the same type of decision: doing what is best for the patient. There is one exception. In a study of decision-making in a tertiary level intensive care neonatal nursery the nursing staff provided a familiar story of a baby born with severe necrotizing enterocolitis (short gut syndrome) who was deemed too ill to survive. He did not have enough intestines to absorb food successfully. The doctors placed him in a private area to die. But they kept checking on him. In five hours there were no discernible changes. In fact he looked good. In subsequent checks he seemed to be getting better. At some later galvanizing moment the staff suddenly opted for a dramatic resuscitation. The child survived, and he developed into a healthy adult. In the words of the staff, he had declared himself, and the declaration was for life. If he had been helped along earlier with a generous shot of potassium for humane reasons, he obviously would not have made it. Letting him die disclosed the diagnostic mistake and allowed the compensation efforts to succeed.[2]

These are almost never the cases in properly administered assisted suicide, however, for the candidates for lethal assistance are terminally ill per-

2. The study is my own *Special Care* (Chicago: University of Chicago Press, 1986). The story of the misdiagnosed infant was told to me by several persons within the first few days of my stay in the nursery. Or see the case study in the book of the child who was too badly damaged to warrant treatment (in the eyes of the staff and conceded by the parents) but was treated anyway because in-house attorneys were fearful of general legal action by outside sources (the case occurred during the litigious days of the Reagan administration's "hotline" reporting service). Again, the child survived to a reasonably healthy mature life. Such cases do not denigrate staff judgments so much as they put into relief the uncertainty of prognosis in the early days of life, and precisely this uncertainty argues for the importance of maintaining a fairly rigid distinction between killing and letting die *in these conditions*.

sons with little hope for a different diagnosis. These individuals, who know with certainty that they are going to die, want a good death (surveys indicate this again and again), and they mean by that declaration a death that is quick, without suffering and dependency, and certainly without a prolongation of morbidity. In most polls a majority of individuals also favor physician-assisted suicide, presumably on the assumption that a good death sometimes, maybe often today, requires the help of a good doctor. A 1998 survey of physicians in the United States reported that over 18 percent had received requests for assistance in dying, and over 11 percent had received requests for a lethal injection. These requests are not being completely ignored, even where the practice is illegal. In the same survey 11 percent of the physicians who responded said that there were circumstances in which they would hasten death, and 4.7 percent said that they had administered a lethal injection at least once.[3]

Securing consent for assisted suicide is complex. One of the important moral burdens in physician-assisted suicide is to ensure that the patient is the author of her own actions and that the actions represent her own interests. The critical distinction between acceptable and unacceptable euthanasia turns on whether the action is (a) decided upon by the patient or others and (b) in the interests of the patient or others. A euthanasia program that terminates lives without consent for the social good is the nightmare extreme that is outside the parameters of discussions in *Washington* or *Vacco*, or any other forum that is licit. But to separate the issues from the morally unthinkable requires at the start a precise sense of consent that can be realized in medical settings *with strong reliability*. If one doubts this sense and realization, then physician-assisted suicide is commensurately less attractive. Again, the surrounding concepts are vital in setting down the right practice.

3. A *USA Today*/CNN Gallup poll has reported growing support in the United States for physician-assisted suicide. In 1973, 65 percent of respondents favored having physicians assist terminally ill patients to die. In 1990, 75 percent of the respondents favored the idea whereas only 22 percent opposed it (3 percent were undecided). This poll was presented in Carol J. Castaneda, "Agonizing Over the Right to Die," *USA Today*, 7 June 1996. The author of a survey of patients admitted to a community hospital who have filled out advanced directives reports that the "overwhelming desire expressed by the patients in the ADs (advanced directives) was not to have their lives prolonged if their medical condition were such that treatment would merely delay death" (Mortimer D. Gross, "What Do Patients Express as Their Preferences in Advance Directives?" *Archives of Internal Medicine* 158 [February 23, 1998]: 363–365). The physician survey cited in the text is Diane E. Maier, Carol-Ann Emmons, Sylvan Wallenstein, Timothy Quill, R. Sean Morrison, and Christine K. Cassal, "A National Survey of Physician-Assisted Suicide and Euthanasia in the United States," *New England Journal of Medicine* 338 no. 1 (April 23, 1998): 1193–1201.

The abandonment of the distinction between killing and letting die in *Vacco* places an unusually heavy burden on consent. Doubts about the capacity of this concept to accept these burdens will support resistance to the Court's arguments in favor of physician-assisted suicide. For example, consent may be seen as a nexus of two other concepts: negative liberty and competence. Absent a genuine free choice of suicide or competence on the patient's side and consent has failed. Yet those who oppose physician-assisted suicide report that one of the more frequently cited fears of death among both the healthy and the dying is not pain, or loss of the conscious self, but being a burden on others. If others unduly trade on this fear by influencing the selection of death, then the patient may not be properly shielded from the type of persuasion that compromises negative liberty. Concerns over the satisfaction of competence may also translate into resistance to physician-assisted suicide. Or the arguments on the issues may turn on the confidence that the adversaries have in the relevant concepts. Optimistic readings of consent allow the rejection of the distinction between killing and letting die. Pessimistic views of consent in medical practice may require an acceptance and tightening of alternative checks from the area of medical norms, including the distinctions between killing and letting die.

Opponents of assisted suicide are especially pessimistic about introducing the practice in systems driven by cost efficiency. The highest costs in medical care are at the end of life. Care in the last year of life consumes 10 to 12 percent of the total health budget and 27 percent of the Medicare budget, and the last month of life absorbs 40 percent of Medicare money spent in the last year of life. How convenient and efficient it would be if the elderly were to be convinced of a graceful exit. In 1984 then governor of Colorado Richard Lamm—an intelligent and innovative leader, on most accounts—in a speech to health care lawyers in Colorado reminded all of us of the obvious: that there is a natural span to all forms of life, and that funds spent on the terminally ill may be misdirected. His words were, however, incendiary: "We've got a duty to die and get out of the way."[4] In his 1987 book, *Setting Limits*, Daniel Callahan proposed rationing publicly

4. As quoted in the *New York Times* (March 29, 1984). Lamm clarified his views in the following days, but no clarification denied that he was raising concerns about funds spent on the terminally ill. The clarifications also did not stop various pro-life groups from demonstrating against Lamm in his public appearances over the next several years. The figures or costs of medical care at the end of life are drawn from Ezekiel J. Emanuel, "Cost Savings at the End of Life," *Journal of the American Medical Association* 275 no. 4 (June 26, 1996): 1907–1914, and Ezekiel Emanuel and Linda Emanuel, "The Economics of Dying," *New England Journal of Medicine* 330 no. 8 (February 24, 1994): 540–578.

funded life-extending medical treatment after a certain age.[5] These views, which sometimes sound like commodity values run wild, are (in both cases) more nuanced thoughts than the sound bites indicate. They effectively highlight the *artificial* extension of natural life. But they have raised the concerns of those who oppose assisted suicide, who have referred to such views in reminding us that a market driven system, where cost and efficiency are trump cards, may not be the best context in which to plant the seeds of limits and assisted suicide.

The arguments over assisted suicide also extend to concepts and practices with even broader implications.[6] Among the concerns expressed by various groups arguing before the Supreme Court and in public forums were whether the legal acceptance of physician-assisted suicide would move the medical profession even marginally to a different and less respectful view of life, whether the trust between the patient and doctor would erode if the traditional goal of maintaining life could be suspended in medicine for any reason however compelling, what might be the possibilities of abuse of the practice among family, surrogates, health care professionals, and whether and how the acceptance of assisted suicide would shape the practices of health care and the distributions of resources for health among different groups in society, especially the infirm and very old. Then there are the meanings accepted for death itself. If death is a passage to another (higher) reality, is physician-assisted suicide more or less acceptable? Suppose that death is a final and complete end to the conscious individual. What does this sense of death do to the standing of physician-assisted suicide?

One generalizable observation in assisted suicide is that the dying experience is unavoidably mysterious. The meaning of one's own death cannot be fully absorbed, for it contains the prospect that consciousness will end, or at least be radically transformed. Hospice workers tend to the needs of the dying with comfort care. This care is a communal effort to mediate pain and discomfort, and provide some understanding of death to those who are terminally ill. For many a version of dualism is eminently comforting inasmuch as it suggests that death attends to the body. The soul or spirit lives on after death. For others death means the eternal peace of oblivion.

Proponents of assisted suicide offer a strong case for a version of the practice in a narrative of empowerment over this experience, not death

5. Daniel Callahan, *Setting Limits* (Washington, D.C.: Georgetown University Press, 1995).

6. These concerns are part of Peter Steinfel's reflections in his *Beliefs* column, *New York Times* (February 8, 1997).

with dignity. Hospice professionals tell us that those who are terminally ill want to own the resources to end their lives if conditions become intolerable, to have control over matters at the end of life. This very human impulse places the definition of life—whether gift or stewardship, for example—with the one living the life, and assigns an importance to palliative care as a mitigating force against the use of lethal drugs: if treatment of the dying is effective then humane lethal drugs may not be used by the dying even when they are available. The ideal good death sought by patients then becomes a combination of individual control and compassionate medical care, and assisted suicide recedes as an important issue. One also finds in this account a narrative that fulfills the long common law traditions that affirm individuals as the locus of meaning and authority in human communities.

These more comprehensive considerations are not reducible to any of the merit terms of public reasoning, whether represented by rights, principles, or utility simpliciter. Nor are they entirely captured by distinctions between "procedural liberalism" and "formative republicanism."[7] The view of public reasoning within which they are contained is a procedural holism that relies on background considerations textured by a variety of arguments and conditions. At explicit levels this reasoning invites examination of the ways in which one wants the political society to be organized at the relevant historical time. The skills required of the participants are compositional, in the best sense of weighing, balancing, and critically examining arguments from disparate areas of discourse. The type of public reasoning is political in the classical sense, with oversight and overriding powers drawn from a concern for proper collective arrangements.

The issue before the U.S. Supreme Court was whether states have the authority to prohibit physician-assisted suicide. On June 26, 1997, the Court held that states may continue to ban physician-assisted suicide. The Court ruled that "the asserted 'right' to assistance in committing suicide is not a fundamental liberty interest protected by the due-process clause" (Chief Justice William H. Rehnquist speaking for a unanimous Court). The Court also held that "the distinction between assisted suicide and withdrawing life-sustaining treatment . . . is both important and logical" (Rehnquist). The opinion suggested that states were free to permit doctor-assisted suicide (in Rehnquist's observation that the Court should "stay its hand to allow reasonable legislative consideration"). But the Court refused to grant terminally ill adults a constitutional right to a doctor's assistance in dying.

7. Michael J. Sandel, *Democracy's Discontent: America in Search of a Public Philosophy* (Cambridge: Harvard University Press, 1996).

The rulings in both the Second and Ninth circuit were unanimously (9–0) reversed.

3

Uncoerced dialogue is a common model for political conversations. It is also common in this model to partition talk into various levels, and types of communication.[8] The arguments here do not so much resist these richly examined distinctions as claim that they have little bearing in actual political conversations. The capacity of dialectics to scrutinize and welcome (at least for a time) all possibilities makes a universal pragmatics and a universality of comprehensibility, truthfulness, and rightness contrary to political conversations. Liberal democracy requires that indigenous languages be given a full hearing in political conversations, and the acceptance of a universal version of rationality is hostile to the fullness of this hearing. Persons can be rational (as Winch and others have demonstrated) in different ways, and in all procedural ways, and the imposition of a universal rationality threatens to eliminate this reality. It is the task of the mediator to translate (with a variety of devices) the different languages of persons without forcing these languages into a single frame of reasoning. It is precisely the sign of a good political conversation that all persons can gain access to the dialogue on their own linguistic terms.

The tongues of public reason are often those of niches and maxims, the tribal formulas that trigger trading vocabularies across subcultures. These trading terms can forge a wider recognition of procedures for managing issues and problems without falling into the false traps of universal values. By trading I do not mean exchanges, which are notoriously tied to problems of optimality and equity. I mean to identify the ways in which information is sent back and forth among radically disparate subcultures. The methods seem to involve the development and use of indigenous vocabularies that may be little more than signs and signals to some outsiders, but which can be appropriated and crafted for internal *and* external use. The outcome of this use-and-return set of transactions may be a rough holistic language that is itself exquisitely sensitive to indigenous influences, and

8. Habermas, for example, works with distinctions between constitutive (theoretical) and argumentative (vindication of validity claims) language, discourse and practical dialogue, types of speech acts (constative, regulative, representative), speaker and hearer, strategic and truth-seeking speech, and comprehensive versus partial (or particular) rationality (among other distinctions). These distinctions orient our understandings of speech and discourse, and carve experience into the categories that philosophers use to organize communication.

must even originate in local sources. But the language can still be effective as a communication framework binding the subcultures.[9]

The absence of an overarching theory effectively removes case studies from a discussion of public reason. But the issues and problems of physician assisted suicide illustrate the forms, and formlessness, of such reasoning. Communication among participants in these conversations (plaintiffs, friends of the court, the justices, and others) is not expressed in languages with generalizing powers introduced by means of some foundational device (such as Rawls's original position), but rather in terms of multiple and local languages crafted by groups and individuals. The numerical unanimity of the U.S. Supreme Court decision on physician-assisted suicide, for example, belies some important differences in the use of legal terms by the justices, in this case Constitutional phrases. In particular the justices differed in their interpretations of the due process clause of the Fourteenth Amendment (which prohibits states from depriving "any person of life, liberty or property without due process of law"). Ronald Dworkin locates Rehnquist and David H. Souter on opposite sides in interpreting the clause. Rehnquist is more historicist, prepared to condemn all and *only* those laws that curtail deeply rooted liberties. Souter, by contrast, has a more expansive view that scans a wider variety of traditions in terms of reasoned interpretations of liberty. So Rehnquist in the Supreme Court decision allowed state prohibitions of assisted suicide on the grounds that there is no tradition of legal protection for such assistance. Withdrawal of treatment, on the other hand, is supported by the common law. Souter, though also refusing to recognize a right to assisted suicide, invoked traditions of medical care and counsel at the time of death, and cited legal protections for withdrawing life support and granting pain relief that advances death. Like so many Court decisions, the divisions among the justices extended to the sense and reference of primary languages.[10]

Several devices in public reasoning shape both theory and information in ways that permit communication and governance across divergent understandings of terms. Maxims elaborate incomplete forms of reasoning, mainly as devices to connect primary or first-order rules and principles to experience. Maxims are succinct principles or rules of conduct. In practice

9. Peter Galison uses work in anthropology on trading languages to explain communication and consensus building in the arcane worlds of elementary particle physics. In *Image and Logic* (Chicago: University of Chicago Press, 1997). I am making similar claims for the arcane worlds of politics.

10. Ronald Dworkin, "Assisted Suicide: What the Court Really Said," *New York Review of Books* (September 25, 1997), 40–44. The opinions of the Justices are presented in the usual adumbrated (though helpful) form in the *New York Times* (June 27, 1997).

they amount to brief rulelike sayings that provide taxonomies to locate, define, and give moral identity to cases. But, unlike rules and principles in liberal theories, maxims are indigenous devices. They typically cannot be expressed in formal terminology. The precise maxim is one that has evolved within a practice, and in its confined development has sharpened its effects in cases that fall naturally within the practice. The saying in medicine that when you hear hoofbeats you should look for horses, not zebras, is a pithy guide that sums up diagnostic success in looking for the common rather than the rare in inferring disease from symptoms.

Maxims cannot be insulated from the interpretive powers of the open society. In any reasonably complex setting, one certainly found in the pluralism anticipated in liberal governance, a variety of maxims will fit a given case and there will be no formal rule to select one over the others. The judgments that allow a maxim to influence a case, and to what extent, are the starting mechanisms in collateral political reasoning. The advantage that maxims have over rules and principles is that they are low maintenance items, relatively stable in conditions that permit variable and rival interpretations of more formal languages. The stabilizing force on maxims is the stability of practical situations. These closer ties between maxims and experience shield maxims from the wider scope of interpretation that more abstract items seem to invite. Maxims stand for routines of thought and action that limit the liberty of persons in practical contexts even when the alternatives are conceivable within a web of rules and principles. Maxims represent an inertia at the edges of experience that grants stability to political reasoning in a state that must be open, not closed.

Political maxims seem to be the obvious practical warrants that indemnify claims and judgments when first-order terms underdetermine practical judgments. Their role as warrants seems to be a function of their status as embedded guides to action. If a political maxim is shaped over time by the culture of a political society, an ideographic expression that is dense with the practical wisdom and foolishness of a particular history, then it is summoned rather than created by decisions. The interpretation of an embedded warrant is also unavoidably affected, and often restricted, by the historical and conceptual setting of a particular time and place. This setting is exceedingly complex and important. How a situation is described and explained, for example, will affect the definition of issues drawn from the situation. Unfortunately for those with a need for the neat and tidy there is no single noncontroversial framework to provide background descriptions and explanations. The formal structure of a situation includes causality, contiguity, and temporality—in general, a sense of the real that delimits the possible and impossible in experience. The more practical rendering of a situation includes the depiction of relevant persons, facts, relationships, timing, and means and ends—in general, the factors that make a situation intelligible to those who are a part of the situation. The relationships between the formal and practical are not clear, though they do bear on one another in important ways. The public reasoning in assisted suicide illustrates these various dimensions of situations by easily moving over and within definitions and considerations.

Another device is analogy. Analogy allows participants in a discussion to apply incompletely theorized assertions by using a relevant similarity among cases without examining the cases in detail. But analogy can also be successful without substantial commitments to information. Analogies seem to be especially effective when they are linked to the powers of narratives to connect experience in unanticipated ways. One need not identify any rational considerations, nor use any form of deductive reasoning in using stories to establish analogies. The only requirement is that bridge rules connect the analogical with the issue story. If successful, these rules establish the dominance of the analogical story. The reasons for this dominance are varied. The analogical story may be clearer, less obscure, or perhaps simply a better, more powerful story than the issue story. But the result is always the same when this type of reasoning succeeds. The analogical story provides a revisionist conclusion that is transferred to the issue story through a kind of recognition. One sees that the story at issue is different than one thought. One is morally persuaded to reach a new conclusion about a practice on the basis of an apt analogy.[11]

The uncertainty of empirical studies of physician-assisted suicide, and the recognition by the justices that a court of law is unsuited to undertake such studies or even evaluate them properly, made the use of empirical work on the issues an interesting use of maxims and analogies. A number of what might be called reasoned sidebars were decisive for particular justices. Some justices seemed to be content with their knowledge of states of affairs. Sandra Day O'Connor, for example, saw no need to decide the question of "whether a mentally competent person who is experiencing great suffering has a constitutionally cognizable interest in controlling the cir-

11. One of the more vivid analogical stories in recent times is Judith Jarvis Thomson's famous-violinist rendition of abortion issues in "A Defense of Abortion," *Philosophy and Public Affairs* 1 (1971): 47–66. It has generated a sporadically interesting literature challenging and supporting the plausibility of the analogy to abortion issues (critical to the success of any analogy in public reasoning). A recent argument in favor of the parallels linking the story with abortion is David Boonin-Vail's "Death Comes for the Violinist: On Two Objections to Thomson's 'Defense of Abortion,'" *Social Theory and Practice* (Fall 1997): 329–364.

cumstances of his or her own death" because states already allow control of the circumstances of death by the administration of pain-relieving drugs that hasten death. Other justices were more tentative. Souter was concerned with studies that seem to indicate abuses of assisted suicide in countries where the practice is legal, even when these studies are themselves controversial. But he pointed out that disputed judgments of fact are best resolved by legislators, which stays the Court's hand when there are legitimate questions about the methodological soundness of the empirical work on these practices. Then, in the wider public reasoning *on* the Court decision, there is Dworkin's reflection that the high levels of morphine currently administered in medical treatment at the end of life is carried out without the regulations that could be expected in a legal practice of assisted suicide. Speculation, rather persuasive in this remark, elaborates a rich merger of actual and possible fact.

The main source of facts on the practice of assisted suicide is the Dutch experiment. But cautions in generalizing data from one culture to another make the interpretation of the story of the Netherlands unsettled, as an interesting case but perhaps limited as a moral lesson. Still, there are abuses in the Dutch system that instantiate at least some of the counternarrative. Euthanasia is illegal in the Netherlands but has been practiced for the last two decades on the basis of an agreement between the Royal Dutch Medical Society and Dutch prosecutors representing the state. The agreement sets up strict guidelines for physician assisted suicide. These guidelines require that the patient (not the doctor) make the request, and make it repeatedly, that the patient be experiencing unbearable suffering that cannot be relieved, that the attending physician consult with another independent physician, and that the attending physician report the facts of the case later to the coroner as part of an oversight procedure. A study reviewed in 1996 for a House Judiciary Committee's subcommittee found that the acceptance of assisted suicide in the Netherlands has indeed opened the door to active euthanasia. In 1995 almost half of doctor-assisted suicides were not voluntary, and roughly 25 percent of the physicians admit to ending their patients' lives without their consent. There are roughly one thousand cases of nonvoluntary euthanasia in the Netherlands (where patients are incompetent or unconscious, and so cannot give consent). In 15 percent of the cases of assisted suicide the patient did not initiate the request, in 15 percent there was no consultation with another physician. And 60 percent of Dutch physicians involved in these practices do not report their cases of assisted suicide and euthanasia. Euthanasia of badly defective newborns is acknowledged, and seemingly justified by a statement by the Dutch Minister of

Health that euthanasia is a kind of healing in some situations. In a commentary on the Dutch data in the *Journal of the American Medical Association* published in the summer of 1997 the definition of those eligible for assisted suicide has been expanded to include the chronically ill and the emotionally disturbed. These reports, and on the admission that some of the methodologies are difficult to evaluate, are a bit chilling even accepting differences between the political cultures of the United States and the Netherlands.[12]

The New York Task Force on Life and the Law in 1994 urged that physician assisted suicide be kept illegal (as it is in New York) because (among other reasons) the likelihood of abuse of the practice would be greater if it were legalized. Some of the members of the Task Force also maintained that legal prohibitions of the act would require assisted suicide to be a private act demanding caution and reflection, and one which would prevent abuse.[13] This last argument enters public reasoning as Machiavellian simplicity: one reason to legally prohibit an act is an understanding that it will be practiced better than if the act were legal. Thrasymachus in Plato's *Republic* could not do better. Do we gain or lose without the oversight functions of law? Administering high levels of morphine in pain management at the end of life is a medical practice carried out without the regulations that could be expected in a legal practice of assisted suicide. Pain-management euthanasia was described in the AMA amicus curiae brief as a humane alternative to assisted suicide, and accepted by the Court as such. But it is difficult to say with confidence how illegal end-stage euthanasia works in actuality because underground practices are notorious for obscuring data.

All arguments in public reasoning seem to take some items for granted, as deep background, in order to contest other items. The background constant in assisted suicide is the sanctity of life, which has now been retrieved and moved to front and center. At this center location may be a need to balance the sanctity of life against the empowerment of persons to establish human dignity over the conditions at the end of life without compromising life's sanctity. This center then requires an examination of the law as an instrument to govern or not govern this delicate and complex balance. Hovering near are a range of political considerations, including the very real

12. *The Journal of the American Medical Association* (Summer 1997).
13. The suggestion, and the physician-assisted suicide case study, can be found in the volume produced by the New York Task Force on Life and the Law entitled *When Death is Sought: Assisted Suicide and Euthanasia in the Medical Context* (New York: New York Task Force, 1994). The oddly intriguing equilibrium is on pp. 140–141.

possibility that a morally justified practice might still be undesirable when legalized because of the potential for abuse, and that an open and legally regulated practice might have more restricted access for those in need than one that is unregulated and largely underground.

The range of considerations in the Supreme Court decision, and the reasoning of the justices, is agreeably robust for a unanimous decision on so complex a set of issues. The same phrase, "due process," is given different interpretations and used to retrieve quite different traditions. The justices also rely on different empirical studies, and use these studies in different ways. They can and do communicate with one another, in part because they share reasonably similar cultures and are thinking within a reasonably common framework of rules and principles. They also are constrained in what arguments they can introduce to the deliberations and conclusions of the Court. But they are free within these constraints to move among the interstices of reason and produce various forms of arguments even as they agree on a legal outcome. Note also that the conclusions of the justices seem to be provisional settlements, which is indicated by the arguments and the occasional references to temporality (Stevens's refusal to recognize a right to assisted suicide "at this time"). Dworkin sees five of the six justices as suggesting that the Court might change its mind in a future case.[14] The arguments of the Court are characteristic of public reasoning in the open use of language within constraints, and the recognition that good practical reasoning is typically provisional and incomplete.

4

Indeterminate relationships between the availability of knowledge and agreeable conclusions sometimes argue for a restriction of forms and amounts of knowledge in practical reasoning. These arguments complement general understandings in liberal political theory that agreement at all levels of an issue is unnecessary and pathological in a system represented by rival theories and different definitions of the good life in human experience. If partial yet effective settlements can be negotiated by pragmatically excluding theory and information, then a reduction in knowledge may be advisable. The standing problem is what and how much to exclude, and on what criteria.

Cass Sunstein has argued that discussants will be more successful in resolving their disagreements if they seek incompletely theorized agree-

14. Dworkin, "Assisted Suicide," p. 40.

ments, which seems to mean agreements that focus on particulars rather than abstractions. These agreements prepare the ground for a variety of reasoning forms that do not require large amounts of information. In Sunstein's version of pragmatism, public reasoning occupies positions of comfort very near the descriptive surfaces of rational considerations. The proposal to restrict discussions from a full exploration of theory recognizes those layers of issues that permit agreements at one level while not requiring agreements at other levels. Individuals may agree on the particular resolution of a dispute, for example, while disagreeing on the full set of reasons that support the resolution. This kind of incomplete agreement may not count as a full moral accord but can still secure a practical consensus on what is needed to manage a dispute. The general program is an invitation to exclude a range of theory from practical reasoning in order to reach an outcome fugitive to the discussants if inquiry cuts too deeply into exactly what may make the issues intelligible in a wider framework.[15]

Many practices and institutions today attempt to achieve closure on internal considerations by systematically excluding irrelevant knowledge. Though the full rationale for restrictions of theory and information differs across conventions and practices, the shared justifications typically include the thought that decisions are more in accord with the rational norms and purposes of a theory or practice (and more likely to be reached) if they are confined to relevant knowledge. In legal trials the restriction of evidence is designed to help secure accurate and sound judgments and avoid bias and error. In all instances it is thought that decisions are more accurately focused on the matters at hand if theory and information are presented in the frame of evidence, which is knowledge secured and presented by the rules of a practice. Rules of evidence control theory and information by establishing relevance. The intended narrowing of a range of inquiry increases the likelihood that internal rules will help participants reach the conclusions sought in the practice. The attempts in science and law to accept only evidence that meets certain criteria also help define each of these practices as a particular inquiry. One of the shaping features of public reasoning may be the set of rules for excluding knowledge *and* truth. Rawls maintains that the whole truth may have to be kept out of public reasoning on the same general logic used in legal trials: a fair trial may require that certain types of knowledge and true statements be excluded.[16]

15. Sunstein, *Legal Reasoning and Political Conflict* (Oxford: Oxford University Press, 1996).

16. Rawls uses a court of law to illustrate the logic of exclusionary rules in public reason in Lecture VI, *Political Liberalism* (New York: Columbia University Press, 1993), p. 218. On the

Justifications and explanations for rules that exclude principles and information in a practice are initially tied to what that practice is about. Look, for example, at the changing use of the exclusionary rule drawn from the Fourth Amendment. The Fourth Amendment prohibits "unreasonable searches and seizures." This prohibition is a principle of the legal system and is extended in the form of a rule used to include or exclude evidence in a trial. But what one means by the exclusionary rule is dependent on how one views a trial. If (as Justice Brennan did) we regard a trial as a kind of contest between prosecutor and defendant, then the exclusionary rule might be used as a mechanism to ensure an equilibrium between the adversaries. On the other hand, if a trial is seen as a search for truth (a more recent view), then the exclusionary rule will be used in a different way (more recently to allow evidence secured through a tainted process). The rule cannot be used independent of considerations outside the rule proper, in this case a definition of a trial.[17]

But there are problems in a designed reduction of theory and information in the larger arenas where public reasoning is conducted. They begin with the recognition that disputes occur at various levels of communication and sometimes are not located at any of the abstract levels of reasoning. For example, partisans in the abortion disputes seem to agree on first principles and to disagree on the extension of these principles to experience. Reducing the primary level of theory is unnecessary in that the disputes are located at the descriptive references in the minor premise. The pragmatic success of incomplete theory requires a more measured set of techniques that recognize levels of theory and the locus of disputes.

The need to sort out and rank various strategies of reduction can be illustrated with a map of conflicts along the complex axes of principles and actions. Let P designate a principle (in either moral or political reasoning) and a an action that reasonably follows the principle. Four patterns can be

point about objectivity: Both utilitarianism and the social contract rely on consensual objectivity. The dominance of arithmetical composition rules, and the reliance on formal rationalities and shared reasonableness, are attempts to reach objectivity in political arrangements. In both approaches a publicly accessible political system is generated through some formula known and useable (in principle) by all persons. The resulting state is to be rationally visible in all respects.

17. For a helpful distinction between adversarial and truth-seeking practices, Jerome Frank, "The 'Fight' Theory Versus the 'Truth' Theory," in Frank, *Courts on Trial: Myth and Reality in American Justice* (Princeton, N.J.: Princeton University Press, 1976), 80–85, and then Jeffrey Toobin's lucid distinctions on the exclusionary rule in "Ito and the Truth School," *The New Yorker* (March 27, 1995).

found in these two axes. (1) Full consistency: Morality and politics are consistent at both the principled and action levels. Example: homicide prohibitions in noncontroversial areas. (2) Full conflict: Contrary principles and actions endorsed in morality and politics. Example: creationism versus evolution in the curriculum of public schools. (3) Partial conflict (where principles are contrary and actions are identical). Example: The principles of moral autonomy and medical economy leading to an acceptance of voluntary euthanasia. (4) Partial conflict (where the same principle yields contrary actions). Example: The sanctity of human life producing both pro-choice and pro-life perspectives on abortion.

The resolution strategies that are available to address the conflicts in (2)–(4) include a range of ordinary interventions: rank order the principles and their interpretations through dialogues (persuasion, convincing, argument), change the conditions on which principles and actions occur, and/or allow a dominant story to redefine persons and backgrounds. In some of these interventions an avoidance of abstract matters (theories, principles) may be useful. The partial conflict in (3), for example, is manageable with minimal references to principle. But other interventions may be more helpfully served by shifting the factual domains of the conflict. The well-known conflict in (4) may be more tractable with changes in the acceptable conditions for realizing the principle. The full conflict represented by (2) may require attention to both principles and the conditions of action, with no assurances that reductions in theory or changes in empirical venues will be the more effective strategy. The links between theory and information may simply be unavoidable in some issues. Certain principles of life and liberty are needed in abortion and creationism issues, for example, in order to make the disputes intelligible to the participants. Excluding these principles would distort the issues even if a settlement were secured.

Also, and more generally, the test of a proper type and level of exclusion cannot be simply whatever secures an agreement, for this risks the abuse of other relevant considerations and invites the modus vivendi settlements that Rawls excludes from a genuine political consensus. Suppose that bracketing all theories of human development and natural equality leads to an endorsement of slavery. Or that shedding all moral dimensions of procreation, including both fetal characteristics and women's rights, allows population concerns to produce an agreement on family planning that requires state coercion of women to have abortions. The possibilities of unjust or biased outcomes, and their obvious fragility, leads Sunstein to reintroduce principles as limits on agreements. But then the problem of how to relate the side constraints of principle to the discussions occurs, as do questions about the logic of metarules—bridge rules in analogies, rules that connect agreements to sparer sets of rational considerations, and of most importance the criteria that justify exclusions of data and theories. It is also not certain that the theories or facts that define an issue can be controlled. Their absence might render the issue incoherent, or they might have an inertia that overrides all efforts at exclusion. We might simply conclude that such issues are intractable. But these may be exactly the issues that public reason is charged with managing.[18]

One is reminded in an odd way of the restrictions on knowledge that the veil of ignorance imposes on reasoning parties in Rawls's original position of choice. But Rawls provides a philosophical justification and a working explanation for the theory of exclusions. Incomplete forms of reasoning are just that, and need more development to meet the terms of public reasoning. That incomplete reasoning permits political settlements indicates a practical effectiveness that invites fuller explanations. A theory must be provided that explains how to tailor information, why items are to be excluded, and how the exclusion is to work, even when the exclusions are successful at a pragmatic level.

5

Theory and information are ordered and presented in different ways, and many strategies for expanding and contracting knowledge in public reason vary on differences among logical forms or modes of expression. For example, the two prominent ways of ordering and presenting knowledge in the modern world are science and narrative. These two ways of framing and shaping experience are closer to one another than often realized, but they also differ profoundly. Jerome Bruner has proposed that science (as a formal or logical exercise) and narrative represent two forms of knowing, of cognitive functioning, of constructing reality. Science is driven by observations and possible realities to explain experience in generalizable ways. Narratives render experience intelligible by combining the grammar and inventory of a story with the consciousness of protagonists. Science is a truth-functional inquiry. Narratives need not be.[19]

18. Sunstein offers a better (and less strident) defense of incomplete theory than the account I am developing in the text, *and* a justification of analogy as it is used with other devices.

19. Jerome Bruner, "Two Modes of Thought," in *Actual Minds, Possible Worlds* (Cambridge: Harvard University Press, 1986).

Scientific and narrative accounts of experience define and use knowledge in different ways. Scientific practices are typically presented as fully visible, and appropriate for the incorporation of the unknown into the realms of the known. To reduce or exclude from public reasoning relevant theory and formal data drawn up in sound scientific research is by definition a kind of obfuscation (and possibly dishonest), and can only be justified as a tactical means to secure agreement that is likely to be fragile in almost all senses. Imagine, for example, excluding the latest theories and data on abortion rates in the United States in order to persuade pro-choice representatives that the uses of abortion therapy are in need of state regulation. It is first, very difficult to exclude this type of knowledge from dispute management given the public nature of such studies, and, second, the exclusion would be cause for overturning the agreement inasmuch as it was secured on known distortions of empirical practices. There are also the close relationships of theory and data in science. A reduction in one will have complex effects on the other, and the reductions stipulated in a pragmatic attempt at an agreement must be sensitive to the possibility that unilateral alterations in one may make the other unintelligible. Consider, for example, what happens to data on voting when theories of voting behavior are systematically reduced (for any reason).

Narratives present different issues. First, it is not easy to say what an exclusion of theory or a reduction in information means in a narrative. It cannot always mean (as it does in science) that the theory or information excluded deprives the listener of some knowledge. One can tell only some of a story, but the adumbrated story may tell more than that told by the omitted part, and it may tell more than the full story does with the part left in. Narratives can use a kind of controlled obscurity that indicates background conditions that may be instructive precisely because they are not fully accessible. Bruner observes that "psychic reality dominates narrative." A narrative often makes use of realities that exist "beyond the awareness of those involved in the story."[20] The deepest and least accessible domains of the human intellect may contain such background realities, unknown and unknowable in any complete sense to the subjects who use them, but which make human experiences intelligible to reasoning persons. Second, because narratives can present experience in nonliteral ways, changes in the symbolic frameworks that order and interpret information may be more important than the theories and amounts of information made available to

20. Bruner, "Two Modes of Thought," p. 14.

participants. A new synthesis that reduces or reorders fragmentary information can provide greater enlightenment. Less may be more because it carries a different meaning.

6

Instead of a programmatic reduction in what and how we know, it can be better to let relevant knowledge be a function of public reason itself. The broad scope of public reason suggests a variety of methods within which theory and information are processed differently. The adversarial techniques that Mill offers as a method to arrive at the best opinions are variations on public reasoning. But so too are the cooperative searches for common ground represented by nonadversarial dialogue.[21] The eminently pragmatic approaches of mediated dialogue range over a variety of techniques largely judged by their multiple and varied uses of knowledge controlled by success in reaching an accord. If one is thinking that "the ends justify the means" in this epistemological pragmatism, the insouciant response is that of course ends must justify means in mediation because settlements are the aim of the effort. The serious response simply reminds the reader that moral knowledge in dialogue provides the list of acceptable means within which a ranking is established on the best way to reach agreeable ends.

One of the more impressive (and *very* tentative) resolutions of what many regarded as an intractable dispute is the peace agreement in Northern Ireland. It is a case study in the pragmatic uses of obfuscation and indirection in public reason. For thirty years the partisans of this small section of the British political system had been violently opposed to one another. The conflict had taken the lives of more than 3,200 people and injured roughly 37,000 others. From 1996 to 1998 the British and Irish governments, led by former U.S. senator George Mitchell, crafted a peace agreement that literally redefined the issues by reworking the language of the conflict. The goal of the mediators seems to have been to abandon all inflammatory terms ("terrorism" is not mentioned, though frequently used by Protestants to describe the paramilitary Irish Republican Army over the last three decades) and to find alternative language on which all parties could agree as a basis for initiating an effective peace process. Key terms such as "self-determination" and "united" were softened to the point that a

21. P. W. Bridgman once described the scientific method as a scientist "doing his damndest," which might fit the aims of mediation. Bridgman is quoted in Abraham Kaplan's *The Conduct of Inquiry* (San Francisco: Chandler Publishing Company, 1964), p. 27.

linguist would throw up his hands and walk out. But the very ambiguity of the controlling phrases, when coupled with some elaborate institutional machinery, has allowed people at war with one another to move toward political accommodation. The outline for peace was a political structure to be formed in three strands over time: one, an assembly (108 members elected by proportional representation) and a twelve-member executive committee; two, a north/south ministerial council; and three, a Council of the Isles consisting of representatives from Ireland, Northern Ireland, England, Scotland, and Wales. The agreement was dominated by the pragmatic outcome of peace, not the requirements of justice forged by a moral or political philosophy. The result is a document that attempts imprecision at critical points. These "right" words were presented to the people of Northern Ireland and the Republic of Ireland on May 22, 1998. The referendum passed by a majority of 71 percent.[22]

Abortion issues in the United States have created another long-standing dispute that also illustrates how the pragmatic uses of principles and facts can serve mediated dialogue. A dominant word in describing and explaining the abortion disputes is polarization. We hear and read of the divisiveness of abortion, the opposition of extreme groups, the intractable wasteland between pro-life and pro-choice. One might say (in the dramatic terms that seem always to fit the rhetoric) that the political divides in abortion are cut by a system of moral ellipses, nonintersecting orbits where the disputing parties do not and cannot reach one another except by abruptly violating the laws of motion that establish their isolation.

Polls have consistently identified polar groupings. A Gallup poll tracking attitudes on abortion issues found in January 1998 that 17 percent of the American public said that abortion should be illegal under any circumstances, and 23 percent said that it should be legal under any circumstances. This distribution is remarkably stable. In 1980, for example, 18 percent of the respondents expressed an illegal-under-any-circumstances view and 25 percent expressed a legal-under-any-circumstances view. It is worth noting that the largest number of respondents said that abortion should be legal under some circumstances (59 percent in 1998; 53 percent in 1980). But the polls also indicate complex views on abortion, some in the form of anomalies that testify to the contradictions that abortion crafts in our moral vocabularies and sensibilities. In the 1998 Gallup poll 48 percent agreed and 45

22. The subsequent violence in July of 1998 over traditional Orange marches through largely Catholic areas, and the mysterious bombing of the town of Omagh in Northern Ireland by an apparently renegade IRA faction on August 15, 1998, underscore the fragility of these peace arrangements.

percent disagreed that abortion is an act of murder. These numbers tell us that some people believe that abortion should be legal even though they believe that the act is murder.

Members of pro-life and pro-choice organizations at least occasionally pursue what military officers might call a scorched earth campaign. For core pro-life there is (almost) never a reason to justify an abortion. For core pro-choice there is never a need to offer a reason for an abortion. Each of these polar domains burns away the apparatus of justification that typically produces discourse on an issue. The extreme groups on abortion occupy separate orbits because they are free of the thick languages of explanation, judgment, and argument that ground moral matters, even as people seem to want to talk about the circumstances that might introduce noncombat zones between the extremes of pro-life and pro-choice.

In one way abortion disputes are natural items in any inventory of issues populating a contract version of liberal democracy. The moral primacy of governing rules and principles in contract democracy rests on a kind of primordial consent. The U.S. Constitution, for example, is an historical agreement that confers legitimacy on the political system. This narrative of contractual beginnings is the source of the inertia of the political system over time. Contract democracies require institutions to monitor the drift of laws and periodically to interpret the meaning of the contract.

But contract foundations also set agendas for political interactions. Put simply, they favor a logic of in-or-out, of members versus nonmembers, and eventually of categorical alignments. If you show up at my door wanting to buy my house, either you present a purchase agreement or you do not. There are always conditions to any contract, and many contracts contain maintenance and termination provisions (often with sanctions attached for contract violations). But a contractual agreement, once consummated, identifies the parties to the agreement and describes their obligations in a precise language. When this logic is used as a metaphor for the state it often leads to the "tough love" liberalism that extends from John Locke through John Rawls and Antonin Scalia: citizens must fulfill the terms of mutual cooperation without important exemptions from the contract's requirements. Failing to comply risks sanctions.

The problem is that social contracts are loosely written even as metaphors. Governing principles (as we have seen) are notoriously elastic, capable of rival interpretations on reasonable grounds, and secondary terms such as *harm, life, security,* and *property* are too vague to resolve disputes by enforcing an original contract. Because pro-life and pro-choice subscribe to the basic tenet that life is to be protected from harm, but disagree on the extension of the term *life* to embryonic conditions, the dispute may be presented as a broken agreement. Each reasonably thinks that the other side has abrogated the terms of the social contract in (a) failing to protect the most vulnerable forms of life, or (b) overriding basic rights to control one's body.

There is another way. Let the contract metaphor die a natural death. Forget consent and legal sanctions. Politics is basically an exercise in unco-erced dialogue. Classical philosophers elevated *logos*—reason in words—as the instrument of reconciliation and the locus of justice. If talk is dialectical then the conversation never ends. People can explore gradations of convictions in talk, discover nuances in beliefs, and attend to arguments that support and deny more subtle distinctions than the blunt and even crude positions on abortion represented by pro-life and pro-choice.

Think of a series of group meeting (not just one National Issues Forum) in which participants cannot stop at mere discussions, but are compelled to examine critically their own settled convictions on abortion as well as the opponent's views, to attain extended sympathy by entering the arguments and narratives of the adversary through role playing, to break down all proposals to more basic components and rebuild toward a resolution. In short, to explore abortion issues by means of dialectics that cannot by definition end, but that may reach provisional closure by transforming abortion extremes into thought experiments that yield a moral and political synthesis.

An associate has likened a politician on abortion issues to a person caught outside a locked window on a ledge near the top of a high rise building: All he wants to do is flatten against the wall and not move until help arrives.[23] The trouble with this vivid image is that the trapped ledge explorer has to initiate the rescue effort by talking, beginning with a well-known sentence delivered to another person: "Help me."

7

We can imagine three types of dispute entering the arrangements of public reason at almost any stage of a political system's development. One is a type that demands on the surface that one of the competing claims be recognized as true. The demand is typically a function of the way in which truth envelopes the claims. If, for example, one community asserts that the earth is flat, and another that the earth is round, it seems that the simple declarative form of the statements requires that only one of the assertions

23. I heard David Mathews use this image at a conference on citizenship at the University of Chicago in March 1985.

can be true. Another type of dispute expresses multiple truth conditions. If one group claims that God cures spinal meningitis, another that antibiotics cure this disease, then causal origins and auxiliary hypotheses are in dispute as they relate to a dependent effect that is recognized as true (the cancer is cured). Only the causal origins and auxiliary hypotheses require a settlement. Still another type of dispute is mainly interpretive, not depending on truth. A dispute over the assignment of human predicates to inchoate stages of life is one such dispute.

Governing among communities with even roughly incommensurable beliefs can only be a truth functional activity (it has been argued here) in the epistemic sense of truth. In cases where the claims seem to demand a realist settlement (either the earth is flat or it is round) this assignment is not easy to negotiate. Yet identifying some epistemic grounds for a resolution is part of the logic of liberal governance. On occasion alternatives can be found even for realist contradictions. (In the traditional story, the mediators allow that while the earth is round, it is also flat in certain areas.) The most common adjudication of rival theories in science is conducted by identifying the domains within which theories are valid and outside of which they are not. A discredited theory may still be useful as a local theory even when its scope is restricted. Claims that express multiple truths only some of which are disputed can also be managed, as can be interpretive claims, by establishing validity domains as the primary considerations in ranking.

The closest political correlates of domain identification are the avoidance mechanisms known as jurisdictional change and maintenance. Both slavery and abortion are examples of moral disputes that have entered political space. In the first case a war was fought in the United States that had at least as one of its goals the eradication of slavery. Force was used to alter the social and economic basis of slavery. No moral or political conversion occurred. In the second case it is still possible that a change in the technological conditions of abortion will redefine the dispute so that political resolutions are no longer possible (RU486 making abortion a private act, for example). On the reasonable assumption that all disputes occur on conditions, one oblique way of managing disputes is by addressing these conditions in such a way that the dispute is altered or made to disappear.

The political approaches of partitioning and regulation yield additional jurisdictional strategies. Partitioning is an approach that addresses structures rather than beliefs. As a filter for regulation various types of partition can combine authority and liberty in helpful ways. One type of partitioning can be called domain heterogeneity. The state prohibits *a* as an institutional practice but permits *a* as private activity. Here the suggestion by some members of the New York State Task Force on Life and the Law is clarifying: that the legal prohibition of physician-assisted suicide may be preferable because it allows private instances of the act that are humane and at acceptably low frequencies. The underground practice of assisted suicide in principle might be calibrated on an understanding that instances of *a* will not exceed some numerical threshold, and continue only on the consent of relevant parties. Domain heterogeneity maintains both *a* and *−a* in a tolerated equilibrium. The frequencies of *a*, and the moral and non-moral reasons for private tolerance of *a*, may combine to yield a coherent social practice.

Another jurisdictional strategy is vertical heterogeneity. Here *a* is legally prohibited or allowed among sectors in the political system. A rough version of this type of partitioning will likely follow the complete dismantling of *Roe v. Wade* in the United States legal system and the reduction of abortion law to state statutes. The variety of state approaches to abortion suggests that the United States will be a patchwork quilt of abortion laws if state hegemony is the source of abortion law. Yet another pattern is personnel heterogeneity. Here the state prohibits *a* generally, but permits specialists licensed by the state to do *a*. This type of partition is of course quite widespread, covering most professional activity. But often underestimated is the power of this mechanism to resolve disputes by authorizing only credentialed persons to engage in a disputed practice.

In all of these mechanisms power is mediated by institutional arrangements. Coercion may seem an odd avoidance technique, requiring as it often does the direct control of a respondent by a subject. But coercion is also oblique on occasion, and consistent with some measure of freedom. Legal power may be directed at the conditions in which individuals act, modifying their agendas and resources. Freedom can be enhanced, not limited, by a state that provides those conditions in the absence of which desired action is impossible. Partitioning distributes power, directing regulation along certain dimensions that simultaneously prohibit and permit actions.

Any liberal state will represent a variety of compartments designed to contain and address different issues and problems, often segregated along functional lines. The traditional distinctions along executive, legislative, and judicial lines are amplified and refined, and sometimes frustrated, by multiple divisions and subdivisions of institutions. A rich variety of domains contain local authorities with power over types of issues that have found their way into their niches. This description is baroque, but the labyrinth of governance is amply confirmed. The assignment and reassignment of disputes to jurisdictions is not neutral, for disputes will occur over the assignment (witness the dispute between pro-life and pro-choice over whether legislatures or courts are the appropriate venue for resolving their dispute), but the lateral concern with jurisdiction is a shift away from direct confrontation *and* truth.

The abortion decisions by the U.S. Supreme Court illustrate an oblique form of legal reasoning. Ian Shapiro has pointed out that one version of the abortion disputes holds that they are intractable, lost to rational deliberations due to the incommensurability of the debate's guiding premises and concepts. Against this philosophical pessimism are the constant efforts by partisans to argue the superiority of their own views, and the apparent needs of the public to discuss and resolve abortion disputes rationally. The U.S. Supreme Court also deliberates about abortion issues presumably on the expectation that public reasoning can help manage the disputes.[24]

In tracking the reasoning of the Court from *Roe* through *Casey* Shapiro delineates the practical and sometimes haphazard evolution of the Court's abortion decisions and opinions on these disputes. The most important of these changes is a gradual move from the privacy considerations in *Roe* to those of due burdens (and their arguable reliance on equality) drawn mainly from the due process clause of the Fourteenth Amendment. A center position crafted on due burdens is suggested as early as *Bellotti v. Baird* (1976) in the Court's reference to "undue burdens upon a minor capable of giving informed consent," and is crystallized in the *Casey* decision, which accepted what Shapiro labels Justice Blackmun's "throwaway line" in *Roe* that the state has an interest in "the potentiality of human life."[25] The Court in *Casey* allowed certain regulations of abortion but limited the state's interest by affirming the woman's Constitutional right to an abortion and using an "undue burden" test which prohibits regulations that impose

24. In this part of the text I am drawing on my review in *Journal of Church and State* 39 (Spring 1997: 375–376)of Ian Shapiro's *Abortion: The Supreme Court Decisions* (Indianapolis: Hackett, 1995). Shapiro develops the account I describe in the text in his introduction. He tracks the Court decisions from *Griswold v. Connecticut* (1965) to *Planned Parenthood (of Pennsylvania) v. Casey* (1992)—a span of time that covers two other principal cases, *Roe v. Wade* (1973) and *Webster v. Reproductive Health Services* (1989), as well as relevant cases like *Doe v. Boulton* (1973) and *Maher v. Doe* (1977). Shapiro's description of the Supreme Court's evolution in thinking from polarizing issues to areas where compromise and accommodation are possible, combined as it is with the opinions of the justices in providing judgments and dissents in the abortion cases, makes this book an excellent case study of what I am calling oblique forms of public reasoning.

25. Shapiro, *Abortion*, p. 7.

"substantial obstacles" on women's choices to terminate their pregnancies. Shapiro maintains that the increasing reliance by the Court on "undue burden" in evaluating state laws on abortion has shifted debate away from incommensurable terms to the manner in which abortions are performed, and encouraged discussions in the democratic process on the proper regulations that will meet Supreme Court standards.

The tactics of avoidance mechanisms are almost a prototypical way to avoid intractable disputes and stop infinite regresses. They are forms of indirection that concede the failures of *direct* public reason, and amount to the use of institutional or deliberative partitions in noncomputational reasoning. Avoidance mechanisms govern without fixed or consensual settlements, or perhaps any settlements at all. These mechanisms are a pluralistic set of methods that accommodate the critical powers of democratic subjects. It also does not matter for theories of avoidance mechanisms that the state is to avoid moral judgments in carrying out its activities. The logic of oblique power may be coded with moral predicates at the origin of governance. But state neutrality and even impartiality give way to the empirical strategies that shape and even control moral and political reasoning. Avoidance strategies in public reasoning use restrictions in principles and information to concentrate on amenable rather than intractable areas, and in doing so they pay homage to legitimate pluralism.[26]

Public reason defined by the use of practical devices and avoidance mechanisms is constrained by a shifting arrangement of conceptual items in varying relationships with experience. The logic is inductive, from cases to abstractions, and is subject to the coherence tests of pragmatic reasoning. The form of practical reasoning that best depicts this arrangement is known as *casuistry*: the thick set of skills (not values) that locates reason in an arrangement of subjective beliefs and cultural contexts that are normally known as political realities. Casuistry invites agents to look

26. Note also how legal dialectics can be the discourse equivalent of jurisdictional change and maintenance. In the case of *Rosenberger v. The Rector and Board of Visitors of the University of Virginia* (1995) the U.S. Supreme Court addressed the issue of whether the university had to subsidize a student magazine providing a Christian perspective. In oral arguments before the Court each of the opposing lawyers attempted to ground the case in different sets of considerations. The lawyer representing the students presented the case as one of discrimination against religion because the university's refusal violated neutrality requirements. The University of Virginia lawyer ignored the standard establishment clause that might support the denial of funds. Instead he defined the case as one in which institutions have the right to refuse to spend money on various causes without violating the Constitution. These commonplace efforts in law to establish *conceptual* jurisdiction are well within comfort zones in dialectical conversations.

at the circumstances that surround issues and problems, and the analogies and maxims that give moral or political identity to events. A political form of casuistry bearing on liberal governance would use precepts drawn from the operating vocabularies of authority, sovereignty, power, liberty, and the like, to craft interpretations and meanings in the pluralistic settings of the modern world. In abortion disputes, for example, the harm thesis is relevant but useless without a method to rationally *and* reasonably set its scope and meaning. The interpretation and meaning of the principle, in turn, can only be fixed in the mutable circumstances of abortion disputes, the stability of institutions, the inertia of law, the kinetic effects of cases filed in the same taxonomy, the weight of relevant principles, the proper scope of discretion, the limits and opportunities of power, and a variety of other practical considerations that inform and justify judgments.[27]

Casuistry abandons the thought that languages can guide actions directly. The postmodern inclinations to deconstruct texts, to reduce words to contexts, to exhibit the influence of power and interests on language, is an assault on the Protestant elevation of text to decisive authority in human experience. One of the key features of the Reformation was the replacement of an authoritative interpretation of sacred texts with a text directly accessible to the congregation. No mediating authorities are to intervene between the reader and the text, the believer and God, because the text and God can speak directly to the individual person. But if reason provides a text that is open, yielding rival meanings so various that there may be no text "there," then the direct authority of language is illusory. One is invited to reconsider the Roman (or Hobbesian) recognition of authoritative *figures* who intervene between citizen and government in interpreting and applying the languages of the state. Governing becomes more a matter of persons than words, guides rather than an evident and authoritative text, and the state is best understood in terms of mediation rather than authoritative principles. Oblique forms of reasoning testify to the elasticities of texts, and

27. Albert R. Jonsen, "Casuistry As Methodology In Clinical Ethics," *Theoretical Medicine* 12 no. 4 (December 1991): 295–307, for a good close look at casuistry in medicine, and Jonsen and Stephen Toulmin, *The Abuse of Casuistry* (Berkeley: University of California Press, 1988), and Edmund Leiter, ed., *Conscience and Casuistry in Early Modern Europe* (Cambridge: Cambridge University Press, 1988) for more detailed inspections of the history and theory of casuistry, which also includes a treatment of maxims in reasoning. An excellent summary and critique of several types of practical reasoning is provided by Tom L. Beauchamp and James F. Childress in *Principles of Biomedical Ethics* (New York: Oxford University Press, 1994), especially in the first two chapters.

indicate the logic of casuistry in the intermediate contexts of public reasoning.

The message for liberal theorists that this program delivers may not be entirely welcome. It states that rational deliberations must shift their ground from the derivations and identifications of principles to the intermediate conceptual areas where collateral reasoning occurs. The primary rules and principles of reason do not matter all that much. On the pluralism that occasions the liberal state the pragmatic and diverse use of these principles in political realities is what counts most of all.

8

One central responsibility of any political system is to attend to the collective arrangements of the society in which it governs. The legacy of this definition is found among both the ancients and the moderns. One way to express Aristotle's opening observation in the *Politics* that the state aims at the highest good, meaning the most inclusive and sovereign of goods, is to regard the political as that sector of communal life deliberating on the entire set of governing arrangements. This concern with the highest communal functions also represents the sovereignty assigned to the state by the early contract theorists. The dominant common thread is eminently readable: the logic of the political undertaking is located at the collective level.

The boundaries that frame arguments throughout the cases used here to illustrate public reasoning are collective references. These references do not offer a strong sense of a purpose in public reasoning, certainly not one that could be used to identify an exclusionary rule to keep principles and evidence out of public reasoning, and sometimes the references are not fully or even partially obvious in the cases. But the references do help demarcate the private senses of practical reasoning from public reasoning by reminding us that the state attends to collective arrangements. In this way collective terms transform mediated speech acts into forms of public reasoning. The thematic connections then invite certain questions: what are holistic terms, and how are they used in public reason?

On the first question: Different types of collective terms shape deliberations in political philosophy. Classical theorists regard the whole political community as the primary unit in human experience, and they elaborate the structures and practices of the political society as resources to adjudicate individual claims for justice. Modern utilitarian theory relies on the total or average good of aggregate wholes to order individual actions. In all of these theories rational agents are encouraged to use the extensive arrangements or arithmetical outcomes of collective actions to define and evaluate issues and problems. The use of these various types of holistic conditions opens all versions of public reasoning to the interests and needs of the larger community, though in different ways.[28]

Answers to the second question on the use of collective nouns are provided by surveying cases in public reasoning. Numerical and structural references are found throughout law and politics. They lead us away from merit forms of public reasoning to those larger considerations that have always been a part of theories of the state. In *Wisconsin v. Yoder* (a case that has become a critical test for rival understandings of the scope of the liberal state), the Supreme Court addressed the issue of balancing the state's interests in universal education against the free exercise clause of the First Amendment and the interests of parents in rearing their children. The Amish argued that enforcement of the compulsory attendance law after the eighth grade would endanger, if not destroy, their religious beliefs and hence their community. The state argued that the critical skills taught in secular public schools are needed for citizenship in a liberal democracy and to survive economically in the modern world.[29]

Amish practices represent a separate way of life. The abandonment of violence and most accouterments of modern life are tokens for an independent cultural existence in distinct geographic regions. But the Amish are also members of the American liberal political system. They presented themselves in court during *Yoder* through their attorneys, argued their case according to rules of evidence and argument stipulated by the legal system, and indicated that they were willing to abide by the court's decision. The gravity of the issue for them is dramatized by data indicating that their

28. A parsimonious holistic framework separates collective nouns into three types: numerical, in which the whole is produced with arithmetical composition rules; practice or structural, where the whole is designated by arrangements (such as rules or power relations); and holistic, where the whole is described and defined by features that are not derivative from its constituent parts. As examples, "The large crowd" is a description of a whole in which the holistic attribute is a simple product of arithmetic assigned to the numbers of the crowd; "The dense crowd" refers to a collection (or arrangement) of individuals in a fixed space; and (1) "The dangerous crowd" is a generalizable attribute that may be an emergent property of the crowd when no member of the crowd is dangerous, and (2) "The warring crowd" is an attribute that can be assigned only to collectives (because in common usage only communities can go to war, not individuals). It is in this last sense (with the last two examples) that collective nouns are strongly holistic. The initial distinctions among these types of collectives is in Virginia Held, *The Public Interest and Individual Interest* (New York: Basic Books, 1970).

29. *Wisconsin v. Yoder* 406 US 205 (May 15, 1972). I have also used Jesse H. Cooper's "Defining Religion in the First Amendment," *University of Illinois Law Review* (1984): 579–613, in my description of the case in the text.

young may be increasingly inclined to drift away into Western culture.[30] But even more important, the meaning of Amish culture is fixed in part from its existence in Western societies. The Amish, as an insular community opposed to many Western values and beliefs, are premodern in their resistance to such technologies as television and the telephone. None of these observations could be made if the Amish were a community geographically isolated from Western culture.

A similar context-dependent definition of Christian Science is persuasive. If the core belief of Christian Science were expressed in a theistic society that had little contact with secular views on medicine, especially if the dominant and perhaps exclusive religion were Christian Science, the meanings of the defining religious statements would be different. The current expression of the belief that illness is an illusion with no ontological standing is semantically linked to the existence of modern medicine. The concepts of disease, the body, and health on which the claims of Christian Science are developed rely on the vocabularies of medical practices. The disease that is illusory, for example, is not a version of spiritual possession prominent in scripture but is the empirical sense of disease found in current medical theory and practice. Understanding the full import of Christian Science also requires that one be conversant with recent medical practices. Even the radical standing of Christian Science views on illness and health depend on medical advances. Imagine, for example, how prosaic these views might have been at a time prior to the impressive advances of modern medicine. Community beliefs, even as tokens of moral realism, depend on conventions for their full meanings.

Semantics are not the full story. The effects of arguments drawn from beliefs vary with context. To see this pattern of influence, look at two of the opposing forms of argument found in disputes like *Yoder*. Let the presentations drawn from religious beliefs be called *exclusive*, meaning that the arguments move in one way to one truth that is regarded as generalizable to all reasoning persons. Those who make such arguments can express their

---

30. Donald B. Kraybill, *The Riddle of Amish Culture* (Baltimore, Md.: Johns Hopkins University Press, 1989), especially chapter 12, for a discussion of the Amish and modernity. Data on trends in the rate of leaving the Amish is categorized and tracked in terms of population pressures and higher land prices in Lancaster County, Pennsylvania, in Eugene P. Ericksen, Julia A. Ericksen, and John Hostetler, "The Cultivation of the Soil as a Moral Directive: Population Growth, Family Ties, and the Maintenance of Community Among the Old Order Amish' " *Rural Sociology* 45 no. 1 (Spring 1980): 46–98. Data on the Amish population by state and district is provided in John Hostetler, *Amish Society* (Baltimore, Md.: Johns Hopkins University Press, 1993), in a table on p. 98. See also Hostetler's views on Amish adaptation to change in chapter 14.

identity in the argument and the truth that the argument presents.[31] Let presentations from critical perspectives be called *inclusive* presentations. These entertain a menu of possible arguments leading to similar conclusions and the possibility of multiple truths from different arguments. The person making the argument and drawing the conclusion may remain distant from method or outcome in maintaining an impartial or objective stance. In this type of presentation the person is invited to develop argumentative skills that provide entree without commitment to various truths and concepts of truth. The antagonism between these forms of arguments is undeniable. If one maintains, for example, that only an uncritical immersion in religion will provide for religious experiences, then the critical thinking of liberal institutions of learning (which require a distance from subject matter that avoids commitment) would be hostile to one's religious needs. Similarly, the invitation to immerse oneself in a belief would be repugnant to anyone who is merely surveying religious experiences from a detached point of view.

Now let a political society be homogeneous or heterogeneous with respect to types of presentations. Society *a* has a membership consisting only of religious persons (who, for the convenience of this thought experiment, have common arguments and truths). Another *b* has only supporters of critical perspectives as its members. A third, *c*, is mixed—both believers and critics (let these terms represent religious and critical perspectives) are found in the political domain. The standing of each type of presentation will vary across these societies. In-house presentations, such as those from believers in *a*, will be reinforcing, while external presentations, a believer's presentation in *b*, for example, will be overriding or undermining. The value of presentations also varies among the societies. Critics may find their presentations more important when they visit *a*, less important in *b*. Believers may present a mirror image of this evaluation, assigning a higher standing to proselytizing among the critics in *b* than re-

---

31. A passage in Robert Bolt's play *A Man for All Seasons* illustrates the point. The playwright has Thomas More say the following words on truth and identity: "When a man takes an oath, Meg [More's daughter], he's holding his own self in his own hands. Like water. And if he opens his hands *then*—he needn't hope to find himself again" (p. 81). Earlier the playwright's version of More speaks of certain beliefs and the self: "But what matters to me is not whether it's true or not but that I believe it to be true, or rather, not that I *believe* it, but that *I* believe it" (p. 53). Whether Bolt is accurate in his reconstruction of More is irrelevant to the illustration of a widely held view. It is that the identity of the self can be a part of realist versions of truth. Epistemic discourses, by contrast, require the distance between self and reasoning that allows for critical stances toward truth and belief. Quotes from the Vintage Books edition (New York, 1962).

inforcing the faith in *a*. But whatever the particular assignments, in both *a* and *b* the presentations of each perspective will have different functions and values.

Society *c* is more complex, with a subtle range of functions and values. In this society, which represents more adequately the setting for the liberal state, state exemptions and regulations turn on proportions and equilibriums between exclusive and inclusive presentations. In *Yoder* the Court examined the scope and location of the Amish community in the political system. The fact that the Amish are a relatively small and passive community with little capacity to disrupt or alter secular values probably was a factor in the decision to grant an exemption for their educational needs. If a fundamentalist sect of impressive size had petitioned the Court similarly, then the same utilitarian considerations would have provided the justices with considerations against granting an exemption.

A form of public reason that accommodates a more complete range of human experience could provide for both exclusive and inclusive presentations in social arrangements. Pluralism, remember, can be satisfied along several dimensions. One is *b*, a society of those who are uncommitted to a single overriding truth and prepared to tolerate a diverse set of community beliefs and ways of life. This type is the liberal society through and through, in which pluralism is secured through epistemology. We might label this *intellectual pluralism*. Another type of pluralism is found in the social arrangements of *c*, which can also include dissimilar moral communities. This might be called *institutional pluralism*. Now, if both exclusive and inclusive presentations, religious beliefs and critical perspectives, are devices widely used to render human experience intelligible, a judgment exceeding the simple merits of cases can select the second type of pluralism on the grounds that it is more effective in meeting human needs. Decisions on exemptions or regulations might be guided accordingly. The arrangements of communities—their relationships to one another, the set of beliefs and claims emerging from then, their relative size and distribution, the political implications of beliefs—are the primary considerations in this type of public reasoning. They enter public reason as holistic considerations and as semantic contexts for the presentations that each philosophy makes. Knowledge is restricted in public reason to the landscapes of collective arrangements.

It is an axiom of liberal realities that some communities in the liberal state do not meet the standards of liberalism. Churches and the military are two prominent examples of nonliberal institutions that may flourish in liberal settings. The standing issue in liberal political societies is the extent to which liberal values, especially autonomy, are to be protected by the state. A shift to collective considerations allows the state to permit nonliberal practices if the arrangements of the larger society are enriched or not threatened by these arrangements *and* the practices pass minimal thresholds identified by moral reasoning. For example, a liberal state may allow gender-based hierarchies in consensual religious communities, but not a coercive exploitation of one sex by another. The logic of collective reasoning allows the acceptance of values that one would not generalize to the entire society if these values are conducive to the productive flourishing of diverse human communities. A state governed by such considerations is charged with the protection of diversity rather than the enhancement of liberal values.[32]

Public reason oriented to the organization of collective life will not be contained within a juridical form of reasoning that shields its deliberations from external considerations, such as the needs of the political society. In its place will be an expanded public reasoning that can permit more general considerations to dominate merit-based arguments, with the consequent loss of the impartial face that models liberal expectations. But, then, it is the vain effort to secure impartiality by attending exclusively to merit that paralyzes public reason in those divisive conditions when it is most needed. Collective terms may be the first anchor in a version of public reason that succeeds in considering both moral and political arguments.

The similarities between the account of public reasoning developed in this work, and the main reference for power and morality in Machiavelli, are remarkable. The story of power Machiavelli tells the Medicis and the world requires the political leader to set aside ordinary morality for reasons of state. In both *The Prince* and *The Discourses* Machiavelli suggests, and sometimes argues, that effective political rule and the demands of morality are not fully compatible, and when they are not morality must give way to political needs. The view that political and moral domains are independent, and that the political must dominate the moral, parallels the liberal view that public reasoning must bracket certain moral beliefs, though different reasons support the separation in each theory. In Machiavelli's work the prince cannot either maintain his power or secure the general good with an unqualified and uninterrupted allegiance to the requirements of morality. A reason of power or state requires the occa-

32. William Galston's point in "Value Pluralism and Political Liberalism," *Philosophy and Public Policy* 16 no. 2 (Spring 1996): 7–13.

sional suspension of a morality that might govern the lives of ordinary citizens effectively.[33] The suspension of moral beliefs in political liberalism occurs deep within a vocabulary of politics that is widely viewed as effective insofar as it is independent of the moral values it must both tolerate and contain to meet the needs of civic order. Both arguments conclude that the political must dominate the moral in the civil society, at least on occasion.

The important difference is that Machiavelli confines such reasoning to a state that guarantees a higher moral good, the orderly security of the human community. Liberal theorists extend public reasoning to the populace and are more cautious in assigning an overriding moral position to civic order.[34] Not present in Machiavelli's work is the modern awareness of pluralism across basic values, which is the main impetus in liberal thought for localizing morals and subscribing to a political system outside ordinary morality. But even cautious liberal theorists are prepared to say that the wide political domain has responsibilities drawn from the peculiar moral imperatives of governing in a pluralistic society, and that these moral imperatives cannot be identical in all respects to the ordinary morality that governs the private life of the individual. The critical variable identifying public reasoning is exactly the reference Machiavelli uses to demarcate reason of state, which is a consideration for the collective arrangements of the political society.

33. *The Prince* (as we all know) is mainly about securing and holding power, with virtually no concerns for a distinction between the interests of the ruler and those of the state. Well, with one possible exception. In the famous chapter 18 there is this sentence: "To preserve the state, he (the ruler) often has to do things against his word, against charity, against humanity, against religion" (p. 50). This is thin stuff given all the other things that Machiavelli says in *The Prince*, and not very effective as a demarcation of interests given that the Prince is the decisive interpreter of state interests. But, still, there is that one statement to suggest that the interests of the ruler and the state are not identical and might yield different reasons to override morality. *The Discourses* provides more substantial distinctions between interests, with observations like this one: that the prudent ruler governs "not in his own interests but for the common good" (p. 132). This distinction presents a possibility not found in *The Prince*, which is that state interests might require the dismissal of the ruler. Reason-of-power is not the same as reason-of-state. The result (which is my modest point, finally) is that *The Discourses* proposes a separation between political and moral discourses that is the initial design for the liberal state, which must trump morality *on occasion* for political purposes. References are to Machiavelli, *The Prince*, Robert M. Adams, translator and editor (New York: W. W. Norton, 1977); and *The Discourses*, Bernard Crick, editor, Leslie J. Walker, translator (New York: Penguin Books, 1983). Because this work begins with a concern about speakers, symmetry requires that I note the different audience for each book. *The Prince* must be directed at the moral person, *The Discourses* at both the moral and amoral person.

34. Though see (again) Rawls, *Political Liberalism*, Lecture V, section 4, for the moral standing of the political domain.

9

Dialogue reasoning meets the terms of coherence with methods and outcomes found in neither arithmetical nor adjudicative mechanisms.[35] The outcomes of dialogues are conclusions that follow mutual understandings, and they must be regarded as provisional settlements open to renegotiation at any stage. This fluidity of both technique and conclusion is anathema to the more settled practices of consolidation. In traditional liberal arrangements the state enforces the outcomes of those practices (elections and courts are examples) that use aggregation and/or deliberative methods. In the dialogue version of public reason developed here even the state is open to redefinition on a continuing basis. Nothing can be outside the interpretive powers of those who are members of the dialogue.

The spectacle of a political system satisfying the open requirements of reason at the expense of those continuities that have always informed reason may seem like a painful contradiction that must be quickly set aside and forgotten. Reason, after all, requires minimally treating like cases alike, using the generalizing powers of logic to extend judgments across particular cases, excluding special interests on the grounds that reason is controlled by general criteria, and setting aside the arbitrary and the random in favor of rules and principles that ensure consistency in judgments. None of these tests and expectations can be met if collective outcomes are the products of shifting sentiments and preferences.

But the concerns follow misunderstandings of the logic of dialogue. There are first the realities of tradeoffs in arrangements of concepts. The maintenance schedule in a dialogue theory of public reason assigns priority to liberty combined with coercion at the expense of generality, consistency, and the maintenance of the same governing imperatives over time. The arguments in favor of this schedule succeed by demonstrating the illusory

---

35. A dialogue version of public reason works with different criteria of success than found in either aggregation or adjudication. In both of these latter forms of consolidation, consistency and generality are basic norms. But there are problems in realizing the norms in either addition or deliberation. Arithmetic cannot consolidate reasons, for example, which produces the infamous conflicts between the arithmetical version of the consolidation machine and the needs of moral reasoning sketched by Richard Wollheim, "A Paradox in the Theory of Democracy," in Peter Laslett and William Runciman, eds., *Philosophy, Politics and Society*, Second Edition (Oxford: Basil Blackwell, 1962). I discuss some of these problems in my *Rational Association* (Syracuse, N.Y.: Syracuse University Press, 1987). Dialogue (see the text) does not require the senses of consistency and generality that produce many of these problems. Note that the distinction between numerical and deliberative outcomes is a quasi-formal variation on Ronald Dworkin's distinction between policy and principled outcomes, in *Taking Rights Seriously* (Cambridge: Harvard University Press, 1977).

standing of the latter set of terms: that they cannot function in the way that they are designed to do so in political theory. From this demonstration of failure the case for a tradeoff that favors the former set of terms is more plausible. Remember that even on those occasions when impartiality and objectivity can be secured the purchase comes with an insensitivity to diversity in the meanings of governing terms. Dialogue can still meet tests of completeness in answering all fundamental questions in public reasoning, and fulfill mutuality while stressing the contextual interpretation of principles and allowing for constant re-orderings of values. *These* tests are arguable more important in public reasoning than those sacrificed.

Second, however, a dialogue theory of public reason cannot function in the same way that other normative theories do in political philosophy: as a practical ideal that primarily explains and justifies empirical practices. Contract theory, for example, is a thought experiment that grants a certain standing to principles and rules. No one supposes the theory requires that persons actually contract with one another, or the government. Rather, the acceptance of a contract origin for the state means that governing principles are to be regarded *as if* justified by some consent formula. The selection and legislating powers of the principles must be at least imperfectly mappable back to hypothetical conditions of consent. A dialogue account of public reason cannot employ an *as if* type of guiding logic. Persons must actually engage in dialogue with one another for the account to be maintained. Political outcomes resist evaluation on the hypothetical exercise: that they are justified as they can be shown to have originated in a hypothetical uncoerced dialogue.

The reason for this difference is that there are different roles for ideals and hypothetical conditions in dialogue and contract theory. The dominating model in my version of dialogue is the practice of dialogue itself, the actual talk that represents political discussions. Dialogue employs the historical insights of situated persons in the process of ongoing and repetitive politics. Contract theory, by contrast, represents an assignment of ideal universality to rational powers. This ideal may be embedded in the practices indicated by contracts but is still a normative standard in legitimizing actions. The practice of dialogue is eminently contextual. It accepts an ideal rationality only in the secondary sense, by means of the thought experiments that take the actual practice to an abstract level for purposes of explanation and evaluation. This difference is considerable and locates dialogue in indigenous conditions. No ideal rationality or communicative structure legitimizes dialogue on the terms set out here.

This qualification is another way of saying that dialogue is in all regards closer to the actualities of politics than are the other mechanisms used in liberal theory to justify governing principles. *Talk* is a defining street activity. It is the medium of exchange for ideas and actions. Its importance in political philosophy is intact at the very beginnings of the discipline. A world without talk is not a political, or a human, world. Contract, by contrast, is an artifact assigned to communities. It is not empirically universal, not a core property of politics, and must be developed at more abstract levels of inquiry. Uncoerced dialogue is a concept that requires precise specification. But its natural home is in the activity of politics as we have always understood it.

But third, it is a mistake to think that a dialectical conversation cannot discover conclusions that have retentive power. Dialogue must always permit the reexamination of conclusions and methods. But it also can produce provisional truths with a standing that stabilizes discussion, allowing practices to be governed by conclusions with the coercive powers that reason can exert. Reflection and random change are obviously distinct, and there are reasons to think that they may be contraries as well. Uncoerced dialogue may yield and justify an eminently stable set of political practices, not least because they are grounded in the kind of deliberations that produce fundamental agreements.

Dialogue redefines public reasoning by negotiating the central problem in liberal theory in a different way. All liberal theories of public reason must provide a method for negotiating the space between individual persons and collective outcomes. The standard methods for doing this in Western thought are arithmetical and deliberative. One collects and aggregates individual preferences, or adjudicates claims on the basis of reasoned inquiry, to reach collective states. Dialogue is a deliberative method that abandons the flawed reliance on governing principles. Collective outcomes are the results of sustained dialectical conversations among political figures. The conceptual space between individual and collective is collapsed to the activity of organized talk. This activity, nonneutral in both method and effect, requires a dialogue that uses both linear and narrative means of communication. The state is a vital entry in this activity even though distinct from other actors by virtue of possessing coercive powers that sanction deliberative outcomes, however provisional they may be.

The addition of mediation as a generic form of third-party assistance structures dialogue in mild ways. Mediation, first, is outcome oriented. Without rights and principles the traditional exercises of blame-assignments and justifications have no cash value. One practical effect is to dismiss any strong sense of history in deliberations and calculations. Mediation is a form of dispute resolution that utilizes the past only as an instrument to negotiate the future. A mediated solution to the various abortion disputes, for example, would elicit from the disputants views on what would be needed to establish a workable arrangement that can politically contain pro-life and pro-choice values.

Second, outcomes of mediated sessions are emergent states. They are produced from dialogue, and may not be listed in any prior inventory of possible collective outcomes. Mediated reasoning must allow a wide range of views into discussions, and it succeeds as it can accommodate and revise these views in mediated dialogue. This benign "smothering" can be both transforming and redemptive: views introduced to public reason that may be recalcitrant in a rights or principled orientation to reason can be malleable. When nothing is certain then everything is fluid, and even the conditions of reasoning are items to be mediated.

Mediated dialogue in conditions of deep pluralism is more tolerant of diverse perspectives. Another way to phrase this statement is to say that effective public reason must allow the wild-card alternative, the counterhistory, the rewritten narrative, the idiosyncratic proposal that sends negotiations off the charts but does not divide the participants. The creativity of open conversations provides for the unexpected turn in dialogue. In the film *The Crossing Guard* a man accidentally kills a child while driving intoxicated and spends time in prison for the offense. After being released he cannot forget his crime. One evening he tells his girlfriend about the accident. After listening she tells him that his guilt is a little too much competition for her. He should call her when he wants life. The next day he comes to her home and they begin a conversation. He asks her to tell him what guilt is. Define guilt, he demands. Her response is to ask him if he wants to dance. She turns on the tape deck and begins dancing to the tune "What a Man." The invitation to dance is completely unexpected. Yet when it is issued it seems perfectly natural. The dancing the man tries, hesitant and halting, suits his troubles and his character. It is a brilliant depiction of the stochastic possibilities of conversation, and the ways in which we sometimes know truths only after they emerge in dialogue. It is also an acceptable *form* of expression in mediated speech acts.

6 Consolidations

The appellate powers of reason, cited and assumed throughout the history of political thought, are invariably associated with concepts of the self or person. These concepts often rely on some form of dualism. In his treatise *Defensor minor* Marsiglio de Padua outlines the realms of divine and human law. The levels of being he uses are commonplace in medieval philosophy: divine law is located in a higher level of reality, human law in the domain of secular authority. Then Marsiglio assigns the loci of punishment that represent his own special emphases in the discussions of the period. Transgressions against God are punishable in the afterlife, those against the state are punished with coercive sanctions in the here and now. But he also elaborates another distinction in sanctions. There is a persecution of the body, and of the soul. He quotes Corinthians: "I have already judged who has done this, delivering his body to Satan for destruction so that his spirit may be cured." Later, in another context, Marsiglio observes, "God permitted Satan to persecute Job in his possessions and children and body, yet He always forbade to Satan the persecution of his soul."[1]

Marsiglio is not introducing a distinction between mind and body within recent understandings of either substance or property dualism. The traditions in which he is working have no understandings of body in the modern sense of a material extension devoid of spirit. Ionian scientists accept an animated nature, and it is used appropriately in classical philosophy. When Plato speaks of a ordered relation among reason, spirit, and appetite he is referring to the soul. Spiritual infestations of objects are

1. Marsiglio de Padua, *Defensor minor and De translatione Imperii*, edited by Cary J. Nederman (Cambridge: Cambridge University Press, 1993). The quote from Corinthians is on page 30. The observation on Job is on page 32. All page numbers for the Marsiglio quotes in the text refer to this volume.

common until Descartes's separation of mind and body. The dualisms of St. Paul represent areas of the self, separations of domains infused with mental categories of various types. Job's soul is jurisdictionally distinct from his body, but the body is not the spiritually inert material of post-Cartesian thought.

Yet the medieval distinctions between mind and body are sufficiently profound in their own intellectual settings. Divine law for Marsiglio (and others) is "handed down in order to animate the human spirit or soul" (p. 45). It is this spiritual dimension of the self that can enter transactions sanctified by God. A vow, for example, "is or should be the voluntary or uncoerced swearing of a promise about the committing or omitting of some act which is known rather than unknown" (p. 26). Elsewhere Marsiglio describes vows as "made by the mind or in words or both by a person of a suitable age" (p. 24). All vows are witnessed by God or made to God. The obligation following a vow can only be set aside on the grounds of good conscience. This language—of voluntary or coerced acts, of promises, knowledge, obligations, even the compelling energies of conscience—relies on a concept of *mind* that is the locus for the reflective self. This side of the self can be tempted and corrupted by "flesh," by the corporeal sides of experience. The hierarchical dualism in these arrangements is beyond dispute. Persons are ordered in terms of a soul with at least partial access to a spiritual reality, and a body governed primarily by empirical laws. This body may still be housed in a nature filled with spirits. But it must be distinct from the human mind, which has at least provisional membership in a transcendent realm.

The inchoate binary self of Marsiglio's philosophy is an intellectual compulsion that follows the languages of conscience and divided realities. The self driven by rational considerations must be a self-reflective creature not entirely reducible to material components. The voluntary and deliberative powers of spiritual matters must be distinct from the coercive domains of body. No classical or medieval theory could avoid a binary self once these differences are accepted. But also the belief in a transcendent reality at least partially accessible to the soul requires dual levels of the self. Because the body resides primarily in a temporal world governed by natural laws there must be a different aspect of the self that can gain entry into the realm where divine law originates.

Classical and medieval understandings of mind assign reason to this dimension of the self. The proper expressions of these mental powers are words, the *logos* that Greek philosophers believed was the center and expression of intelligence, *nous*. Persons use language to engage each other and God in transactions, commitments, and understandings. No insensate creature can join these discussions, these thoughts and communications. The human person is the sentient power that animates these mental activities. Distinctions among forms of animal life follow the acceptance of linguistic sentient powers. But the most important feature of deliberative language is that it opens experience to higher appeals. Plato challenges conventional authority with the use of reason. Marsiglio allows oversight even for a vow to God. The appeal is to *conscience*: "Those repudiating a vow on the grounds of good conscience should do so, as we have said, on account of doing what is better or avoiding what is worse, which could not be carried out by them by holding fast to the vow" (p. 27). The source in the text for conscience, and for better or worse, is God, which is true to the spirit of the times and nullifies any inclination to assign a modern utilitarian justification to these repudiations. But the acknowledgment of exceptions even to sacred vows is testimony to the appellate powers of reason that must be admitted (by Marsiglio and others) to deliberations expressed in language.

The standing question—then and now—is how the appeals of reason are to be ordered when they diverge. The standard answer in classical philosophy is that reason itself—the term used to represent the higher powers of a mental or spiritual domain of the self—will lead to a dominant truth as permanent and universal principles are discovered. The modern view is that pluralism in truth must be tolerated within an orderly political experience. For Marsiglio, intent on contracting both the scope and the authority of the Roman Catholic church, the individual person must make first-order judgments and accept the punishments in the next life if wrong. Marsiglio maintains that the relationship of the person to God is sealed from the full understanding of any other person, including religious authorities. This privileged relationship of person to God is the post-Reformation standard for a church organized on the authority of the individual parishioner. But it still leaves undefined the proper model for a state addressing pluralism in both thought and action, when only some of the set of pursued actions can be realized. The modern problem (as it has been raised here) is how public reason can order the various understandings of the good that can follow critical reflection among reasoning persons.

2

Many of the problems of closure in public reasoning are byproducts of the conscious self. The critical and reflective powers of consciousness are undeniable, and seem to have no obvious limits. The person in political settings can always shift conceptual venues, appropriate different frameworks, and undermine computational systems with an unlimited inventory of external perspectives. This undermining power seems to occur in all settings and within all theories of knowledge and reality.

Consciousness has many puzzling features. It is individual in its locus yet collective in its scope and reference. Persons are conscious, not groups or institutions. The conscious self achieves identity in part through an awareness of "owned" subjectivity that is distinct from other subjects and the objective world. But the main stuff of consciousness is that which it is not. Consciousness incorporates, in ways that are not clearly understood, ranges of experiences that seem to constitute worlds in some sense. The arrangements of experience also have a shaping effect on consciousness. In our explorations here we have seen how liberal states require various binary selves. The organization of consciousness seems to depend at least to some extent on the larger contexts in which selves are located.

Dominant physiological accounts of consciousness speculate that sensory data are transmitted to the thalamus (a central brain structure) where it is relayed to the cerebral cortex. There the data are somehow scanned and organized by a wave of nerve impulses transmitted from the thalamus. The now synchronized cells in the cerebral cortex send messages back to the thalamus. These messages constitute images. Consciousness is in some sense this system of communication between the thalamus and the cerebral cortex. The notion of an abstraction would seem to be a product of this neurological activity, which is triggered and modulated by data secured through the sense organs. The problem (as John Searle has persuasively argued) is that simple physiological accounts fail to explain consciousness, which seems to be a biological condition that is yet subjective and capable of critical reflection on its own physiological state.[2]

Nowhere are the influences of physical states on consciousness described in more intriguing ways than in recent speculations on the implications of quantum mechanics for the structure of consciousness. The micro world of quantum theory appears on the maps of continuous or linear thinking as an unintelligible experience. The two-slit experiments, Schrödinger's cat, Heisenberg's principle—a variety of data and theory pre-

2. For physiology summaries see Wendell Krieg, *Brain Mechanisms in Diachrome* (Evanston, Ill.: Brain Books, 1957). Summary in the *New York Times*, Science Times (March 21, 1995). A helpful discussion of subjectivity is in John Searle's "The Mystery of Consciousness," *The New York Review of Books* (November 2, 1995): 60–85, and the exchange with his critics in the issue on December 21, 1995. Also instructive (and great fun to read) is Searle's review of David Chalmers's book *The Conscious Mind* (see note 3) in "Consciousness and the Philosophers," *The New York Review of Books* (March 6, 1997).

sent considerations that simply cannot be managed by the organizing categories of a thinking that seems to work well at the level of ordinary experiences (which is what makes the data, thought experiments, and principles counterintuitive). One radical way around these paradoxes is to assume that the experiences of quantum phenomena impose a division on consciousness itself. Thus a binary consciousness can understand that light is simultaneously a wave and a particle by presenting two states of the brain, or domains of cognition, that correspond to the two positions in the quantum field. Among the important consequences of this kind of bifurcation are that the continuous thinking of human experiences is an illusion (of sorts), and that individual identity cannot be singular.[3] These consequences, though radical, are not unthinkable as possibilities, and the latter is a more extreme version of the need for binary selves that liberal political arrangements introduce.

But the properties of consciousness also assign possibilities and limitations to contexts. The reflective capacities of consciousness render public reasoning noncomputable. Granting appellate powers to reason establishes the chain of reflection upon reflection that produces infinite regresses and the halting problem. Understanding consciousness as a layered arrangement capable of reflective chains leads to the constant interpretation and reinterpretation that defeats merit versions of public reasoning. But also the extension of consciousness to language invites the familiar reliance on discourse as both the means to reach the provisional conclusions of a public reason based on special types of conversation, and as the organized expression of the self.

One way to state these ideas is to think of assumptions and theories as devices to simplify and organize experience. Liberal principles help make political experience manageable by establishing the scope of the state and (by default) domains of social and individual life. These principles also require a certain binary organization of the self. The difficulties with this

3. This is a view attributed to H. Everett, " 'Relative State' Formulations of Quantum Mechanics," *Reviews of Modern Physics* 29 (1957): 454–462. I have relied on the discussion of this view by David Chalmers, in his *The Conscious Mind* (New York: Oxford University Press, 1996). Recent reports from physicists seem to have strengthened rather than weakened the paradoxes of quantum mechanics. In the latest variation on the two-slit experiments physicists at the University of Geneva (in June 1997) sent pairs of "entangled" photons in opposite directions to destinations nearly seven miles apart. No communication between the sets of photons was possible. Yet the paths and states of each pair were matched even though there was no physical connection between them. A recent discussion of "tunneling" (at the June 1997 meeting of the Nobel Symposium on quantum physics in Sweden) failed to explain the strange ability of subatomic particles to penetrate impenetrable barriers, leaving intact yet another quantum mystery. Summary in the *New York Times*, Science Times (July 22, 1997).

program of management begin with the internal implications of the arrangements. The concept of an autonomous self with critical powers introduces the halting problems that we have been concerned with here: the liberal attempt to make political experience manageable results in a devolution of governing terms to individual interpretation, and it elevates the model of a conversation to a preeminent form of public reasoning.

The natural anchor for liberal governance is process of a certain type. If we conceive of the self as both malleable and emptied of fixed content, a version of Sartre's sense of nonbeing, then the creative use of language in discourse is the unruly and proper representation of the human person. The self just *is* the free and open use of language in the public domains of reasoning. A unity of self and conditions is found in the dominance of the discourse method of governance that expresses noncomputation. The merger of self with process redirects the reflective powers of consciousness by means of a representational act: a public self can be unified by the mechanisms and practices that reenact consciousness. The liberal use of impartial principles is a limited form of this kind of merger. The person who submits to fair procedures allows a set of acts and their outcomes to dominate self-interest. The public self of traditional liberal thought subscribes to collective actions and the processes that represent them. But more can be required in the discourse of public reason. Here the self can *be* the process, and in merging with process can collapse the binary arrangements required in liberal political theory.

3

Any number of organizational forms require individuals to submit to a collective state of affairs in order both to know and secure a good that is of benefit both to the organization and the individual.[4] This submission is often an entry in a graded slope from the radical individualism of methodological individualism to the complete holism of various collective experiences. The fact that the slope is graded testifies to the possibility of nondual experiences that only partially fulfill a union of self with reality. But polar

4. Michael J. Sandel, in the concluding words in *Liberalism and the Limits of Justice* (New York: Cambridge University Press, 1998), allows that "when politics goes well, we can know a good in common that we cannot know alone" (p. 183). Sandel seems to mean by "know" here only the more general sense of "experience," and he is referring in the passage simply to the good of *peace*. I want to introduce the more general epistemological point that only in states of unity may certain goods be revealed to individuals. That some goods can be secured only with a group action is part of the canonical literature on the logic of public goods. Note also that *war* is also an experience that can be known only as a type of collective action.

extremes exist. Any general program of merging individual identity with larger wholes proposes a union between one and all that is opposed to the main ideas of political liberalism. In political liberalism individuals join a political order by subscribing to the mechanisms that adjudicate differences. Individual identity is maintained, and at times competes with the political self formed from the endorsement of an adjudicative mechanism. Traditions of mysticism urge a union of self with collective that extinguishes the person in the larger action.[5]

Methods of union are arrayed along these extremes. Aggregation is a method of consolidation that maintains the integrity of individual units. Deliberation more nearly collapses distinctions among individuals. In voting, for example, individuals feed preferences into aggregation machines, and these machines combine the entries by using one or more of a variety of arithmetical rules to produce collective outcomes. Voters are not required to commit to anything other than the mechanism of voting, and this commitment may be particular to each voter. One of the main powers of the secret ballot is that each voter may have private preferences *and* reasons in voting, and even support the practice of voting for different reasons. The mechanism itself excludes larger commitments in its incapacity to accommodate the supporting considerations for a vote. Preferences or choices—not arguments, justifications, reasons—are arithmetically combined in voting.

A judicial finding, by contrast, is a tiered arrangement. The collective outcome is supervenient on the arguments that justify the outcome. Individual members of a judicial practice must subscribe to roughly the same rules of evidence, inference and argument if the practice is to succeed. The fusion of person and collective is more complete than in voting, with individuals absorbed to some degree in the collective arrangements throughout the process. Judicial deliberations are to be impartial, ideally shielded from the particular interests of persons. Members of the judiciary are expected to be disinterested members of a deliberative process. Electorates, by contrast, stand as testaments to self-interest, which is then to be transformed by arithmetic into a collective outcome that allows individual voters to remain as egoists.

5. A helpful treatment of nondual philosophies is David Loy, *Nonduality: A Study in Comparative Philosophy* (New Haven, Conn.: Yale University Press, 1988). Three helpful books on mysticism overview the fusions of self with whole: Robert Ellwood, *Mysticism and Religion* (Englewood Cliffs, N.J.: Prentice Hall, 1980), Richard H. Jones, *Science and Mysticism* (Lewisburg, Pa.: Bucknell University Press, 1956), and (especially) Agahananda Bharati, *The Light at the Center* (Santa Barbara, Calif.: Ross-Erikson, 1976).

The concept of the public tracks in many ways the contrasting shapes of communal organization. Numerical senses of the public are found in the discussions of liberal democracy that mark the modern era. Numerical interpretations of the public offer sliding or graded scales, often designating an item as a public issue or problem if it affects enough people. This sense of the public requires setting a threshold, which in practical terms means that some numerical magnitude must be identified that grants public standing to an item. The term *public* is also assigned to the practices, institutions, and sometimes the rules or principles that represent the organization of a community. We often speak of public business, for example, to describe items that deal with the community's procedures for resolving disputes. These structures can be regarded as public without counting the number of individuals affected by them. Then there are holistic senses of the public, which attend to the common or universal properties of communal life. In the modern age this sense of the public often refers to generalizable interests.[6]

There is a simpler, or at least more direct, beginning to an understanding of the concept. It is helpful to remember that *public* is the term we often use as the opposite for *private*. An action is private in a strong sense when information that defines the action is shielded from others, and the person who is the author of the action (the actor, in an older language) has discretionary authority to act, meaning in practical terms without interference from others. For example, abortion is strongly private when it can be carried out by a woman without the knowledge or influence of others (as with a safe "morning-after" pill). A weaker sense of the private would be cases where one but not the other of these properties is present. Abortion that is chosen (without coercion) by the woman but which is yet reported in the media can only be weakly private. The same must be said about an abortion that is forced on a woman in complete secrecy.

An action can be regarded as minimally public when it joins two or more persons in an undertaking. A joint undertaking loses the two features of privacy: both information about the act and the autonomy of the individual are given up to the collective action, which ordinarily requires shared information and mutual influence. Taken as the opposite of privacy

6. See Virginia Held, *The Public Interest and Individual Interests* (New York: Basic Books, 1970). Other extensions on the term *public* are found in the literatures. Perhaps the most frequent is accessibility or transparency. A discussion, for example, is public in some sense if it is viewable by others. (Rawls mentions this sense of *public* in his definition of public reasoning.)

a public action represents communal action, and may be the more common occurrence in political societies. It is interesting that privacy is a more recent principle, and coincides with the assignment of independent standing to individuals. Public action is the older species of action, with a pedigree originating in the communal undertakings that probably are concomitant with the origins of human communities.

The strong version of public that marks off public reasoning in the political sense is one that also refers to collective (or joint) arrangements for human communities. Persons must not only reason together but also reason about the most general arrangements that specify how they are to live together in a political order. In this way public reasoning is both radically open and modestly constrained: the reflective powers of the conscious self can critically examine every item in the political domain, but the core or structure of politics offers a framework for organizing these discourses.

More recent concepts of the public elaborate different patterns that join person and whole. Habermas offers a main definition of the public sphere as a "network for communicating information and points of view."[7] Nancy Fraser, reflecting on stratified societies, identifies (following Habermas) strong publics, constituted by opinion-making and decision making institutions, and weak publics consisting of persons who are involved in opinion formation but not in making binding political decisions. She also recognizes a subdivision of the concept of public she labels subaltern counterpublics, particular publics open only to subgroups within society. These smaller publics maintain the particular cultural identities of their members while creating parallel discursive arenas, in this way fulfilling the communication demands of broader public domains.[8] The assignment of the term *public* to various levels of communal life represent the expectations of pluralism while acknowledging the multiple sites for mergers of person and various forms of collective experiences.

The main issues in the forms of union found in concepts of the public are scaled along degrees of individual fusion with collectives, and the types

7. Jürgen Habermas, *Between Facts and Norms: Contributions to a Discourse Theory of Law and Democracy*, trans. William Rehg (Cambridge: MIT Press, 1996). The main definition of the public as a network for communicating ideas is developed on pages 360–366. Also worth inspecting are different types of the public (drawn up from a discussion of civil society) on pages 373–379, and what Habermas labels "arranged" publics on pages 304–308.

8. Nancy Fraser, "Rethinking the Public Sphere," in Craig Calhoun, ed., *Habermas and the Public Sphere* (Cambridge: MIT Press, 1992), 109–142. Consider the main alternative meaning of a subaltern. In logic it is the relation of a particular proposition to a universal with the same subject, predicate, and quality. The logical sense of the term also enlightens the relationships Fraser identifies for politics.

of collectives that absorb persons. There is no single set of distinctions among collectives. Hannah Arendt's theories of citizenship depend on differences among the public sphere, political agency and collective identity, and political culture. Her use of the term *public* (at least in *The Human Condition*) generally follows the classical recognition of a common space designating the political.[9] Modern political theory permits (but does not require) distinctions among private, social, and political domains. One convenient set of categories might allow individual and family practices under a private category, institutions such as churches and businesses in the social category, and the state (and its corollary activities) in the political category. The term *public* might then be assigned to social and political categories. The classical meaning of the public leads to one sense of the collective self: the person who merges with the political. The more elaborate modern set of categories requires a more complex collective self. Persons can be holistic in both the social and political domains, collapsing identity to social and/or political. Practice dualism is then required to depict persons as members of both private groupings and public spheres.

The pluralism of liberal conditions offers multiple possibilities for the introduction of individuals to collective spheres. The immediate and perhaps obvious patterns are the partial alignments with overlapping and distinct practices. These multiple connections between self and practice are the mainstay of liberal democracies, guaranteeing the partitions in the self that mirror social and political pluralism, and ensuring that persons will not merge with the holistic organizations that have undermined democracy in the present century. But there are also benign forms of holism. If we follow Habermas in allowing discourses to be the reflective and open examinations of terms that occur when speech breaks down, then we should consider the possibility that the special communications of discourse offer a union of self with process. This union is not typically found in the ordinary talk of political life, but is still *not* an extraordinary experience.

4

These preoccupations can be turned in a different direction by examining the ways in which groups reach collective outcomes, and identifying the

---

9. Hannah Arendt, *The Human Condition* (Chicago: University of Chicago Press, 1974), chapter 11, especially 50–58. Seyla Benhabib sees a different "associational" sense of the public in Arendt's *The Origins of Totalitarianism*, where the term refers only to a space where persons can act together in concert. In Benhabib, "Models of Public Space," in Craig Calhoun, ed., *Habermas and the Public Sphere*, pp. 73–98.

requirements for individual-whole relationships in these group dynamics. In the simplest sense a collective outcome can be reached with only minimal expectations from, and effects on, the persons who constitute the group. The arithmetical composition rules that produce utilitarian outcomes and define numerically grounded social practices like voting anticipate only that persons will introduce some variable, typically preferences, to an aggregation device. The summed total represents a collective outcome that may not require anything more of persons than that they stand to one another as numerical units. Reasoned outcomes, by contrast, demand of persons that they engage one another in dialogue of some sort. This engagement at least offers the possibility of a more intimate connection between person and collective outcome.

I have argued that the connections among persons and outcomes in deliberative procedures often require third parties, figures who are to some degree outside of the relationships among persons seeking a collective outcome but are vital to a successful outcome. These persons are present in all varieties of groups, from the liberal maintenance of individuals to the fusion of individuals and wholes characteristic of mystical experiences. But those groups that seek reasoned outcomes apparently have special needs for third parties. The vocabularies that (again) describe such roles testify to the range and importance of such figures: healer, practitioner, mentor, counselor, and (as the more general designation here) mediator.

Imagine a type of reasoned settlement that is often found in divorce proceedings. Suppose that, instead of the adversarial proceedings of a legal setting, the divorcing couple has used a mediator. Various settlement patterns are common in such proceedings. One is the kind of surface settlement that represents liberal governance. Here the issues are typically who owns the car and furniture, who is to get custody of the children, and so on. When successful this kind of settlement can leave the persons who are divorcing unchanged. Another settlement pattern is more demanding. The mediator can move the conversation to a deeper inquiry: what are we arguing about when we argue about the car and furniture, and custody of the children? If successful this discussion discloses something important about the persons who are divorcing. They must change as the negotiations reach a conclusion.

The requirement that individuals change as part of the movement toward a collective outcome is found in several group dynamics. But the scale of involvement and the methods for individual change differ. Charismatic religious experiences are regarded as successful only as individuals are transformed, typically in dramatic and often in permanent ways. In these collective movements the person is collapsed into the holistic movement represented by the group. The methods for bringing about this transformation include a reliance on what members of the movement believe is a higher power outside the normal limits of human experience. At its extremes these methods seek an outcome in which the individual is extinguished completely, at least for a period of time, and a holistic state dominates procedures and reality. The modest beginnings for these moments of fusion are found in dialogue and discourse, where language and self can be inextricably bound.

5

The encouraging fact is that mediated dialogue itself is a powerful source of collective experience. Imagine a two-person political society in which the citizens are in a state of radical disagreement *and* are committed to finding a mutually agreeable solution to their differences. As persons they are rational agents, and so capable of deliberation and the advancement of conclusions that are grounded in reasons. Suppose further in this thought experiment that the two persons engage one another in dialogue. If they have brought to the engagement a thoughtful proposal to resolve their differences they can each offer reasons in support of their conclusions for the other to consider and accept. A rational beginning of public dialogue in this setting is direct: proffered reasons are (a) grounded on the expectation that the other is capable of considering reasons, and (b) invitations for the other to accept the thinking and conclusions of the speaker. Put simply, my reasons introduced to dialogue can be, and should be, your reasons as well.

Persons who share the same culture and framework for reasoning can rationally secure agreeable outcomes, and if they cannot then the coercive powers of the state can adjudicate disputes successfully on impartial criteria of public reasoning. In conditions of strong and comfortable consensus the two persons can talk to one another, listen to competing proposals, mutually adjust the ordering of partisan and political values, and arrive at an ordering of collective goods that can meet their respective and joint interests. Perhaps these dialogues are political tokens for what Rawls means by a well-ordered society. Public reason is a civil proceeding governed by values that everyone can reasonably endorse.

But we must remember that the differences that lead to the exercise of public reason are not of the type that are easily resolved with a mutual exploration of reasons. We can imagine two mathematicians examining proofs and conclusions, and settling their differences with discussions and insights. But political differences are as likely to be about the system of rules and principles that settle differences as the issues and problems that directly represent differences. The additional layers of complexity require the participants in public reason to bifurcate their reasons with the political plane of reasonableness: reasons that take into account the views of the other and the arrangements that house the two persons must find their way into the dialogue. Mathematicians can attend to methods and the solutions that are correct in terms of these methods. Public reasoning must be attentive to the needs of the participants to secure *some* settlement, and the political conditions required in arranging an agreeable outcome among adversaries seeking an agreement or accommodation.

If the persons in the thought experiment are radically opposed to one another a more difficult scenario unfolds. In these conditions the participants in public reasoning do not have a common language for resolving differences. The invitation to accept both partisan and political proposals is flawed. The persons may not agree on what counts as a reason, and the deliberative processes leading to the conclusions that each is offering to the other may not be generalizable across their differences. The use of coercion is difficult in these conditions since its justification to the affected party is impossible. One of the persons may regard the society as not well ordered, and so amenable to the less compromising influences of moral doctrines that attempt to put things right, or bring public reason and its background conditions into a more appropriate setting. The abolitionist and civil rights movements are acknowledged as having this legitimate purpose.

Two arguments that I have introduced on these distinctions are important in understanding the version of public reason developed here. One is that the differences between societies that are and are not well ordered are variables of perspectives often formed by partisan values. The civil rights movement began in social conditions that most of the United States viewed as well ordered. That we now widely recognize the injustice of those conditions is strong testimony for the moral and political effectiveness of the movement. The essentially subjective and partisan standing of the concept of a well ordered society indicates that the concept cannot be used as an impartial arbitrator to allow and disallow the influence of comprehensive doctrines. Certainly many members of the pro-life movement regard the 1.2 million abortions performed every year in the United States as a form of genocide that undermines the legitimacy of at least a segment of the legal system. From *their* point of view the society is badly ordered on these practices.[10] Second, there is no reason to think that the distinctions between settled and unsettled states of society, or between high and low consensus, are stable. If perceptions of order and justice are items of disagreement, then public reason may be a dialogue conducted in a flux so constant that the conclusions and reasons of the participants slide easily among various fulcrums. Even the controlling ordering of political values may be functions of collective terms that are themselves variables.

The two persons in the thought experiment may have to confront an uncomfortable truth: talking to one another with the best and most sincere intentions will not succeed in resolving their differences exactly in those conditions when the differences are most in need of resolution. Other devices are required. Ideal speech situations are not likely inclusions in the inventory of these devices. The fairness logically required for ideal speech is not a condition for political talk but among its topics: in discourse the indigenous languages of the participants can transform the structure of communication. The openness of languages requires that every item be subject to critical inspection, and every definition be the working product of immediate discourse (including the frames for ideal speech situations). One result is a pragmatics that is balkanized, the universal reduced to local dimensions. The participants may discover foundational arguments, what I have called the circuit breakers of language. A different rhythm attends to these sectors of thought and expression. But all arguments must be discussed, and used as the talk requires. A considerable distinction separates

10. John Rawls allows the abolitionists the political use of moral (comprehensive) doctrines because the society of their time and place was not well ordered. This option is not permitted for the pro-life movement because the society is well ordered. See *Political Liberalism*, paperback edition (New York: Columbia University Press, 1996), 240–254. But if the notion of "well ordered" is contestable then the distinction cannot be imposed. There seems to be a "protective belt" (to steal a phrase from Imre Lakatos) in use here that shields concepts from political interpretation when they should be out in the open for critical discussion. A more robust appreciation of contestability might have produced a different footnote 32 (p. 243) in *Political Liberalism*, which elaborates a criticism in the text of comprehensive doctrines on the abortion dispute that cannot support a reasonable balance among three political values: "the due respect for human life, the ordered reproduction of political society over time, including the family in some form, and finally the equality of women as equal citizens." For Rawls a reasonable balance among these three values gives to a woman a right in the first trimester to choose whether to continue or terminate her pregnancy. But surely there is a suppressed belief in this ordering of political values, which is that the human predicates at issue cannot be assigned to early pregnancy for political purposes. Also, it is difficult to see how and at what points these political values, especially the first, can be demarcated from moral domains. This (essentially pro-choice) ordering at the very least misses the urgency attached to the central moral claim of pro-life: the *moral* standing of the "unborn child" trumps the three political values by assimilating abortion to infanticide. See also Rawls's more cautious discussion of this note in the introduction to the paperback edition, pp. lv–lvi.

norms that are imposed as ideals to structure a situation, and those that emerge as empirical patterns whenever a practice is continued. It is the latter sense of a norm that is appropriate to the version of public reason proposed here.

The only formal devices that do restrict public reasoning are boundary requirements: all discussion requires a sense of relevance that distinguishes licit and illicit topics. If one or both of the persons in the thought experiment rambles on about fashionable attire, or introduces considerations about gourmet food, these items may be ruled as irrelevant to the discussions. The collective nouns that refer to political arrangements, the needs of the larger society, are the governing frames for public reasoning. Notice, however, that these frames limit what can be said only in the required sense of relevance, not in the stronger sense of moral values restricting unthinkable alternatives. Everything is thinkable in a workable form of public reasoning, though some things are not relevant. It goes without saying that if attire and food can be shown to be relevant to collective arrangements then these items are appropriate topics as well.

At some moment the two persons in the experiment will require a third party. The transformation of a lateral discussion to a tripartite arrangement is one of the more familiar of human experiences. If persons cannot agree, then someone who is not a direct part of the discussions may be able to provide direction in bringing the talk to a successful conclusion. Classical liberal theory presents the state as this third party, and the form of the resolution process as binding arbitration. I have argued for a different type of third party as a model for public reasoning: the mediator who guides the discussions to provisional closure with the consent of the participants. It is in the action of mediation that texts are interpreted for the purposes at hand, and disputes absorbed and taken to resolutions that sometimes require a pragmatic redefinition of conditions and languages. It is also the mediator who can move the discussions to the collateral reasoning that seems to be more effective in resolving disputes that are at the essential center of beliefs. Collateral reasoning is an empirical part of the theory of public reason. It is the typical *political* sideshow that traditionally allows discussions to reach agreeable conclusions when the primary levels of political languages and the main participants cannot do so.

Return to the two persons in the thought experiment. Can mediated speech acts framed by collective considerations produce immoral or unjust outcomes? Of course. But so too can binding arbitration and juridical processes strongly controlled by rights and principles. Public reason cannot be an insurance policy that protects against undesirable conclusions. It is a form of joint reasoning oriented toward the collective arrangements of communal life. Whether the two person society, or any society, secures just or moral outcomes probably has a lot to do with the culture and circumstances of the participants. It cannot be assured through the mechanism of public reason, which is finally no more or less than the instrument that expresses what is best and worst about the political society in which it is practiced.

An account of public reason that relies on mediated speech acts is an extremely weak though complex version of procedural liberalism. The main commitment of the two persons in the thought experiment is to an agreeable outcome. The defining statement of mediation is toleration of a wide variety of methods to reach conclusions that the participants can accept. These procedures include scientific and narrative forms of discourse, and any number of approaches that use truth and rhetoric in effective ways. The procedural holism noted here is simply a recognition that property dualism is inadequate to express the capacities of persons to identify with the talk that produces settlements. In both the telling of stories and the rendition of empirical theories, persons can, and sometimes must, surrender the partitions in the self that seem to represent liberal views of human experience. These transient moments of identification with a successful procedure are no more or less than a representation (in brief form) of the strong unifications that seem to fill all political theories except liberalism. The two persons in the thought experiment would find the holism described here as both routine and benign.

6

Political discourse seems to be a kind of complex adaptive system, partially ordering and in turn being modified by its environment. If a text is malleable, and dominated by its environment, then it matters less whether any particular set of assumptions is written into the document. A governing language that can be manipulated by the background beliefs of a time and place has ceded authority to political movements, not to the theories of society that justify its authority. Malleable texts can be abandoned, modified, maintained with less concern and perhaps kept safe from random effects (as is sometimes the case in Britain, where constitutional boundaries and change are also complicated by the trumping power of the House of Commons). But if a political text is a kind of ordering grammar, a genotype that yields and constrains phenotypes, then its social and theoretical content matters a great deal. Codes inserted into grammars (by historical accidents, mutations, and human interventions) have fundamental implications for phenomena. Even to be able to regard changes as in or outside of a text seems to depend in part on what we mean by the standing of languages that govern the relations we have with one another.

Governing languages are more accurately defined as evolving grammars that carry into political settings a range of assumptions on the powers of reason and the nature of the persons who exercise these powers. The extremes at either end of a political text are never successful: a governing document that is too restrictive cannot accommodate the sharp changes in society that produce new meanings of terms; a text that is too open cannot be authoritative. Texts that endure seem to capture the middle conceptual ground that constrains discretion without extinguishing freedom of interpretation. Grammars that restrict and are altered by the phenomena of politics seem to represent the realities of political logics.

The devolution of authority by freedom of interpretation suggests that the assumptions of liberal texts require substantial modifications if the grammars of authoritative languages are to be maintained. I have argued that the political principles of liberal thought cannot govern in any fashion that makes the liberal state coherent, and that the type of reasoned closure reconciling authority and interpretive freedom is found in discourses of a special sort: the informal street conversations that have always marked political activity, and that are the sources for both political stability and working definitions of reason and persons. One implication of these arguments is that the grammar of a constitution is formed from the bottom up, by those dialectical exchanges that offer provisional stopping points on the adaptive logic of political life.

But the absence of an Archimedean point for reasoning does not mean that perspectives are free-floating, without positions and assumptions. All reasoning is from a point of view, and so contains both explicit and tacit knowledge. The foundational values of noncomputation are those that support the provisional standing of all values, including those of noncomputation, and permit the exit reasoning that leads to regresses and the halting problem. The subscription to dialogue also depends on understandings about the person and languages that contribute to the dense stock of assumptions in public reasoning. These collections of statements, arranged at the various levels found in all perspectives and theories, present a complex package of items that helps stabilize public reasoning in ways that escape the relativism haunting postmodern views of the text.

The specter of relativism defines the micro worlds of physics. Quantum mechanics suggests that a particle can travel along all paths and exist in all states simultaneously. In some bizarre way entities seem both to exist and not exist at the same time in this potential or premeasurement state. But when particles are measured their wave functions instantaneously collapse into a definite state. This metaphor of open possibilities transformed into definite states of affairs through an action by an observer or agent is more accurate for my purposes than the Newtonian metaphor of fixed states rendered intelligible by the right theories. The version of public reasoning delineated here is an exercise in dialogue or discourse that assigns definite states to conditions that have no discernible form or meaning prior to the exercise. Whatever stability is found in political experience follows rather than precedes the uses of public reason.

Experience is filled with relationships of necessity, sufficiency, contextual influence, and a variety of dependencies that render singular events virtually unintelligible. The arguments offered here take a two-pronged form of dependency as a beginning grammar for public reason. The first prong is the elevation of perspective over many other variables. Suppose that the definition of p can only be settled by determining the perspectives represented by a, b, and c, in that the sense and range of p can be a matter of the views found in a, b, or c (or some combination of these). The variables of a, b, and c are community perspectives, and p is public reason. On this account variations in p are parallax: differences in the logic or outcomes of public reasoning are explained in terms of the positions represented by community views. A complete rendition of public reason must then express its dependency on the communities that constitute the state.

But a parallax sense of differences is constrained by a provisional (and nonideal) logic of public reason. Experience also provides several actions with dependencies that resist a collapse to local perspectives. To do x may require doing y, as we seem to recognize when we say that teaching requires some fidelity to truth-telling. Or sometimes to do x successfully requires some y, as teaching well requires knowledge of the subject matter taught. The arguments here maintain that any exercise of public reasoning requires a reference to collective considerations. So even if a complete account of reasoning must include attending to the background perspectives of communities, the grammar of public reason still cannot be entirely reduced to community interpretations. The second prong of dependency is the logic expressed by the statement that to do x (public reasoning) requires y (a consideration of collective arrangements).

The core presence and theoretical constraints of collective terms introduce braking actions on interpretations, though not closure. Quine's metaphor of a web, or set of concentric circles, helps mark what I call the retentive powers of various statements. One point here is that collective terms are closer to the center of this image than are political principles. Recall that at the retentive core of any cluster of statements are analytic statements, rigid designators, synthetic a priori statements—in general, those statements that seem to have some generalizing powers across cultures and possible worlds. The collective languages of politics, minimally expressed in logical and spatial terms, are more appropriately located at the core of political concepts, even as other political languages are not.[11] If this assertion is correct, then the braking powers of languages assign a frame to interpretation in the domains of collective arrangements. The main frames for political dialogue and discourse are the referential powers of collective terms, but these frames are aimed at governing the forms of arguments rather than political actions (and so do not function either as political rules and principles, nor as logical norms).

The dense conceptual package of public reason can be represented by the metaphor of a core with spokes that extend the internal concepts of the core in different ways to different circumstances. In this representation public reasoning is a kind of layered arrangement, with a set of statements that can be maintained across different issues and problems, and other statements that vary as the topics addressed by public reason change. The separation among levels allows for a single generalizable form of public reason that yet assumes different expression in different sectors of the political system. On the periphery of this arrangement might be found the practices of casuistry, where pragmatic considerations close to the practical side of politics dominate. Closer to the core might be the mediated dialogue that models the deliberative settlements of politics. At the core are framing devices, including those that instruct on the uses of theory and information, and the deeper assumptions that form the tacit dimensions of dialogue (such as the concept of the person or self in reasoning). Perhaps at the icy center are the shifting typologies that organize collective considerations.

Reductions of knowledge, either from necessity or stipulation, will have a different logic and pace as one moves across the arrangement. A selective reduction in the magnitude of information is appropriate in casuistry, where pragmatic means and ends tend to dominate proceedings. But the advisability and possibility of reducing information in mediated dialogue are more complex. The mediator is guided by the mandate to reach closure in discussions, but the guidelines are defined by the legitimate needs of the

11. See my own early contribution, "The Structure of 'Politics.'" *American Political Science Review* 72 (September 1978): 859–870.

participants to know and the features of the practice in which the mediation occurs. Practice rules that specify evidence and proper inferences are typically found in the procedures. The logic of boundaries is different again at the core. Here the efforts are restricted by the natural limitations of what we can know. Justifications for epistemic and realist approaches to knowledge invariably turn on what is accessible to the human intellect and its mediating instruments.

Three implications follow this arrangement of public reasoning. First, the division of reason into (a) core terms with a retentive power that provides constancy across issues and problems, and (b) the peripheral terms that vary with circumstances, allows both the general and the particular into public reasoning. The minimal structure of mediated dialogue can be retained in general form even as its practical form varies across the content of reason. Or, there are many types of public reasoning, but a minimal or necessary core is common to all of the variations.

Second, mediated dialogue does not offer a single magic bullet to manage all political disputes and problems. Mediated dialogue if offered here as a *model* to replace the contract model that informs juridical versions of public reasoning. The substitution requires a revision of the governing logic of the liberal state, in part by modifying the concept of persons and the adversarial relations among political participants. But these substitute strategies are theoretical proposals, intended to shift the references of reasoning. The extension of mediation to different sectors and difficulties may still tolerate a heterogeneous set of practices, so long as the variety of forms is linked to a centering notion. This linkage occurs with many political and moral concepts. Consent, for example, is routinely extended within medical practices today, in adumbrated form, to substituted judgment and surrogate consent. These practical modifications require a clear initial concept of consent. Without the concept of mediated dialogue the extensions and amendments of public reasoning similarly may be unintelligible.

Third, holistic terms introduce a stability to all versions of public reasoning. The core standing of collective arrangements in politics offers an inventory of reasonably fixed terms to craft the practical applications of public reason. Collective frames can function as minimal guidance systems in the conversations of public reasoning.

The conditions of public reasoning are replete with both critical and closed forms of social life, where the skeptical perspectives of critical beliefs coexist and compete with commitments to singular and dominant truths. The contemporary landscapes of Western liberal societies contain varieties of secular and religious organizations that represent this heterogeneous set of beliefs. The ordinary observation is that liberal societies are constituted in part by nonliberal communities. The more complex proposition is that there is no persuasive case for anything else. Both facts and justifications rule out any powers of exclusion for noncomputational or computational reasoning in the organization of human communities.

In an odd and yet familiar way, however, noncomputational reasoning trumps by default in the domains of public reason. If there is no natural point of closure for public reasoning, and the deep pluralism of modern societies is the natural concomitant of this admission, then noncomputation must be the dominant form of public reasoning even as this dominance requires the acceptance of communities organized by various types of computational reasoning. But the dominance of critical and reflective reason occurs as an exit strategy, requiring that the rational person move to a perspective outside the range of beliefs at issue. In political terms this exit strategy amounts to a viewing of collective arrangements and a determination of the acceptable distributions of beliefs at the collective levels of society. The provisional nature of these determinations, and the acceptance of all forms of reasoning in human communities, grants a privileged standing to noncomputation only as an instrument of public reasoning, not in the larger society of communities that constitute the liberal state. The liberal state that relies on collective considerations can still favor a distribution of beliefs and communities dense with closed forms of organization.[12]

It is a fact of political life that open and critical forms of reasoning are simply one among several species of reasoning in human communities. Like science, religion, law, and any other practice, types of reasoning compete with one another, which is what one would expect in a world populated by conscious and reflective forms of life. That the governing reason of a diverse society must express a creative tolerance for multiple forms of thinking is simple testament to the distinctive needs of a public form of reasoning in conditions of pluralism.

12. In this sense the arguments here both align with and dissent from liberal critics who reject "the universalist pretensions of liberal theory." No privilege can be assigned to noncomputational reasoning in the larger society. John Gray's view that "liberal forms of life enjoy no special privileges of any kind" is acceptable in my account of the conditions for public reasoning. But from the remarks in the text it is obvious that I am less optimistic about the equal viability of computational and noncomputational reasoning in the domains of state, and inclined to grant immunity to noncomputation in the areas of public reasoning from this welcome leveling of perspectives. See Gray, "From Post-Liberalism to Pluralism," in Ian Shapiro and Russell Hardin, eds., *Political Order* (New York: New York University Press, 1996). (The two quotes are on page 360.) Also note that the exercise of noncomputational public reason can support a preponderance of closed forms of organization even as the state installs and protects conditions that permit critical reasoning to flourish.

7

This account of public reason is presented as a coherent set of concepts, and so it is vulnerable to pressures and tradeoffs as the items in the set are made to fit together in some acceptable arrangement. One source of stress is the lacunae seemingly created by the abandonment of the normative powers of rights and principles. The very thought that all political settlements are provisional closures, without the binding force we traditionally recognize in the modern state, must be puzzling to those who regard a settled framework of rights and immunities as necessary for authoritative governing and democratic practices. It might even be argued that all dialogue requires elementary protections for participants, for example that they not be, or risk being turned into, slaves.

But two very different arguments must be recognized in understanding the prospect of a chronically open public reason. The first is the disabusing argument: however desirable rights and principles may be in political domains, there is no language that can provide the fixed and general foundations needed for any form of enduring political or moral authority. We simply do not have reasonably closed and stable terms, and the unattainable cannot be a foundation for public reason simply because it would be a good thing to have.[13] Rights and principles do work on many occasions. But the work done is largely due to background consensus, a point that is dramatically shown when these terms are employed in conditions of deep pluralism. The governing terms of the liberal state are just another set of partisan instruments when individuals and groups are severely divided. The second argument is that the only constraints on political dialogue just are those found in the political languages of dialogue itself, in the logic of mediated speech acts, and in the background conditions that frame dialogue. These constraints can be considerable, and they indicate that the conditions of liberal human experience can be ensured by public reasoning. Certainly the thought that participants in a dialogue cannot be slaves is a defining part of any mediated conversation. But (again) the checks and balances of good liberal politics must be sought within the logics of public dia-

13. The persistence of political philosophers in hanging on to terms (and ways of thinking) that cannot establish distinctions and resolve differences is remarkable. See Stanley Fish's discussion of Locke's strategy in identifying religious doctrines that the government will not tolerate by relying (finally) on "the judgment of all mankind." Fish is persuasive in showing that the phrase is empty and even self-referential at critical moments. Yet, in spite of its illegitimacy, Fish points out that "this imaginary Lockean move is made over and over again by every liberal theorist including those who write today." In Fish's "Mission Impossible: Settling the Just Bounds Between Church and State," *Columbia Law Review* 97 no. 3 (December 1997): 2255–2333. The quote is in the abstract of the article.

logues. They are not to be found in the vocabularies of rights and principles that, among other things, try to establish political legitimacy.

Richard Rorty and others have described the rich inventory of linguistic devices used by members of the civil society in identifying, dissecting, and reconstructing the political terms that feed into public reasoning.[14] There is little doubt that this inventory is a kind of vast spreadsheet encompassing the items expected in any wide-ranging conversation. A dialectical treatment of truth is part of the common currency of ideas when political rules, principles, issues, problems, and more are negotiated in civil dialogue, and the tactics designed to explore the meanings of things political can include a full range of rhetorical instruments to persuade audiences. One might say that the techniques can and do exceed the bounds of civility, and that the excess is completely appropriate. But the chroniclers of this merry sideshow in political talk generally want to consider it as just that, a sideshow funneling into the more controlled setting of public reason. Where everything is up for grabs, after all, it does not seem that one can have deliberative examinations and thoughtful outcomes. Again, the image of a well-run courtroom, with acknowledged *judicious* rules of evidence, inference and argument, seems best as a model for public reasoning.[15] Let street or dinner conversations be unbridled. The reasoning of state officials must be deliberative.

One of the central arguments of this work is that the properties of political actions and events cannot demarcate the conversations of civil (and uncivil) society from the domains of public reason. It is true that the dialogues found in well-defined practices and institutions typically contain rules for proper talk, and the purpose of the practices or institutions can help interpret the rules. A trial (as illustrated earlier) may be regarded as either proposing to balance the rights of the defendant and the authority of the state, or as an inquiry to determine the guilt or innocence of defen-

---

14. Richard Rorty, *Contingency, Irony and Solidarity* (New York: Cambridge University Press, 1989).

15. I have cited Rawls, *Political Liberalism*, on this point. Rawls allows that citizens are proper figures to exercise public reason, but the ideal is still a deliberative mode of talk that is above all else *judicious*: "The ideal is that citizens are to conduct their public political conceptions of constitutional essentials and matters of basic justice within the framework of what each sincerely regards as a reasonable political conception of justice, a conception that expresses political values that others as free and equal also might reasonably be expected reasonably to endorse. Thus each of us must have principles and guidelines to which we appeal in such a way that the criterion of reciprocity is satisfied." In the paperback edition of the book, pp. l–li. The triple use of "reasonable" communicates the message: We must be well behaved within a common structure of discourse. A dialectical approach, by contrast, reminds us that endorsements are often stochastic outcomes of unbridled conversations.

dants, and which purpose one assigns will influence the use of the exclusionary rule for the introduction of evidence. The acceptance of science as a practice that seeks a type of truth establishes scientific methods of inquiry. The more varied goals of different art forms help craft a set of rules and tactics for composition.

But politics cannot run so tight a ship. I have argued that the defining point or purpose of public reason is to compose or attend to arrangements for the entire society. This point or purpose will frame talk along certain lines, ruling some considerations as illicit, others as appropriate. Nothing in this logic, however, can shield public reasoning from the unruly dialogues of civil society. Political languages can always appropriate whatever references are needed to negotiate views on the proper arrangements for the larger society, including the most wretched considerations possible. The possibility of admitting the morally unthinkable may be precisely what is needed in public reasoning to control the real and hypothetical extremes in human experiences. But it is a clearly a property of such reasoning that the range of items that can be considered and the arguments used are limited only by the frames of collective arrangements.

One might think that the restriction of public reason to constitutional essentials will insulate deliberations from unruly talk. But a separation between constitutional and practical issues is not a strong presence even in legal reasoning. One of the clearest indications that this distinction is ignored in public reason is the welcome tendencies of even strict constitutional champions to address practical matters. John Rawls has stipulated that public reasoning deals with basic structures. But the account of this reasoning in *Political Liberalism* is filled with talk about issues of school prayer, abortion, education, just wars, and in general the practical stuff of real-world politics.[16] All constitutional scholars also know the elementary truth that constitutional essentials are always discussed by the courts in terms of actual cases. In addition, any study of courts will reveal that the legal treatment of cases is hardly free of rhetorical flourishes and vivid arguments.[17] It is a modest observation to say that public reasoning is unlikely to be separated from civil dialogues by any distinction between constitutional and practical issues. But the most important point is that there

16. Rawls, *Political Liberalism*, especially the introduction to the paperback edition.
17. Most of the literatures I have looked at concentrate on the trial levels of the legal system to describe the rhetorical flavor of legal arguments. A helpful work is W. Lance Bennett and Martha Feldman, *Reconstructing Reality in the Courtroom* (New Brunswick, N.J.: Rutgers University Press, 1981). I am told by colleagues in various fields of law that the great study of conversational reasoning in the U.S. Supreme Court has yet to be written.

is no reason for the separation. Public reasoning is not simply about constitutions, but about the arrangements that represent a political system. These arrangements invite talk that can exceed all legal boundaries.

The image communicated in my arguments is one of continuities and overlaps across communities, and between communities and the state. The discussions of physician-assisted suicide illustrate the several senses of comprehensive references found in public reason. We have seen that these discussions range over an open set of items and argumentative forms (the meaning of life and death; concepts of the person; the constitutional standing of liberty interests and due process for those seeking physician assistance in hastening death; the justice and utility of various arrangements; the roles of religion, medical practices, and the family in these issues; and more). The formal ruling of the U.S. Supreme Court on the constitutional particulars, in particular whether states can proscribe the practice, is one expression of public reason in one venue. There is evidence that even this more deliberative venue is privately enriched with the less formal conversations that represent noncomputational dialogue.[18] But the point here is that no realistic demarcations can be established between communal conversations and any kinds of formal deliberations. Public reason just *is* the give-and-take of dialogue, structured only by a concern for collective arrangements.

My arguments require the abandonment of certain illusions, in particular the belief that the disputes of deep pluralism can somehow be managed by the traditional languages of the liberal state. The rejection is supported by another plain observation: open versions of public reasoning are found in abundance in democratic political societies. Almost all political processes rely on informal and persuasive languages to find creative solutions not countenanced by rules and principles. The main variables of public reason are not in the justifications prominent in liberal theory (including the original position) but in the conduct of mediated reasoning in political settings. These forms of reasoning offer certain advantages that meet many of the goals and terms of liberal political theory. Mediation, for example,

18. Or so we are told in that gossipy report of conversations among the justices: Bob Woodward and Scott Armstrong, *The Brethren: Inside the Supreme Court* (New York: Simon and Schuster, 1979). Or see the more recent and darker story of in-chambers dialogues marked by both acrimony *and* ineptness in Edward Lazarus, *Closed Chambers* (New York: Times Books, 1998). Lazarus describes the justices as they engage each other in *political* terms that do not at all resemble the deliberative and formal discourses that some may expect from individuals working in a marble temple wearing black robes. See the review of *Closed Chambers* by Kathleen M. Sullivan, "Behind the Crimson Curtain," *New York Review of Books* (October 8, 1998): 15–18.

precludes the possibility that the adversaries on an issue can harden into implacable opposition. They have to keep talking and exploring settlement options. It should also be more than obvious that freedom must be granted priority standing in a dialogue theory of public reason, and that the abandonment of property dualism invites a closer connection of self and process than is provided in liberal theory. But these patterns and standings follow the maintenance logic of all theoretical provisions in political governance, which is that they are the conditions and/or the results of open conversations.

8

Two influential theories of state and society support accounts of collective reasoning. One is the theory of justice elaborated by John Rawls, which specifies public reason within the boundaries of the political. In this theory the deliberations that both constitute and manage the political system are freestanding uses of governing principles that owe little or nothing to the comprehensive doctrines found naturally in a pluralistic society, nor to any metaphysical doctrines familiar in philosophical discussions. The political domain for Rawls can and must be sealed off from those synoptic theories that propose complete accounts of human experience. Public reasoning is instead to be guided by various political principles drawn up from the representative device that Rawls labels the original position, and by precepts like reasonableness that set out the terms for successful cooperation among persons who are members of the political system.

A second is the theory of communicative action introduced by Jürgen Habermas. In this theory reason attains its sense and reference in the collective conditions represented by the ideal speech situation. The theory is comprehensive, in that it offers a full account of epistemology, and of theoretical and practical reasoning, as forms of modifiable communication. Habermas provides the governing rules of both speech and discourse, including those of grammar, syntax, communicative forms, and other items that delineate the structure of various types of reasoning. Public reasoning in this theoretical framework must be one or more of the types of deliberation and discussion defined by the analytic properties of ideal communication. In recent work Habermas has expanded political reasoning to include a variety of rational forms variable with different conditions.[19]

19. Read the exchange between Habermas and Rawls ("Remarks on Rawls's *Political Liberalism*" and "Reply to Habermas") in *The Journal of Philosophy* XCII no. 3 (March 1995): 109–180. Rawls has republished his article (with editing) as Lecture IX in the paperback edi-

The version of public reason developed here draws on both of these theories, but is unlike them in important ways. The arguments in these pages regard the political domain as porous, unavoidably (and helpfully) influenced by morality, metaphysics, and the comprehensive doctrines that seem always to inhabit the political world. The distinguishing mark of the political cannot then be an artifact of its insulation from other social and intellectual discourses. It is instead its orientation to collective arrangements. The powers of mediated dialogue or discourse in public reasoning can also subordinate both principles and structures to its own needs and logic. In this sense the present account of public reason is more comfortable with the latter stages of Rawls's four-stage extension of the original position to the critical reflections of citizen deliberations, and even more comfortable when the original position is itself a malleable subject of street talk rather than its constituting frame. Also, the analytic structure of the ideal speech or discourse situation does not govern political talk in the theory of public reason proposed here. The model representing public reasoning in the arguments here (a) abuses (ignores, overcomes, fuses) theoretical distinctions and categories with an unremitting dialectical form of reasoning, (b) does not have ideal standing, (c) is indigenous at the expense of universality (and so sides with Winch against Habermas, though with reservations that deny full alignment), (d) requires a mediator and so is mildly hierarchical, and (e) is local to political domains, which restricts the discourse to collective references.

The transitions in the modern period from classical to various forms of bounded reasoning have occurred with an increased awareness of intellectual limits. The map that traces the conditions of reasoning from certainty to risk to uncertainty represents a journey from the Platonic convictions that reason can apprehend transcendent truths to the more realistic expectations that reasoning powers are deep within the contexts of human experience. The map is also a chronicle of the communal opening of reason. The solitary reasoning agent gives way to the agent who relies on others for the full and effective use of reason. Groups and institutions are the resources for information and rational strategies, and the singular individual must absorb and use these collateral arrangements (including the networks formalized by computers) to realize intellectual skills. In many ways the transitions from the reflective reasoning of philosophical accounts to the

tion of *Political Liberalism*. The best arguments Habermas offers for communicative instead of philosophically grounded practical reasoning are found in *Between Facts and Norms*, especially Chapter 1.

communicative rationality elaborated by Habermas depicts the extension of reason into communal settings.

My arguments here take reason even further into communal settings, in two senses. One is the introduction of mediated speech acts as the core of public reasoning. The rational person engaged in the political actions described as public reasoning needs the benign assistance of another to negotiate the interpretation and use of political vocabularies, in effect to be politically rational. Mediated speech acts represent the group orientation of politics, and recognize the presence of guides and mentors in reason. A full treatment of the grammar of public reason would require a theory of mediated speech acts comparable to speech act theory in linguistics (which still elaborates speech acts in terms of the singular speaker). The second is the use of community arrangements as the defining focus of public reason. I have argued here that public reasoning must consider collective arrangements in addressing particular cases, and also depends on tacit wholes that help form the contexts of political judgments.

9

In many ways liberalism is a theory of incomplete unions. All versions of the liberal state negotiate a transition from diversity to political unity, from anarchy to governing systems that maintain the integrity of individual persons while producing collective outcomes. Liberal theory ranges over the degree of union and diversity needed for effective and legitimate governance. But even the political liberal expects a governing unit (however thin or fragile) to manage the differences that occasion the formation of the state instead of the acceptance of anarchy. Imagine a consolidation machine into which individuals introduce units of various types (claims, preferences, choices, arguments, judgments, demands, supports). Now suppose that the machine acts on these items to produce collective outcomes. This metaphor, of a mechanism that speaks for society by consolidating individual entries into political outcomes, is the central image in all theories of the liberal state. Public reason is the deliberative side of the metaphor, representing the reasoning powers expected at some point in all democratic consolidations.

One interesting complication is that the metaphor opens public space for three overlapping narratives of public reasoning in democratic forms of governing. One is the populist line that individual entries are to have full and accurate expression in the machine's product. This story requires an algorithmic mechanism that routinely collects and combines, without changing, the preferences of the enfranchised. The collective product of the populist machine is no more and no less than the added totals of the individual entries.[20] The story lines and sayings that accompany this narrative are common ingredients in democratic lore: governance by and for the people, power to the people, citizen rule, and so on. Cinematic versions of this story are common (e.g., *Mr. Smith Goes To Washington*) and the threats to the story are easily identified: boss rule, machine politics (where the algorithms are corrupted by organizations), elite rule, special interests, and so on.

A second narrative is the adjudication story. In this story the more enduring interests of individuals are protected and encouraged by deliberative bodies. Adjudication requires a "thick" machine, one enriched by rules of evidence, inference and argument organized by various criteria of impartiality. Individual entries are to be interpreted and judged, eventually rank ordered, and sometimes flatly denied as they pass from the entrances to the exits of the machine. Though more usually represented in the production of legal outcomes, deliberative bodies are found throughout liberal democracies, from courts to draft boards to juries, and more. The legal trappings are as theatrical as populist symbols: among judges, for example, one finds the deliberative forum replete with ceremonial robes and marble halls. Threats are equally familiar: corruption, moral weakness, flawed or biased rules, favoritism that defeats impartiality.

A third, and minor, story is the Madisonian narrative that artfully protects each of the two major themes from their resident, and dominant, players. In this story any uninterrupted passage from entry to exit doors, whether on aggregation or deliberative mechanisms, is treacherous. The Madisonian story thickens the machine with institutional parts that impede movement by partitioning and complicating the passageways. An equilibrium of sorts is reached that balances interests by distributing them through institutional arrangements. It is interesting that the Madisonian story does not play well in any of a society's dramatic settings. No theatrical symbols attach to the story, no good and bad guys, no clear identification of threats. Perhaps the explanation is found in the

20. This at least is the version of populism that follows a one-person, one-vote universal franchise point of view. See Robert Dahl, *A Preface to Democratic Theory* (Chicago: University of Chicago Press, 1956). The importance of path independence in the derivation of collective outcomes from individual entries is uncritically accepted throughout collective choice theory. One of Arrow's initial conditions—the independence of irrelevant alternatives—prohibits consolidating machines that are creative in interrupting the connections between entries and outcomes.

odd fact that the machine itself is the hero in Madison's story of liberal democracy.

The metaphor of consolidation expresses the liberal belief that the ideal state is to be an instrument of political unity that respects the autonomy and freedom of its citizens. The mechanisms of aggregation and adjudication, and the Madisonian tale of machines that restrain and permit collective opportunities, are variations on the baseline assumption that persons form and accept a state which secures conditions unavailable in conditions of anarchy, and governs with methods that are benign rather than oppressive. A spatial domain of consolidation indicates separate (private) spheres where persons independently craft items to be introduced to the machine. Public reason is located in different sectors of each form of consolidation, but is expected to be a central practice in liberal democracies.

The problem for liberal democracy is that all three narratives fail as complete expressions of both liberal and democratic expectations. A vast body of work in collective choice and game theory has demonstrated how difficult it is to realize equity and rationality in aggregation mechanisms.[21] Various critical theories argue that adjudication fails as a neutral or impartial consolidation device, and some of these failures are among the topics explored throughout this work. Even the more nuanced versions of Madisonian democracy seem to beg the questions that arise in trying to bind individual and political whole, and first-order theory with practical judgments. Public reason, as the objective practice that adjudicates and manages individual claims at the most reflective levels, seems to have no adequate form of consolidation to represent liberal democracies.

These breakdowns in all versions of the liberal story have encouraged the recent tendencies in liberal thought to rely on various types of holism to repair breaches in the consolidation metaphor. Both communitarianism and current rediscoveries of republicanism are heroic (and often persuasive) attempts to make things whole by (a) introducing a generalizable (or collective) normative content to the state in order to close the technical and moral spaces in liberal political arrangements, or (b) elevating the Madisonian narrative to decisive levels with the balancing powers of institutional

21. Kenneth J. Arrow, *Individual Choice and Social Values* (New York: John Wiley, 1963). For a summary of aggregation and combination failures, see William Riker, *Liberalism Against Populism* (San Francisco: William H. Freeman, 1982) and the collection of readings and commentaries in Brian Barry and Russell Hardin, *Rational Man and Irrational Society* (Beverly Hills, Calif.: Sage Publications, 1982). Note that Arrow's theorem is a logical proof, not an empirical theory. But the theorem examines an abstract calculus drawn from empirical democratic theory, and the conclusions in the proof on the relationships among the terms in the calculus bear on democratic theory in reshaping its form.

arrangements.[22] Some collective terms seem required in all versions of liberal public reasoning, though the terms vary considerable as one inspects issues, problems, and theories.

If public reasoning is a mirror of liberal democracies, then the failure of the consolidation metaphor fixes collective terms in public reason. All types of public reason devolve (I have argued) to discursive communications in conditions of deep pluralism. The discursive mode of talking is eminently political (in the populist sense) and leads to the indeterminate and provisional conclusions of public reason. Varied types of rhetoric and interrogations, the verbal firepower of good arguments, and the intermingling of narrative and science are the dominant modes of public reasoning when consensus is not effective. In this type of communication the discursive forms of talk we designate as conversations fashion and express opinions.[23] There is no consolidation metaphor in such reasoning. The two properties of public reason are mediation and a particular type of content: what talk is about. Public reason is a form of mediated conversation that is about the collective arrangements of a political society. Collective nouns enter public reason as the organizing frames for talk, not as derivations from the use of consolidation rules. These nouns provide a sense of relevance for the open conversations that are at the heart of all democratic politics.

10

The histories of political theory are often marked by ambiguities, and transitions, in the conceptual foundations of moral and political reasoning. Though there is no reason to assume an orderly sequence along the lines of paradigm shifts, acknowledgments of conceptual limits have imperfectly led to different definitions and arrangements of basic terms. We understand classical political philosophy as a kind of fusion of virtue and politics: the complete state is one that represents a higher good. The medieval depictions of a political society organized to secure the common good are drawn from an acceptance of moral objectivity, and later distinguished from the church by demarcations between secular and transcendent truths.

22. Michael J. Sandel, *Democracy's Discontent: America in Search of a Public Philosophy* (Cambridge: Harvard University Press, 1996), and a working paper presented to the Maxwell School, Syracuse University, on April 14, 1997.

23. Look at the conversations recorded by William A. Gamson and presented in his *Talking Politics* (Cambridge: Cambridge University Press, 1992). It is clear (even if not stressed by Gamson) that these forms of reasoning are discursive and continuous, not single-event or closing opinions (putatively captured and presented in sequences by opinion polls).

Machiavelli's suggestion that political and moral reasoning can be incompatible on occasion is remarkable as a denial of the classical paradigm without either the sea changes that follow the denial, or a rejection of the challenge. The later development of contract theory is a more complex rearrangement of morality and politics. Moral and political discourses are regarded as distinct, but the state cannot just be another moral community. It is that special arrangement of authority justified in part as a necessary condition for the realization of natural law. The resulting transformations of theory represent changes in ground-floor terms and principles. The emotivist theory of value early in the twentieth century challenged the truth-functional standing of all evaluative statements, and with this challenge all normative political theory. One of the central problems of contemporary political theory has been to construct an intelligible theory of the state on noncognitive theories of value. What transitions can grant reason a location in politics without the stabilizing effects of foundational devices on moral objectivity and truth?

The arguments here on public reason require a sense of political morality that depends on both fusions and distinctions across moral and political domains. The deep pluralism of many liberal democracies, and the postmodern views of language that have followed these divisive conditions, discourage realist versions of truth. But the slope between an abandonment of a higher objectivity and the end point of nihilism is comfortably dense with stopping points shaped from epistemic forms of truth. If warranted beliefs are to effectively replace realist truth, however, it is vital that proper conditions of justification be in place. Truths crafted from human constructs require a demarcation between legitimate and illegitimate warrants. It is on this requirement that my arguments support a type of discourse that can provide provisional areas of reasoned governance in liberal democracies.

The political morality that emerges from this program of unrestricted dialogue is guided by standards of coherence, in almost all senses of that term. Any political community will provide several venues for morality in politics. These include the presence of community morals, and the larger and more diffuse backgrounds found in all political deliberations. The program suggested here requires an acceptance of the state as itself a moral undertaking, and it urges a focus on the skills of composition required in attending to collective arrangements. These skills are not those that permit competent adjudications of right and wrong. They are the virtues that define the capacity to see and order the arrangements of collective life. This species of political morality fills the areas of governance emptied by the failures of governing languages to support merit forms of public reason. It offers a deliberative procedure that is moral in both its effects on participants, and its consequences for communal life.

The success of this form of public reasoning is entirely a matter of balancing and fusing the sometimes disparate variables of moral and political practices. These variables include the concepts, rules and principles, and social structures that mediated dialogue addresses within the organizing frames of collective references. A concept of public reason organized on such open and comprehensive terms cannot be dominated by either a vocabulary of rights nor community values. Its moral sense must be located in efforts to manage differences, establish collective harmony, and exceed thresholds of security, rather than in individual and group interests. We have seen that morality can and must trump politics on occasion on a broad front of issues and problems. But it is also important to record that a public reasoning aimed at establishing the best arrangements of collective life is also eminently moral in its own right.

The moral terms in this version of public reasoning anticipate the redemptive powers of uncoerced dialogue on both subjects and participants. What I have called procedural holism, where the norms of self governance are in the mediated speech acts of public reason rather than in a republican sense of common substantive values and ideals, is a powerful force to unify persons. This force can make whole the citizens of a liberal democracy, folding into a single strand the divided identities of traditional liberal politics. In this sense political morality is expressible as a kind of psychic exercise that absorbs persons into the deliberations of public reasoning. The final magic of establishing a set of processes for resolving differences among individuals and groups may be that the effort can yield a political community with benign rather than malicious powers of union. *These* powers may be the most important resources for political morality in the liberal state.

Index

Abolitionism, 205, 206n
Abortion debate, 43–48, 58–60, 104, 169; avoidance mechanisms and, 177–78; polls, 174–75; social contract and, 175–76; undue burden test, 179–80; well-ordered society and, 205–6
Access, 26, 122–23, 141–42, 144–45
Accommodation, 119
Action-directive, 16
Actions, 169–70, 200–201, 210, 218
Adjudication, 42, 60, 129–30. *See also* Deliberation; Judgment
Adjudication story, 221
Advocacy claims, 110, 112
Aggregation, 199, 222
Algorithms, 62, 66, 68, 116, 220–21
AMA amicus curiae brief, 166
Amendments to the Constitution: First Amendment, 183; Fourteenth Amendment, 13, 46, 160, 162, 179; Fourth Amendment, 169
Amish, 183–84, 186
Analogy, 7, 164
Appellate powers of reason, 193–95
Appetite, 80, 98, 109
Arbitration, 147, 207
Arendt, Hannah, 202
Aristotle, 54, 99, 111, 154, 182
Arrow's theorem, 34
Assistance, 133
Assumptions, 208–9
Athenian democracy, 154
Austin, John, 95–97

Authority, 55, 117, 130, 135–36, 141, 145; texts and, 133, 181–82, 195
Autonomy, 57, 79, 82, 148, 187
Avoidance mechanisms, 104, 112, 150, 177–82

Background conditions, 2, 135, 160, 166–67, 172, 212–14; disputes and, 19–21, 177
Bayesian decision rules, 66
Behavior, 81, 95–97
Beliefs, 18–19, 38–39; clusters of, 45–47; commensurability, 83–84; as context-dependent, 184–86; heterogeneous, 212–13; religious beliefs, 32, 83, 90–91, 95, 124–25; toleration of, 72–73; truth and, 54–55
Bellotti v. Baird, 179
Bias, 141
Binding conclusions, 124–25, 147, 207
Black box, 149n
Blackmun, Harry, 179
Body, 96–97
Bolt, Robert, 129n, 185n
Boundaries, 65, 71–72, 135, 147, 207, 212; collective arrangements as, 182–83. *See also* Halting problem
Bracketing, 43, 80, 170; language and, 61–62, 210–11; morality and, 55–61, 187–88
Bradley, 54
Brain structure, 91–92, 196
Brennan, William J., Jr., 169
Bruner, Jerome, 93, 171, 172
Bruner-Postman experiences, 36
Burkert, Walter, 17

227

Callahan, Daniel, 158–59
Capitalism, 20, 32
Casey, 179
Casuistry, 180–82, 211
Causality, 37–38
Choice, 79, 82, 127–28
Choice theory, 4, 48, 107–8
Christian Science, 48–51, 59, 184
Citizens, 82–83, 87, 202, 215n
Civil rights movement, 205
Civil society, 16–17, 215–16
Classical theory, 2, 74, 80, 99, 182, 223; dualism and, 193–94
Clinton, Bill, 121
Closure, 1–2, 28, 65, 70, 97, 122, 144–46; coercion and, 146–47; consciousness and, 195–96; freedom of expression and, 126–28; identity and, 97–98; knowledge and, 168; mediation and, 132–33; narratives and, 105; noncomputational reasoning and, 213; objectivity and, 116; provisional, 189, 207, 214
Coercion, 32, 63, 142, 178; closure and, 146–47; liberty and, 125–29, 147–48
Coherence, 57, 224
Collateral reasoning, 115, 120, 207–8
Collateral theories, 70, 153–54
Collective arrangements, 74–75, 107–9, 151, 154, 160, 210, 217–19
Collective choice theory, 48, 107–8
Collective references, 182–83
Collectives, 110, 132–33, 201–4. *See also* Communities; Society
Commensurability, 83–84, 143, 179
Commitments, 85–87, 208
Communicative action, 218
Communitarianism, 35, 79, 222
Communities, 2; commensurability and, 83–84, 143; commitments and, 85–86; deliberation and, 199; doctrines and, 83, 85; harm thesis and, 23–24; institutions and, 150–51; language and, 15–16; morality and, 58, 224; persons and, 79–80, 83–88, 107–8; political liberalism and, 51–52; public reason and, 5–6, 41, 72–73, 150–52, 219–20; state, relationship to, 31–32, 84, 87, 138–39, 151–52; values, 55–56, 60. *See also* Public space
Compassion, narrative of, 14

Competence, 124–25, 127, 139–40, 153–54
Competition, 26, 138
Compliance, 52
Comprehensive doctrines, 55–58, 85
Computational reasoning, 6, 62–63, 66, 115
Concepts, 36–37, 214
Conscience, 103, 150–51, 194–95
Consciousness, 37, 92–93, 101, 106, 159; closure and, 195–96; quantum mechanics and, 196–97
Consciousness Explained (Dennett), 92
Consent, 2, 28n, 32–33, 142, 212; physician-assisted suicide and, 157–58; political domain and, 84–85, 87
Consolidation, 189, 222–23
Constitutional issues, 175, 216–17
Contexts, 38, 48, 184–86, 197
Contiguity, 77–78
Contract theory, 5, 32, 33, 71, 86, 120, 224; as thought experiment, 190–91. *See also* Social contract
Conversation. *See* Dialogue
Cooperation, 124, 137–38
Corinthians (St. Paul), 193, 194
Council of the Isles, 174
Creation of the Sacred (Burkert), 17
Crossing Guard, The, 192

Deciphering, 90
Decision theory, 41, 66, 90, 106n
Deconstruction, 181
Deep pluralism, 42, 60, 84, 214, 223
Defection, 44–45, 52–53
Defensor minor (Marsiglio), 193
Deliberation, 21, 40–42, 121, 191, 199, 220; impartiality and, 42, 51, 136. *See also* Adjudication
DeLillo, Don, 100
Democracy, 108, 116–18, 154, 175–76
Dennett, Daniel, 78, 92
Depth, 53–54
Descartes, René, 80, 194
Dialectics, 121–22, 126–27, 145, 219. *See also* Dialogue; Discourse
Dialogue, 6, 118, 145; constraints on, 214–15; deliberation and, 40–41, 191; as form of discourse, 122, 131; logic of, 189–90; mediation and, 121, 151, 211; noncomputational, 63–64, 132; open,

Grammar, 208–9
Gray, John, 22, 213n
Group dynamics, 202–4

Habermas, Jürgen, 71, 115, 118, 142–43, 161n,
    201, 202, 218, 219
Halting problem, 8, 61, 67–71, 145, 197–98
Harm thesis, 23–25, 43, 45, 126
Hart, H. L. A., 62
Hemlock Society, 13
Heterogeneity, 177–78, 212–13
Heuristics, 102
Hobbes, Thomas, 32, 33, 71, 87
Holism, 110, 112, 182–83, 198–202, 208, 212,
    222, 225
House Judiciary Committee, 165
Human Condition, The (Arendt), 202
Human law, 193–94
Hume, David, 50

Ideal speech, 206, 218–19
Idea of a Social Science, The (Winch), 142
Identity, 34, 66, 88, 90–91, 110; closure and,
    97–98
"I Have a Dream" (King), 105
Impartiality, 33, 41–42, 51–52, 136, 198. *See
    also* Neutrality
Impulses, 96–97
Inclusive presentations, 185
Incomplete reasoning, 164, 167–71
Indeterminacy, 15–16, 20–23, 115, 145–46;
    halting problem and, 68–70; ontology
    and, 70–71; political setting for, 29–30;
    radical speakers and, 48–49
Indigenous discourse, 142–43, 161–63, 219
Individualism, 4, 23–24, 32–33, 110; method-
    ological, 76, 106–7, 112
Individuals. *See* Persons
Infinite regresses, 64–66, 68, 70–71, 197
Information, 48, 67, 79–80, 90, 128, 167; me-
    diation and, 145, 151, 211–12; theory and,
    171–73, 211. *See also* Knowledge
Inquiry, 117, 126–28, 142
Institutional pluralism, 186
Institutions, 42–43, 76, 178–79, 215; commu-
    nities and, 85, 150–51; nonliberal, 186–87.
    See also State
Intellect, 80, 219
Intellectual pluralism, 186

Interests, 29
Interpretations, 6–8, 19–20, 27–29, 64–66,
    80, 217–18; dialogue and, 118, 130; of text,
    69–71, 74, 145
Ireland, peace agreement, 172–74
Irish Republican Army, 172

Jehovah's Witnesses, 147
John Paul II, 60
Johnston, David, 30
Judgment, 21–22, 40, 70
Judiciary, 40, 42, 149, 199
Jurisdictions, 27–28, 177–79
Justice, 16, 55n, 118, 218; narrative and, 101–2;
    original position and, 79–80
Justification, 54, 69n, 71, 117

Kahneman, Daniel, 37
Kennedy, Anthony M., 156
Kevorkian, Jack, 13
King, Martin Luther, Jr., 105
Knowledge, 49, 54, 66–67, 71, 90, 128; media-
    tion and, 145, 151; ordering of, 171–73; re-
    ductions of, 211–12; restrictions on,
    167–70. *See also* Information
Kuhn, Thomas, 116, 143

Lamm, Richard, 158
Languages, 3; behavior and, 95–97; bracket-
    ing and, 61–62, 210–11; collateral, 70,
    153–54; communities and, 15–16; disputes
    and, 19, 69–70, 96–97; evaluative, 64–65;
    external perspective and, 90; formal
    properties of, 123–24; of governance, 16,
    20–21, 61–63, 72–73, 144, 208–9; indige-
    nous, 142–43, 161–63, 219; moral, 56–57;
    openness of, 6–7, 19, 206, 217–18; persons
    and, 104–5; pluralism and, 15–16, 61; post-
    modern theories of, 2, 224; self-reflective
    language, 63–67; state and, 72–73, 114. *See
    also* Indeterminacy; Interpretation; Polit-
    ical languages
Laws: divine vs. human, 193–94; hybrid in-
    stitutions and, 150; partisan use of, 27–28;
    property dualism and, 81–82
Legal discourse, 121, 216
Legal reasoning, 179–80
Legitimacy, 175
Lepore, Ernest, 83

Leviathan (Hobbes), 33, 87
Lewin, Kurt, 66
Liability law, 81
Liberalism: classical, 114–15; coercion and, 178; critiques of, 34–35; definitions, 30–31; incomplete unions and, 220; indeterminacy and, 22–23; intractable disputes and, 43–44; mediated reasoning and, 217–18; neutrality and, 136–41; nonliberal institutions and, 186–87; persons and, 137; political liberalism, 4–5, 30, 51–52; values and purposes, 33–34
Liberal principle (LP), 31
Libertarianism, 23n, 127
Liberty, 23, 123; coercion and, 125–29, 147–48; negative, 25–26, 108, 125, 129, 158
Libra (DeLillo), 100
Locke, John, 86n, 175
Logos, 176, 194
LP (liberal principle), 31

Machiavelli, Niccolò, 187–88, 224
Madisonian narrative, 221–23
Maintenance, 177, 189–90
Management of mechanisms, 114
Man for All Seasons, A (Bolt), 129n, 185n
Marsiglio de Padua, 193, 194, 195
Material considerations, 18–20, 80
Mathematics, 68, 116, 133, 191, 203, 220–21
Maxims, 7, 162–64
Meaning, 76, 144, 160
Mediated speech acts, 6–8, 17, 121, 182, 220
Mediation, 17, 73–74, 113, 121, 217–18, 224–25; authority and, 133, 135–36, 141, 145, 181–82; boundaries and, 135, 147; closure and, 132–33; information and, 145, 151, 211–12; as model, 211–12; narratives and, 144–45; neutrality and, 136, 140; as outcome-oriented, 191–92; texts and, 133, 181–82, 195, 207–8. *See also* Dialogue; Discourse; Third parties
Medieval philosophy, 2, 74, 193, 223
Meme evolution, 92
Mental considerations, 81–83
Merit public reasoning, 5–6, 42–48, 115–16, 187, 197
Metaphysics, 49, 77–80, 88–89, 94–95, 218
Metarules, 171

Methodological individualism, 76, 106–7, 112
Methodology, 22, 191
Mill, John Stuart, 24, 25, 124; *On Liberty*, 117, 122, 125–30
Mind, concept of, 194
Mitchell, George, 172
Moore, G. E., 64, 67, 114
Morality, 43, 48, 60–61, 73–74, 76, 148; communities and, 58, 224; political, 224–25; power and, 187–88; state and, 33–34, 55, 57–59, 224
Moral languages, 56–57

Narrative persons, 78–79, 92–93, 100–101, 104–5
Narratives, 14, 119, 171–73, 208; experience and, 102, 105–6, 171–73; justice and, 101–2; mediation and, 144–45; parables, 102–3; physician-assisted suicide and, 159–60; rival ideas, 103–4; unifying powers, 104–6
Native speakers, 43–48, 53
Naturalism, 49–50
Natural law, 155–56, 159
Natural Right and History (Strauss), 55n, 101
Nazis, 109n
Netherlands, physician-assisted suicide and, 165–66
Neutrality, 51; definitions, 136–37; failures of, 139–40, 144; goods and, 137–39; mediation and, 136, 140. *See also* Impartiality
New England Journal of Medicine, 11
New York Attorney General, 155
New York Task Force on Life and the Law, 166, 178
Ninth Circuit Appeals Court, 161
Noncomputational reasoning, 43, 67, 73–74, 122; avoidance mechanisms and, 180; closure and, 213; consciousness and, 197; dialogue and, 63–64, 132; mediation and, 144–45
Nonliberal institutions, 186–87
Nous, 194
Nozick, Robert, 12, 135

Objectivity, 2, 5, 33, 114–16, 128
O'Connor, Sandra Day, 164–65
On Liberty (Mill), 117, 122, 125–30
Ontological dualism, 78, 89–91

Ontology, 110, 112, 138; indeterminacy and, 70–71; radical speakers and, 49–52
OP. *See* Original position
Open society, 116–18
Opinions, 128–29
Oracle, 71
Order, 137–39, 171–73
Original position (OP), 28–29, 71, 171, 218, 219; persons and, 79–80, 82
Outcomes, 51, 69–70, 120, 137, 189–92, 220; collective, 202–3; commitments and, 86–87

Parables, 102–3
Parfit, Derek, 98
Partisanship, 3–4, 27–28, 131–32, 140
Partitioning, 177–78
Paul, Saint, 193, 194
Peirce, Charles, 116
Persons, 6, 31–33, 43; as citizens, 82–83, 87, 202; classical views of, 80, 99, 182; communities and, 79–80, 83–88, 107–8; concepts and, 36–37; consciousness and, 92–93; dualism and, 80–81, 149–50, 193–94; group dynamics and, 202–4; mental considerations, 81–83; metaphysics and, 77–80, 88–89; narrative persons, 78–79, 92–93, 100–101, 104–5; original position and, 79–80, 82; political sense of, 76–78; populism and, 220–21; rationality and, 127, 161; reality and, 35–37; reason and, 97–98, 101; as source of meaning, 76, 160; state and, 136–38; unification of, 111–12
Perspectives, 90, 119, 196, 210
Physician-assisted suicide, 11–15, 134, 154–65, 178, 217; consent and, 157–58; cost-efficiency and, 158–59; Dutch experiment, 165–66
Piaget, Jean, 142
Plato, 2, 54, 71, 80, 98, 102, 105; reason and, 195; *Republic*, 3, 109, 166; soul and, 107, 108–9, 193
Pluralism, 6, 80; beliefs and, 54–55; deep pluralism, 42, 59–60, 84, 214, 223; defection and, 52–53; depth and, 53–54; dimensions of, 186, 188; dualism and, 110–11; language and, 15–16, 61; politics of, 85; scope and, 52–53

Polarization, 174–75
Political culture, 3–4
Political domain, 84–87
Political languages, 16, 56–57; of dialogue, 161, 214–15; dualism and, 93–95; rival interpretations, 6–8, 19–20, 27–29, 64–66, 80, 217–18; translation of, 130–32, 142–44. *See also* Languages
Political liberalism, 4–5, 30, 51–52. *See also* Liberalism
Political Liberalism (Rawls), 4, 16, 56, 206n, 216
Politics (Aristotle), 182
Polls, 174–75
Popper, Karl, 116, 117
Populism, 220–21
Positivism, 112, 116
Postmodernism, 181
Power, 3, 8, 32, 96, 187–88
Practice dualism, 78, 88, 95, 110, 202
Presentations, 184–86
Prichard, H. A., 69n
Prince, The (Machiavelli), 187–88
Principles, 22–23, 58, 169–71, 211, 214; defining, 46–47; dualism and, 197–98; of futility, 118–19; liberal principle (LP), 31; of political domain, 84–85
Prisoners' Dilemma, 133
Privacy, 12–13, 87–88, 128, 200–201
Procedural liberalism, 160–61, 208
Procedures, empty, 31–32, 34, 70, 149, 198
Process, 111, 122, 124–25, 198
Property dualism, 78, 80–82, 88–89n, 91, 95, 99, 110–11, 208
Provisional settlements, 17, 19, 207, 214
Psychology, 107–8
Psychosis, 109–10
Public, 200–201
Public reason: assumptions and, 208–9; authority and, 130; communities and, 5–6, 41, 72–73, 150–52, 219–20; conditions of, 212–13; constitutional essentials and, 216–17; dialogue and, 111–13, 119–22, 129–30, 189–92, 217; indirection and, 172–74, 180–82; as layered arrangement, 211; maxims and, 162–63; merit form of, 5–6, 42–43, 115–16, 187, 197; morality and, 60–61, 73; as ongoing dialogue, 151–52; wide view of, 56. *See also* Computational

State: (*continued*)
neutrality and, 137–40; persons and, 136–38; reason and, 2–3; as third party, 207; translation and, 144; truth and, 32, 72
State regulation, 24–25, 177
Strauss, Leo, 54, 55n, 101
Structures, 18–20, 135, 177
Subjectivity, 80–81, 91, 105–6, 114, 196
Substance, 89
Sunstein, Cass, 167–68, 170
Supreme Court, 13, 121, 217; abortion debate and, 48; education decisions, 183–84; legal reasoning and, 179–80; physician-assisted suicide and, 40, 155, 160, 162, 167; range of considerations, 162, 167

Talk, 191, 223
Tarski's truth schema, 53–54
Taylor, Charles, 110, 111
Texts: grammars and, 208–9; interpretation, 69–71, 74, 145; mediation and, 181–82, 207–8
Theory, 8–9, 65, 71, 117; frameworks, 21–22; information and, 171–73, 211; of justice, 55n, 79–80, 168, 218; metaphysics and, 77–78; reduction of, 169. *See also individual theories*
Theory of Justice, A (Rawls), 4
Third Circuit Appeals Court, 156
Third parties, 133–34, 143–44, 155, 170, 191, 203, 207. *See also* Mediation
Thornburgh, 48, 127n
Thorson, Thomas, 116, 117
Thought experiments, 71, 87, 118–19; contract theory as, 190–91; on merit public reasoning, 43, 45–48; original position and, 79–80. *See also* Abortion debate; Christian Science; Physician-assisted suicide
Tolerance, 72–73, 117

Transcendence, 194–95, 219
Transition rules, 62
Translation, 130–32, 142–44
Trials, 169, 215–16
Tribe, Laurence, 156
Truth, 53–55, 116–18, 121, 195; disputes and, 176–77; freedom of expression and, 126–27, 130; state and, 32, 72
Tucker, Kathryn, 14
Turing, A. M., 71
Tversky, Amos, 36–37
Two-slit experiments, 196, 197n

Uncoerced discourse, 117–18, 176, 191
Undue burden test, 179–80
United States Court of Appeals for the Ninth Circuit, 13
Universalism, 35, 105–6, 142, 161, 219
U.S. Constitution, 175, 216–17
Utilitarianism, 4, 33, 117, 119, 182, 203

Vacco v. Quill, 13, 155, 156, 157, 158
Values: of community, 55–56, 60; of liberalism, 33–34
Value statements, 116–17
Veil of ignorance, 29, 79
Verification, 116–17
Vertical heterogeneity, 178
Voting, 47–48, 199

Walzer, Michael, 75
Washington v. Glucksberg, 13, 57, 155
Weber, Max, 32
Well-ordered society, 204–6
Wertheimer, Alan, 147
Widdershoven, Guy, 93
Winch, Peter, 115, 142, 143, 219
Wisconsin v. Yoder, 183–84, 186
Wittgenstein, Ludwig, 71
Wollheim, Richard, 86